THE
YANKEE WAY

Also by Andy Martino

Cheated

THE
YANKEE WAY

THE UNTOLD INSIDE STORY OF
THE BRIAN CASHMAN ERA

ANDY MARTINO

Doubleday   *New York*

Book design by Michael Collica
Jacket images: *Yankee Stadium* by Rob Tringali / SportsChrome /
Getty Images; (sky) Dove Lee and Katsumi Murouchi, both Getty Images
Jacket design by Michael J. Windsor

Library of Congress Cataloging-in-Publication Data
Name: Martino, Andy, author.
Title: The Yankee way : the untold inside story of the Brian Cashman era / Andy Martino.
Description: First edition. | New York : Doubleday, [2024] |
Includes bibliographical references and index.
Identifiers: LCCN 2023042331 (print) | LCCN 2023042332 (ebook) |
ISBN 9780385549998 (hardcover) | ISBN 9780385550000 (ebook)
Subjects: LCSH: New York Yankees (Baseball team)—History. | Cashman,
Brian, [date] | Baseball managers—United States—Biography.
Classification: LCC GV416.N48 M37 2024 (print) | LCC GV416.N48 (ebook) |
DDC 796.357/64097471—dc23/eng/20231018
LC record available at https://lccn.loc.gov/2023042331
LC ebook record available at https://lccn.loc.gov/2023042332

MANUFACTURED IN THE UNITED STATES OF AMERICA
1 3 5 7 9 10 8 6 4 2
First Edition

This book is for Ruby.

The story that is always told about the Yankees is wrong.
—Brian Cashman, Yankees general manager, 1998–present

Well, why don't I try to get it right?
—me, to Cashman

Contents

Part Three: Dynasty

Part Four: Derek, Alex, and Joe

Part Five: Into a New Age

Author's Note

I have covered New York baseball for more than fifteen years, and this book is derived in part from relationships, firsthand observations, and interviews with players, owners, executives, managers, coaches, scouts, and agents conducted along the way.

Once I began working in earnest on this project in 2021, Brian Cashman—though we were both clear that this was not his book, or a collaboration—did agree to participate in dozens of exclusive interviews on the phone, in his Yankee Stadium office, on the field, in the dugout, and via text message between 2021 and 2023. He only consented to this if I promised to interview many others and not frame this as his book, which was my plan anyway. Some quotes are from an extended interview with Cashman conducted in his office in 2018.

Most other sources agreed to on-record interviews, which are identified throughout the text. Certain sources requested anonymity to discuss sensitive matters, also noted throughout the text. The many books and articles cited in the bibliography were also essential in telling this story.

Through representatives, Derek Jeter and Alex Rodriguez declined to be interviewed.

Introduction

"This Game Is a Monster"

Derek Jeter, at forty-seven years old, maintained the trim physique and imperious gait he had carried since the end of the previous century.

On the morning of September 8, 2021, Jeter strode across the lobby of the Otesaga Resort Hotel in Cooperstown, New York—shoulders back, chin upturned—accompanied by another New York Yankees deity who had never lost confidence, Reggie Jackson.

Jackson was nearly three decades older than Jeter but comparably fit and stylish. He expressed his own self-assurance with a smirk that held when he spoke, the corners of his mouth turned slightly down as if permanently amused. He wore glasses with thin frames and had a neatly trimmed mustache.

The Otesaga itself was a setting worthy of the Hall of Famers who populated it annually for the induction ceremonies. Built in 1909, it had a lobby that stood between a grand, white-columned entrance in the front and a veranda overlooking Lake Otsego—the water nick-named Glimmerglass because of its startling ability to refract light—in the back. Each year, living Hall of Famers gathered for an exclusive reception on that patio.

Standing on the plush rug to the left of the entrance was a man not programmed to notice any of the grandeur around him, but whose mind was forever stuck back in his office or on his phone. Brian Cashman was getting coffee.

He was fifty-four years old, five feet seven, bald on top with hair cropped close on the sides and back. The Yankees, the ballclub he had served as general manager since 1998, were near the end of one of the most stressful seasons Cashman had yet endured.

The night before, the Toronto Blue Jays had squashed his team, 5–1, beating the $324 million ace, Gerrit Cole, and keeping alive the possibility that the Yanks would fail to qualify for the postseason. Game details always rumbled in Cashman's belly. His monotone voice and blank stare hid the inner storm.

But it was Cashman's duty to be here in Cooperstown. Stewardship of an iconic franchise carried many responsibilities, including traveling to see the enshrinement of the player who, above all others, defined Cashman's era—no matter how deep the personal disconnect between championship shortstop and championship executive had grown.

Standing by a stainless steel coffee urn and taking the first sips of his steaming beverage, Cashman spotted Harold Reynolds, a former big-league infielder currently working as a television analyst. The two chatted briefly. Then Cashman noticed the approach of Jeter and Jackson.

"Hey," Jeter said to Cashman. "When you get a chance, can I meet with you for a second?"

Now seemed as good a time as any. The two walked away from Jackson and Reynolds and down a hallway.

Cashman figured that Jeter, in his current role as CEO of the Miami Marlins, was about to request permission to interview a Yankee executive or coach for a job. Jeter had been hiring Cashman's people since crossing over to management four years earlier.

But that wasn't it, not this time. Jeter had a more significant topic on his mind: he wanted, even just for his own sense of peace, a measure of closure.

"He basically said, 'Hey, I just want to thank you for everything you did in my career,'" Cashman says. "'I know we've had issues, but as far as I'm concerned, it's over. I have a whole new appreciation for how things are, being on this side of the fence now, and I want to thank you for everything. As far as I'm concerned, things are cool between us.'"

Jeter's words landed as a pleasant surprise. He and Cashman were titanic figures: one stood with DiMaggio, Mantle, and Berra in Yankee lore; the other was the longest-standing general manager in

Yankees history and had overseen the club's final dynasty before the game changed in ways that made a dynasty nearly impossible.

They had disagreed in public and private, vented about each other, remembered key events differently. Peace did not seem near. Now—suddenly, finally—they were exhaling together.

"From my end, I was like, 'Listen, dude, I just feel bad because I feel like people were lying to you,'" Cashman recalled. "'And all I ever did was be honest with you. And I feel like a lot of people approach you as a superstar and are not willing to be honest because they're afraid to lose their friendship. But I was going to do my job.'"

Cashman didn't say who was allegedly lying. Details didn't have to be made explicit between these two Yankees luminaries who had been through so much together.

"I appreciated it," Cashman later said. "It was a good conversation."

It was also a lot to unpack. More than two decades of emotional churn, in fact. The characters in Cashman's long story at the helm, some of whom happened to be in that gilded hotel at that very moment, included Joe Torre, Mariano Rivera, Alex Rodriguez, and the late George Steinbrenner. Legends all. But also men with egos and feelings and flaws and roles in one of contemporary baseball's greatest stories—men who collaborated on an era of excellence the likes of which we may never see again.

WHAT IS A GENERAL MANAGER, ANYWAY?

The year after his chat with Jeter in Cooperstown, Cashman quietly achieved a significant milestone of his own: he passed Ed Barrow as the longest-tenured general manager in the history of the world's most iconic sports franchise.

The term "general manager" in baseball is actually a bit tricky to define. In the modern game we understand the GM as the person who constructs the team, but in practice job titles and responsibilities have shifted through years and eras.

In the nineteenth and early twentieth centuries, some owners and team presidents like Charles Comiskey of the Chicago White Sox and Barney Dreyfuss of the Pittsburgh Pirates chose the players. In other cases, domineering field managers performed these functions—think John McGraw of the New York Giants.

For much of the twentieth and early twenty-first centuries, "general manager" became the term of fashion for architects of the roster, so much so that the industry gathering that kicks off every Major League Baseball offseason is called the General Managers Meetings.

In recent years, contemporary front offices have added another wrinkle, creating titles like president of baseball operations and chief baseball officer. The men who hold those jobs appoint general managers. But those "GMs" are, in practice, assistants to the "presidents" and "chiefs," who typically act as a GM in the way most of us understand the term.

The best way to understand this evolving nomenclature is to dive a bit deeper into the structure of a contemporary baseball organization.

Directly under the ownership level, there is often a team president. For the Yankees, Randy Levine has served in this role since 2000. Below that sit heads of the various departments: baseball operations, business operations, marketing, communications, and more.

Since 1998, Cashman has led the Yankees' baseball operations department. He took the job when the term "general manager" was standard, and he has kept it. David Stearns, his counterpart for the crosstown New York Mets , entered that organization in 2023 as president of baseball operations.

But both Cashman and Stearns were in charge of the major-league roster, the farm system, the manager, coaches, strength and conditioning, and everything else related to winning and losing ball games. They had the same job.

For the Yankees, Barrow held titles including business manager and team president from 1921 to 1944, but his responsibilities covered what we would now understand to be those of a GM.

None of these shifts in terminology seemed to matter much to the average fan until a monumental development in the early twenty-first century: the publication of Michael Lewis's bestselling book *Moneyball,* which dramatized the Oakland Athletics GM Billy Beane's innovations in utilizing data and creativity to run a team.

That book cast a new spotlight on the baseball general manager. Arriving as it did when fantasy sports were already exploding in popularity, allowing any fan to become a mini-GM, it contributed to the celebrification of the sports executive. Brad Pitt played Beane in the movie.

Because of that, Beane stands as the most famous person to lead a baseball operations department. But he holds the strong opinion that Cashman is the best to ever do the job.

"Based on Brian's accomplishments, I would make the argument that he is the greatest executive in the history of the sport," Beane says. "He has four championships and the longest tenure. It's not unlike Tom Brady's career, from an executive standpoint. He is the Tom Brady of GMs."

Seven executives are enshrined in Cooperstown for their work running teams: Barrow, George Weiss, Branch Rickey, Larry and Lee MacPhail, Pat Gillick, and John Schuerholz. Theo Epstein, who ended long-standing championship curses for the Boston Red Sox and the Chicago Cubs, will join them one day, along perhaps with Brian Sabean, winner of three championships with the San Francisco Giants.

For Beane, Cashman towers above them all. In fact, when asked in a telephone interview if Cashman belonged in the Hall, Beane raised his voice and made clear that he found the question ridiculous.

"If you look at the standard of executives who have been elected into the Hall of Fame, and you look at everyone's accomplishments, he completely blows everybody away," Beane says.

"He has the championships. He has the length of career. He literally checks every single box. So the idea that [his Hall of Fame candidacy] would even be questioned to me seems absurd, based on what I would see as the criteria for being a Hall of Fame executive.

"Why wouldn't he be in the Hall of Fame? You know, that question to me is one that shouldn't be asked. In fact, when you talk about Brian, 'future Hall of Famer' should be part of the sentence every time. That might sound corny, but it just seems crazy to even have to ask. In fact, you can go even further. Why don't you go outside of baseball, find somebody in sports who has done better than Brian."

Beane is not a lone voice. Sabean, who worked alongside a young Cashman with the Yankees of the late 1980s and early 1990s before moving on to San Francisco, became a very different executive from Beane, relying more on traditional scouting than the data and analytics that made *Moneyball* famous. Through a contrasting lens, Sabean sees Cashman the same way.

"Brian is the greatest general manager in the history of the sport,"

Sabean says, without knowing that Beane had uttered practically the exact same sentence.

"The expectations on him are through the roof. They're well established. It's not a city or team that you can take a step back and say, 'Hey, we're going to have to rebuild or even retool,' so to speak. He's had to try to win the division, get deep in the playoffs, get to the World Series, and win the World Series every year. It's amazing how he's navigated that, because he can't lie in wait for a couple of years, like many teams can. The ownership is not going to allow it. The fan base wouldn't stand for it.

"That in itself is a bear. This game is a monster. You've got to deal with it every day. He's got to deal with it 365 days a year. And try to win the day."

Cashman's success astounds competitors, when they stop to really think about it.

Under his watch, the Yankees have never posted a losing record. In fact, the team began a streak of winning seasons in 1993, when Cashman was a key underling in the general manager Gene Michael's front office.

During that span, no other club has had half as many consecutive winning years. In fact, no other major-league franchise has had twenty-five straight winning seasons *at any point in its history.*

Through the 2023 season the Yankees have been mathematically eliminated from postseason contention in just 22 of the 4,108 games during Cashman's tenure as GM. Rivals struggle to even comprehend that one. He is the youngest-ever GM to win a World Series and the only to win championships in each of his first three years on the job.

Cashman's detractors in the fan base note that the Yanks have won just one championship since 2000, and none in more than a decade. This is a serious violation of the longtime owner George Steinbrenner's edict that any season ending without a World Series title is a failure.

As each year passes, tension builds inside and outside the organization. Frustrated fans note bad trades and failed prospects. Cashman has plenty of both on his ledger. The 2023 season, which Cashman himself called a "disaster" in an August news conference, ended with the Yankees missing the playoffs for the first time since 2016. By

September, fan unrest had reached a fever pitch, and at least one paying customer unfurled a "Fire Cashman" banner at the stadium. The Yankees posted a winning record for the thirty-first consecutive year—second-most ever in MLB history, behind only the 1926 and 1964 Yankees—but their 82–80 mark was not nearly good enough for Cashman or his public.

For the twenty-first-century Yankees, the game presents new obstacles that threaten their very identity as a sports behemoth. The context of the sport has changed in a way that will likely leave fans who yearn for the 1950s or 1990s dynasties forever bereft of satisfaction. The postseason field has gradually expanded from two teams to twelve. It is easier than ever to reach the playoffs but an increasingly fraught grind to survive its many rounds.

Since the Yankees won three titles in Cashman's first three years as GM, a run that ended in 2000, no team has captured two in a row, though the Giants, Houston Astros, and Boston Red Sox have won multiple championships in that span. Dynasties, as baseball defined them for more than a century, no longer exist.

But this book isn't about Yankee championships and championship droughts, at least not primarily. It is about the long arc of transformation in the game of baseball itself. There is a broader tale to tell here than the annual success and/or disappointment of one franchise.

Simply put, the story of the Yankees since Cashman arrived as a nineteen-year-old intern in 1986 is the story of the entire game during that time. The Yankees are steeped in more tradition than any team, and now they are also as modern as anyone, immersed in data and technology as well as old-school scouting.

From old school to new, gut feeling to analytics, power in the manager's office to power for the GM, baseball is in many ways unrecognizable from the game that held a claim as the national pastime for more than a century.

In the 1980s, most baseball executives began their careers in the game as players. Now execs come from Wall Street, the Ivy League, and PhD engineering programs. Some are literally rocket scientists. As the industry severs old traditions, new ones arise.

This broader story of baseball's evolution was a reason to pursue writing the story of the Yankees through the lens of its front office.

Plenty of books have chronicled the team on the field; this one aims to capture how a franchise is run on the executive level during a time of dizzying change in the industry.

The Yankees aren't just any franchise, either; love or hate them, they are a dominant global brand. And, according to Cashman himself, their story has been recounted frequently but never correctly.

"The story that is always told about the Yankees is wrong," Cashman has told me on multiple occasions.

"Well," I answered one time, "why don't I try to get it right?"

I have known and covered Cashman for years and have been the beneficiary of countless hours of off-the-record stories about his Yankee adventures. We met during the first decade of his tenure, when I was writing a journalism school master's project about his work with the Yankees. We came to know each other well as I became a reporter for the New York *Daily News* and later a broadcaster for the television network SNY and writer for its website.

Because we enjoy a measure of personal chemistry and he seems to consider my daily coverage generally fair, I figured that it would be easy to persuade Cashman to be interviewed for a book about the Yankees during his time there.

I was wrong. In October 2021, when I called Cashman to explain the idea and ask if he would speak on the record, he transformed back into the version of himself that the public sees, quiet and inscrutable.

"I'd like to write a book about your time with the Yankees, and I would like to interview you," I said.

He paused for a few seconds.

"Okay," he finally said, and not in a tone that signaled agreement. It was more like, "Okay, I acknowledge that you just said that and am choosing not to indicate a reaction."

Eager to fill the silence, I launched into a version of the explanation written above, about how the Yankees tell the story of the sport itself in the years since Cashman arrived.

"Okay," he said again, in the same flat voice.

I stammered something about following up soon.

"Okay," Cashman said.

A few weeks later, Major League Baseball convened its annual General Managers Meetings, the event that kicks off every offseason with preliminary trade and free agency discussions. This year, execs and media decamped to a resort in Carlsbad, California.

On the first day, just past 6:00 a.m., Cashman and I were both still on East Coast time. We bumped into each other at the coffee shop.

"Want to sit down and talk about the book idea?" I asked.

"Sure," he said.

As I made my pitch again, he spent most of his time looking over my shoulder.

"Are there any concerns you want to express?" I asked.

"No," he said. "Just thinking."

"Do you want me to stop bugging you about this and just drop it?"

"No, you can keep asking."

Okey dokey.

A full six months later, after several intermittent follow-ups, I made a final attempt, spelling out for Cashman what I'll make clear now: this is not a biography, and certainly not his memoir or a collaboration between us.

The book would be about Cashman, but also about his Yankees forebears like Gene Michael, Billy Martin, and Bill Livesey and star players—the people who made the Yankees the Yankees and provided the necessary context to understand the Cashman era.

It would be about the entire franchise, the entire era, the entire game. I would speak to current and former Yankee executives, managers, coaches, scouts, players, employees on every rung of the ladder, and rivals from around the league. Cashman would have no control over its contents.

"Well," he finally said. "If that's what you're doing, I don't have the right to tell you not to write a book."

He then agreed to be interviewed at length and quoted on the record.

Cashman's lack of enthusiasm made sense. He was a busy man who now had to talk to me even more frequently than before. He was accepting the risk of entrusting an independent party to tell the story of his career and set his legacy.

Ultimately, though, Cashman was extremely generous with his time and insight. Through Yankees highs and lows over the next two years, he took my calls, often on his morning drives into the stadium from his Connecticut home. We would talk until he pulled in to the garage on 164th Street in the South Bronx or cut me off mid-answer with "I gotta go" or "I've gotta take this call."

Through all those conversations, Cashman unspooled his version of the past thirty-plus years of Yankees and baseball history, our conversations marked by his sharp memory, candor, and the occasional angry edge.

As I promised Cashman, the reporting did not stop there. As much as I spoke with him, I spent many more hours interviewing others, from the clubhouse to the owner, Hal Steinbrenner.

It all felt like privileged access into the inner workings of the franchise, and I'm grateful for it. I hope it's as much fun to read as it was to report.

The result is what I hope will stand as the definitive account of how the Yankees were built and operated—and, by extension, how baseball itself functioned and changed—in the Brian Cashman era.

The team has always featured big characters and big drama: prolific winning, but also Jeter versus Cashman, George Steinbrenner versus everyone, Jeter versus Alex Rodriguez, Cashman publicly telling A-Rod to "shut the fuck up," Gerrit Cole's use of advanced data to become one of the best pitchers in the sport, and Aaron Judge's pursuit of home run records and a massive contract.

There are infinite choices for moments at which to begin this tale, but let's rewind all the way to here: a hotel lobby in Cleveland, 1966, a rock-bottom moment from which the next fifty-plus years of Yankee history would rise.

PART ONE

GENE MICHAEL, GEORGE STEINBRENNER, AND THE FLYING HOT DOG

Rock Bottom

On April 19, 1966, Yankees stars Roger Maris and Elston Howard stood in the lobby of the Sheraton-Cleveland Hotel and discussed the night's opposing pitcher, Sam McDowell.

A woman and her husband approached.

"You're going to lose tonight, you know," the woman told the fading Yankee deities.

"[Is] that right?" Maris said.

"You know the Indians have a better team," the woman said.

"We'll show up," Howard said. "We've been here before."

The woman laughed and continued to tease the players, before asking for an autograph and leaving.

"Stupid broad," Maris said as she walked away. Then he mimicked her. "You're gonna lose," he said.

The "stupid broad" turned out to know of what she spoke. McDowell beat Yankees ace Mel Stottlemyre that night, dropping the Yanks to 1–6 on the season, tumbling toward a deeply unfamiliar void. The year before, New York had posted a losing record for the first time in forty years. Now they were on their way to their first last-place finish in fifty-three seasons.

The first era of Yankee dominance was finally winding down.

It had all begun on January 9, 1903, when Frank Farrell, a Lower East Side native who owned gambling houses and was sometimes referred to as the Pool Room King, and Big Bill Devery, a former New York City police chief who had once been arrested for bribery and extortion, purchased the rights to an AL franchise for $18,000.

The Yankees' official account holds that Farrell and Devery bought a defunct Baltimore club and moved it to New York. Other sources suggest that the pair might have instead purchased the rights to a new franchise—meaning that the Yankees did not, in fact, have roots in Baltimore. That remains inconclusive.

In any case, the ballclub that would become the Yankees played its first game in Manhattan on April 30, 1903, defeating Washington 6–2. In that era, team names were fluid and often determined by newspaper headlines; in recounting the opener, one paper called the New York AL club the "Deveryites," and another labeled them the "Invaders."

In those early years, the Hilltoppers and the Highlanders, references to the elevation of the team's Washington Heights ballpark, were common monikers. An April 7, 1904, headline in the *Evening Journal*—"Yankees Beat Boston"—marked an early appearance of the name that ultimately stuck.

After a largely mediocre first decade, the Yankees entered a new phase in 1915, when the beer baron Colonel Jacob Ruppert purchased the club with a partner, Tillinghast L'Hommedieu Huston (Ruppert bought out Huston in 1923).

Ruppert hired Red Sox manager Ed Barrow to run his front office. Barrow, an adept evaluator of talent, built the Murderers' Row teams of the 1920s and the dynasty of the 1930s and established the Yankee expectation of success that endures to this day.

Ruppert died in 1939. In 1945, his estate sold the team to Dan Topping, Del Webb, and Larry MacPhail. Topping and Webb bought out MacPhail in 1947 and went on to oversee yet another dynastic era in the 1950s before cashing out in 1964.

CBS's purchase of the Yankees that year coincided with a dark period for the franchise. The Yanks had won the World Series three times in the 1920s, five times in the 1930s, four times in the 1940s, and six times in the 1950s. The final gasps of Mickey Mantle and Whitey Ford's Rat Pack–era teams won a pair of titles in the early 1960s; then the franchise slipped into darkness.

The reasons for decline were many. Mantle's health and skills eroded. Maris, hampered by a hand injury, lost his power. Ford and infielders Bobby Richardson and Tony Kubek faded and would soon retire. Younger standouts like Jim Bouton, Joe Pepitone, and Tom Tresh did not find sustained success.

Meanwhile, broader changes to the business of baseball made it more difficult for the Yankees to build another championship core. For decades, New York's scouts had been able to woo high school kids and their parents with promises of pinstripe glory and annual World Series bonuses, and those kids were free to sign with them if they chose. In 1965, the creation of the amateur draft ended all that.

Suddenly the Yankees could not sign any player they wanted, but had to wait their turn in the draft order. With major-league free agency more than a decade away, the team was suddenly forced to behave like everyone else.

The Bronx Bombers had misplaced their mojo and would not find it for years. Still, the CBS ownership under President Mike Burke and GM Lee MacPhail quietly set to work building the next dynasty in ways that have gone largely uncredited in the decades since.

Here is where Yankee myth and Yankee reality begin to diverge. The legend goes that it took George Steinbrenner, scion of a Cleveland shipping family, onetime assistant football coach, and self-styled hard-ass, to rescue the franchise when he purchased it in 1973.

In fact, CBS planted seeds that began to blossom soon after Steinbrenner took over.

Recognizing that the old ways were no longer working, MacPhail initiated a rebuild, trading Maris, Howard, and longtime third baseman Clete Boyer. In 1968, he drafted catcher Thurman Munson, who would later become a Yankee captain. Three years later, he drafted future ace Ron Guidry. In 1972 he traded for reliever Sparky Lyle and third baseman Graig Nettles. All of those players went on to become pillars of the team's upcoming success.

Steinbrenner thus inherited a strong foundation. Then the mid-1970s brought a franchise-changing bit of luck tailored perfectly to his strengths as a recruiter: the advent of free agency. Steinbrenner set about augmenting the team's core with pricey stars like pitcher Catfish Hunter and slugger Reggie Jackson, then won championships in 1977 and 1978.

As MacPhail later wrote, "The general impression of people today is that CBS did not provide good ownership—that it would not spend money to improve the team. Actually CBS did everything in its power—under the baseball rules in force at the time—to improve the club. Scouting and player development budgets were increased and it gladly would have purchased players had there been good players available for purchase. And actually, the team did improve."

Steinbrenner, then, oversaw two dynasties: one in the late 1970s, with a core built under CBS ownership; and one in the late 1990s, with a core built by the legendary GM Gene Michael and staff (including Cashman) while Steinbrenner was banished from the game.

Yankee fans in the 2020s tend to deify Steinbrenner, who died in 2010. Hal Steinbrenner, George's son and successor as the Yankees' managing general partner, knows that prior generations held a different view. He experiences the contrast on a visceral level when fans boo him at the stadium and pine for a resurrection of his father.

"Everybody who criticizes me forgets that George was not well liked," Hal says. "Not at all. Particularly in the '80s."

But so persistent is the myth of Steinbrenner as savior that even Cashman has internalized it. He had no idea that CBS built the core of Steinbrenner's first dynasty.

"Really? Those players were there when George got here? Nettles? Munson?" Cashman said when I filled him in on the reality.

"Yeah."

"Wow."

So who was the actual savior of the Yankees, if it was not Steinbrenner himself?

If we want to be reductive enough to credit an individual for organizational success, we must take a long look at a shortstop who arrived soon after the day when Maris and the fan traded those salty barbs in a Cleveland hotel.

2

Enter Gene Michael

THE PLATFORM ON WHICH Gene Michael stood in Yankees lore is built on the bedrock of a flying hot dog. But first, some background.

Born in 1938 in Kent, Ohio, Eugene Richard "Stick" Michael played ten seasons as an infielder in the big leagues, including seven with the Yankees. He then served as a coach, an executive, a scout, a manager, and, crucially, the GM who oversaw the assemblage and retention of the last Yankee dynasty while mentoring Brian Cashman.

Michael was beloved by colleagues for both his baseball genius and his personal quirks.

"He was like the Nutty Professor," says Buck Showalter, the one-time Yankee farmhand and manager who became one of Michael's best friends. "He would come in with his hair all over the place, kind of off-kilter, and the shit-eating grin on his face."

"You know who he was?" says Billy Eppler, an assistant general manager for the Yankees during Michael's later years who later went on to become GM of the Los Angeles Angels and the New York Mets. "He was Doc Brown from *Back to the Future*. He was this genius who had this wild hair, the whole thing."

Michael came to the industry in an unlikely fashion—as a passionate practitioner of a different sport. He attended Kent State University on a basketball scholarship. After beginning a career as a professional basketball player, Michael in 1958 accepted a $25,000 signing bonus from the Pittsburgh Pirates.

"I don't think he was going to make near the money in basketball that he got in baseball, so he went with baseball," says Ron Brand, who knew Michael longer than anyone in the game. The two played together in the Pirates' minor-league system; decades later, Michael made Brand a top Yankees scout, a perch from which Brand influenced key acquisitions in the 1990s and moments in the team's 2009 World Series run.

Brand says that although Michael never let go of his love for basketball, baseball was more suited to his sharp intellect and ravenous curiosity.

"He regretted that he didn't go into basketball," Brand said. "That being said, when he committed to baseball, he began to really understand it. In basketball, if you've got the natural ability and you're not afraid, you can get pretty good at it. Football is the same way; it's more physical. Baseball is more of a mind game than any of the others. And he had a good mind for it."

Indeed, baseball reveals more to the viewer as his or her eye sharpens. As Michael came to know it, he quickly developed the confidence to advocate for himself in ways that would later disarm the Yankees' owner, George Steinbrenner, as no other manager or executive could. That began when Michael was still a minor leaguer in the 1950s.

"He got into it with a few managers," Brand says. "If they got on him and he didn't think it was right, he stood up for himself—like he was with George. When he felt that something was right, he committed to it."

Shouting matches with the Boss were decades in the future, but Michael foreshadowed that behavior as a Pirates prospect by pushing back on minor-league managers.

"If you don't like it, send me out!" he would shout at his elders when they criticized him.

"Stick was a nasty shortstop," Jim Price, a teammate in those minor-league years, said in an interview conducted shortly before his death in 2023. "If you slid into second base to try to break up a double play on him, he would bean you with the throw. He would be the first one to fight."

(It was Price who bestowed upon Michael the nickname that stuck, which began as a simple description of his six-foot-two, 180-pound frame. "I happened to see him in the shower, and I said, 'Man, you look like a stick,'" Price recalls. "And it stayed with him.")

While still playing in the minors, Michael came to trust his judgment of the strike zone so much that once, when a call went against him, he refused to return to the batter's box.

Finally, the ump told the pitcher to throw the ball. The pitcher obeyed, and the ump called a strike. Michael went nuts and was ejected.

Another time, a third baseman tagged Michael on the stomach, hard, as Michael slid into the bag. Michael shoved his opponent's glove with enough force to knock the ball into deep left field.

But while Michael "didn't take any crap," as Brand puts it, he also came to experience, and recover from, fear and failure in ways that enabled him to recognize which players were capable of doing the same.

In 1967, Pittsburgh traded Michael to the Los Angeles Dodgers in a deal that involved star shortstop Maury Wills. The larger stage rattled Michael in a way he hadn't experienced before.

"Going from Pittsburgh to Dodger Stadium, he told me, 'I locked up so I couldn't do anything—I got scared,'" Brand says.

"From then on he could tell when a player was playing scared, because he knew it. He knew how it felt, and he knew how the results looked. You see it in their actions and in their eyes; there's hesitancy rather than commitment. It's guys that get caught between bases—they change their mind and they're stuck. It's guys that are indecisive. And that's what he was that year. It really bugged him."

In November 1967, the Dodgers sold Michael to the Yankees. The following season, Michael bore witness to Mickey Mantle's physical decline—the sad end of the previous era.

"They talked Mickey into [coming back]," Michael, who died of a heart attack at age seventy-nine in 2017, told me in a 2014 interview. "He was going to retire the year before. He had wanted to retire, but it wasn't tough to talk him into playing. They were paying him $100,000, which was a ton of money back then."

Mantle's final game was at Boston's Fenway Park on September 28. He had survived the season with the help of Butazolidin, a strong anti-inflammatory, but because of side effects had weaned himself off it. As a result, he finished the year barely able to walk.

"The last two days [at Fenway], he could hardly go down the dugout steps," Michael said. "I know because I followed him one time."

The two had bonded that season over card playing, at which Michael proved far better. Even then, Stick knew how to bluff.

When the St. Moritz hotel in New York, where Mantle lived that season, sent the bill, Mantle joked to the manager, "Call Gene Michael. He's got all my cash. He'll write you a check."

With the Mantle era and all the mystique that came with it officially over, Michael was the Yankees' best player in 1969, batting .272 and establishing himself as a solid defender and heady player.

"When he went to the Yankees, he had that good year where he hit .270 and was their MVP," Brand says. "He learned to overcome his fears. And again, if you've done that, then you can see that another player can do that."

Now back to the hot dog.

Michael was still on the Yankees' roster when Steinbrenner announced his purchase of the team on January 3, 1973—almost exactly seventy years after Frank Farrell and Big Bill Devery created the franchise.

"We plan absentee ownership as far as running the Yankees," the soon-to-be Boss said at his introductory news conference. "We're not going to pretend we're something we aren't. I'll stick to building ships."

On an August afternoon in Dallas seven months later, Steinbrenner was nowhere near a shipyard. He had flown in to watch his team play the Rangers and was standing on the field while the players took pregame infield practice.

The drills proceeded as usual, set to the sounds of bats cracking, balls popping in gloves, and light chatter—until a six-foot-two, rail-thin player ran from the dugout to the field, shrieking and throwing his glove in the air.

As reported by his biographer, Bill Madden, Steinbrenner watched, horrified, as a hot dog launched from the glove, spun around in the air, and landed at his feet. He wrote down the player's uniform number in order to report him to the manager, Ralph Houk. He then demanded that Houk either discipline or trade this player for clowning around on the field.

Houk, barely able to keep from laughing, explained that the player's name was Gene Michael and it hadn't been his fault.

Michael, Houk said, suffered from a terrible fear of bugs, snakes, and other creepy-crawlies. A teammate had exploited this by stuffing the hot dog into a finger of Michael's glove and watching him panic once he discovered it.

After the game, Steinbrenner marched through the Yankees' clubhouse with a Texas state trooper, demanding to know who had pulled the prank. It was infielder Hal Lanier, but he was not arrested.

This was an inauspicious beginning with Steinbrenner, but at least the Boss now knew who Gene Michael was. Over time, Steinbrenner would come to trust Stick on a level that ran deeper than perhaps any other relationship he formed during his thirty-seven years running the Yankees.

When Houk quit after that season, he told the owner that Michael was a future GM or manager. Steinbrenner began referring to Michael as a "bright young executive type."

The owner also clearly admired Michael's brash, antiauthoritarian streak. Early in his ownership of the franchise, Steinbrenner established a rule that would survive him: no Yankee could have long hair or facial hair below the lip. Stars like Munson and Lou Piniella obeyed, but Michael pushed back.

"Are you going to pay for the haircut?" he asked.

When Steinbrenner said that he would, Michael pushed it further.

"Well, the least you could do is buy us all new suits, too," he said. "If the goal here is for us to look more presentable."

Steinbrenner nearly blew, but Michael grinned just in time. For some reason, he was able to get away with it, then and countless other times in the future.

By 1975, the two had developed a strong enough personal rapport that when Michael turned down GM Gabe Paul's offer of a $45,000 contract, and Paul countered by telling Michael he would release him, Michael invoked his relationship with the Boss.

"Does Mr. Steinbrenner know about this?" Michael asked.

The Boss did not intervene in that transaction. But when the Boston Red Sox released Michael in 1976, Steinbrenner brought him back for a long career as one of the most impactful employees the Yankees would ever have.

Before Michael ever became a GM, Steinbrenner forced him on his other favorite baseball son—the brilliant and paranoid Billy Martin.

3

Enter Billy; Exit Billy; Repeat

S TICK THIS."
   That was Billy Martin's reaction, expressed to his pitching coach and drinking buddy Art Fowler—and in full view of several Yankees beat reporters—when he learned that Gene Michael would be added to his staff in 1976.

A lifelong Yankee fan from his earliest days of a hardscrabble upbringing in Berkeley, California, Alfred Manuel Martin lived his dream in the 1950s as an infielder under his mentor, manager Casey Stengel. A career .257 hitter in the regular season, Martin rose to meet the moment nearly every October, posting a .333 average, with five home runs, across five World Series.

Always scrappy, Martin would push back on coaches on the field and party hard off it. In 1957, six Yankee players—Martin, Mantle, Ford, Yogi Berra, Hank Bauer, and pitcher Johnny Kucks—became entangled in a controversy involving a brawl at the Copacabana, a New York nightclub.

The front office made Martin the scapegoat of this stain on the Yankee aura and traded him to Kansas City. Martin lived out the rest of his career in outposts that lacked the glitz of Manhattan.

After his playing career ended, Martin managed in Minnesota, Detroit, and Texas before Steinbrenner brought him home on August 1, 1975. Between that day and December 25, 1989, when Martin died in a drunken car crash, the Boss would hire and fire him five times. It was an era marked by managerial brilliance but also booze, violence, and drama.

Forever obsessed with protecting his territory, Martin was no fan of Steinbrenner's decision to force Michael on him. It is a common thread in baseball for a manager to suspect one member of his coaching staff of being the eyes and ears of the front office, and Martin was especially paranoid.

"I wasn't a spy," Michael told author Bill Pennington more than thirty years later. "I know Billy hated me being there. But I was supposed to help implement some things and report to George how they were going. I know it wasn't a usual arrangement but I was not running back to George about things that were none of my business. I wasn't spying. I was trying to help Billy. Not that he believed me."

For the next several years, as Martin came and went and the Yankees won championships in 1977 and 1978, Michael tried on different roles in the organization. Late in the 1979 season, while Michael was managing the Yankees' Triple-A affiliate in Columbus, Ohio, Steinbrenner offered to make him the Yankees' general manager at the end of the season. Michael, just forty-one years old, was excited by the chance to shape an entire organization.

Soon after, Martin nearly derailed that plan. On October 23 of that year, he and a friend were drinking at a hotel bar in Bloomington, Minnesota. Also there was Joseph Cooper, a fifty-two-year-old marshmallow salesman from Illinois.

The group started talking baseball, and Cooper opined that Montreal's Dick Williams was his choice for 1979 Manager of the Year, even though Baltimore's Earl Weaver had done a good job, too.

It never took much to provoke Martin into a fight. This perceived slight did the job.

"They are both assholes, and you're an asshole too for saying it," the Yankee manager said. "I want to go outside and whip your ass."

Martin dug in his pocket for five $100 bills, then smacked them down on the bar.

"Tell you what, Joe," he said. "Here is $500 to your penny I can knock you on your ass."

Cooper placed a penny on top of the bills, and the two headed toward the door. He barely made it that far: as Martin reached the archway that led outside, he turned around and sucker punched Cooper.

Cooper needed fifteen stitches, and Martin lost his job. The day after the incident, Steinbrenner told Michael that he would be the new Yankee manager.

"But you said I was going to be the general manager," Michael said.

"That was before I needed a manager."

Michael had to scramble to keep his new gig in the executive suite. He persuaded Steinbrenner to hire as manager Dick Howser, a highly respected former Yankees coach who was then the head baseball coach at Florida State University. With Howser in place as manager, Michael that fall set to work on the roster for the first time as a GM.

He showed an immediate aptitude for the job. Less than a week into his tenure, Michael traded first baseman Chris Chambliss to Toronto for left-handed pitcher Tom Underwood and catcher Rick Cerone. Cerone had the challenging task of replacing Munson, the Yankee captain who had died in an airplane crash the previous summer. Cerone ultimately stuck with the team for five years.

Michael also signed first baseman Bob Watson and left-handed pitcher Rudy May. All of the players acquired performed well, and the Yankees won 103 games and an American League East title. They fell to the Kansas City Royals in a three-game sweep of the American League Championship Series.

A few days after the ALCS, reporters called Howser to ask him about Steinbrenner's rumored plan to hire one of his Florida racetrack buddies, Don Zimmer, to coach third base.

"I would think I should be given the courtesy of approving or disapproving the coaches that are added to the ballclub," Howser said.

That perceived insubordination was enough for Steinbrenner, who promptly informed Michael that he was the new manager. The Boss later reversed that decision and told Michael to call Howser and ask him to return. Howser refused, citing the stress of working for Steinbrenner.

Howser went on to become a World Series–winning manager for the Royals, and Stick was stuck with the Yankee job.

The 1981 season was a miserable time for both Michael and the sport. On June 12 the players went on strike for fifty days; when they returned, Michael's veteran team struggled, at one point losing six of seven games in August.

Steinbrenner grew itchy, demanding that Michael pinch-hit for the slumping superstar Reggie Jackson. On August 26, Steinbrenner ordered Jackson to undergo a complete physical examination.

"He's just trying to embarrass me," Jackson told the press.

Two days later, after another Yankees loss, Jackson returned to the visitors' clubhouse at Chicago's Comiskey Park after his physical and refused to talk to reporters. As Jackson disappeared into the trainers' room, Michael summoned the writers into his office.

"What can you tell us about Reggie?" asked reporter Moss Klein, who covered the team for the Newark *Star-Ledger*.

"Reggie's fine," Michael said. "But I don't want to talk about Reggie. I have something else to say."

He organized a few sheets of yellow legal paper on his desk, then launched into a monologue that challenged Steinbrenner as no employee ever had in public.

"I heard from George again today," Michael said. "I'm tired of getting the phone calls after games and being told again that it's my fault that we lost. I thought I knew what I was getting into when I accepted this job, but I didn't expect it to be this direct and this constant."

The writers stole glances at one another, wondering if Michael was joking. But he stared back at them, frowning.

"When I was general manager last year, George used to tell me he was going to fire Howser, but he never told Howser," Michael continued.

"But with me, he keeps telling me: 'Stick, I think I'm going to have to let you go.' So when he said it to me again today, I said: 'Fine. Do it now. Don't wait. I don't want to manage under these circumstances. Fire me and get it over with or stop threatening me. I can't manage this way. I've had enough.' I don't think people know what it's like to work for him."

The writers hustled upstairs to the press box to bang out stories about Michael's inflammatory comments. On their way, they found Steinbrenner sitting in the stands with a group of guests.

"Any discussions I would have with my manager are not public," the owner said. "If he thinks talking about it will help, that's his problem."

As columnist Dave Anderson wrote in *The New York Times,* "Not even Billy Martin ever stood up to George Steinbrenner that boldly and that publicly."

For the next eight days, Steinbrenner enacted a punishment worse than firing: he left Michael hanging. He told a national television audience on the NBC Game of the Week that he was mulling it over. Then he finally dismissed Michael and rehired Bob Lemon, who had guided the team to a championship as manager in 1978.

A week later, Steinbrenner summoned Michael to Yankee Stadium, told him that he thought of him "like a son," and offered him a job in the front office.

Michael declined, but his self-imposed exile did not last long: fourteen games into the 1982 season, Steinbrenner fired Lemon and lured Michael back into the dugout.

Did that appointment last long? It did not.

At 1:05 a.m. on August 4, following losses of 1–0 and 14–2 to the White Sox in a doubleheader, Steinbrenner marched into the Yankee Stadium press room and announced that Michael was out after eighty-six games. The on-again/off-again pitching coach Clyde King would become the team's third skipper of the season.

It was the tenth managerial change Steinbrenner had made in his first ten years as owner, the most in baseball during that span.

"I wish sometimes you could let go some of the players instead of the manager," Steinbrenner told the tired writers that night.

"But that's not how the game is structured. We have some players who aren't as good as they think they are. I'm not blaming Stick. I just feel a change is necessary. I'm not going to beat around the bush. I'm just saying the change has been made and I hope Clyde does a good job."

Still riding that Steinbrenner wave, Michael was back in the front office in 1983 and on the coaching staff in 1984. When the two weren't screaming at each other, they bonded over their passion for horses and ate out together in Tampa. It was a complex relationship that, like Brian Cashman in later decades, Michael would find himself unable—or, for some reason, unwilling—to sever.

This pull, on the surface, is confusing. Why did Stick always return?

"The money," Cashman said flatly in 2023. "And while I'm sure in the beginning he didn't like working in that environment, over time there was a bond.

"George, he was the Boss," Cashman continued. "He had a real gift for, when he wanted something, finding a way to get it. He was a charmer. He could touch on all the right notes and say all the right things and be quite convincing. And you know what? It's the New York Yankees, too. It's still the greatest sports franchise. He made them relevant again. It was the epicenter of the baseball world. Obviously no place on this planet is perfect. But it was a combination of his charm, his ability to recruit and close deals, his ability to pay people well.

"Over time, because of working relationships, bonds get developed and loyalties start to take hold, and I think all those would apply [to why Michael stayed]."

"With Stick and my dad, it was almost a Billy Martin–type relationship," says Hal Steinbrenner. "My dad loved Billy Martin, and vice versa. Stick was the kind of guy who was gonna throw it right back in George's face. He was not going to put up with George's stuff, and he was going to give it right back to him. Those are the type of individuals that my dad ended up, through all his businesses, developing relationships with. He liked that."

As Michael himself put it to Pennington shortly before his death, "I taught [Steinbrenner] a lot of baseball, and there was no one he listened to more than me when the topic was baseball. But at the same time, he taught me a lot about hard work and how to use your strengths. He was impatient, difficult and a pain in the butt, but he was a teacher and a mentor, too."

4

The Baseball Philosophies That Would Define a Dynasty

Michael Lewis's 2003 bestseller, *Moneyball,* famously highlighted the Oakland Athletics executives Sandy Alderson and Billy Beane as pioneers of on-base percentage, or a player's ability to draw a walk. Alderson and Beane came to see that walks, long undervalued in the sport, were actually one of the most effective ways to produce runs and, by extension, wins.

Alderson, an attorney and former marine who had no baseball experience before working for the A's, utilized the work of statistician Bill James to bring analytics into a baseball front office beginning in the early 1980s. He was an outsider and came at his ideas from a necessity borne out of an initial ignorance of baseball.

On the other side of the country, Gene Michael—a former ballplayer—was quietly implementing many of the same concepts, without reading James and without the later literary fanfare that found Alderson and especially Beane.

The two organizations rarely discussed their common principles, save for a moment in the fall of 1995 when Oakland met with Buck Showalter for a managerial opening after Steinbrenner fired him as skipper of the Yankees.

"When I went to interview with Oakland, that's all Sandy and Billy Beane wanted to talk about," Showalter says. "All they were interested in was the on-base percentage thing that Stick and I were pushing in New York. And now they act like it was something new."

Indeed, while OBP wouldn't become a point of public discussion around the Yankees for several decades, Michael emphasized it with players as far back as the late 1970s.

In Willie Randolph, a longtime Yankees second baseman, Michael had a prototype for what he would look for in building the 1990s teams.

Back in the 1970s and 1980s, middle infielders were expected to field their positions well, hit singles, bunt, and steal bases. The ability to draw a walk was not a prerequisite. Randolph, though, had a naturally selective eye. He led the league in walks in 1980 and produced an excellent career on-base percentage of .373 across eighteen seasons.

"Stick and I talked about the analytics and on-base percentage back then," Randolph says. "He was one of the first guys to really recognize how important that was to winning. I think the reason we were so close was that he saw me as a guy who understood my role, my job. I was a table setter. I did whatever it took—to get a walk if not a hit, whichever it was—to get on base and set the table.

"Stick was one of the first that really kind of talked to me about the game, about different parts of the game. Middle infielders, we have this little kinship where we look out for each other and learn from each other. That is what I really remember from my earliest time with the Yankees; from a coaching standpoint, Stick was there for me all the time."

Michael and Randolph's bond over baseball values did become awkward at contract time, when Randolph felt compelled to point out that the skills Michael emphasized were not the same ones for which the Yankees were paying.

"We would talk contracts, and we had things back then like at bats that we got paid for in our incentives," Randolph says. "And I remember talking about that: 'We have to change the language in my contract, because if you're telling me I'm getting paid for at bats, I'm not gonna be taking these walks [a walk does not count as an at bat].'

"He said, 'You make a good point, because I don't want you to start swinging away. I want you to do what you do. And if you take the walk, that's good for us.'"

Most of Michael's close friends and associates, including Ron Brand and Cashman, do not recall when, where, or why Michael began to focus on OBP. But Billy Eppler, a co-worker in the Yankees' front office during Michael's later years, managed to extract the answer.

"Where did it come from? Strat-O-Matic," Eppler says, referring to the popular baseball board game invented in the 1960s. "One hundred percent. He said he figured out the game when he was young. He looked at how much the walks were worth relative to trying to get the hit. 'I'm playing the odds, I'm playing the probabilities,' he would say."

Showalter offers his own theory as to why Michael valued OBP.

"Stick would tell you that he wasn't a very good hitter," Showalter says. " 'Okay, so how can I help? Maybe by not striking out. Maybe by playing defense.' Stick could fly, by the way. That man could run. 'Maybe I could walk?' Back then a lot of the guys who hit well didn't walk too much."

For the record, Michael's career OBP as a player was a paltry .288. But if he lacked the ability to draw walks himself, he understood the value of that skill. He also knew how to spot countless other hidden qualities.

"Stick really had a knack for player evaluation," says Brian Sabean, the three-time World Series–winning San Francisco Giants GM who began his professional baseball career in the Yankees' front office in 1985.

"Especially at the major-league level, he had an eye for what he liked and what he wanted to build with the Yankee rosters."

It was that eye, beyond even his identification of on-base percentage as a key stat, that elevated Michael to the status of baseball savant.

5

"Off Ball"

How Stick Scouted

Buck Showalter and Gene Michael met in the late 1970s, when Buck was still a Yankee minor leaguer named William Nathaniel "Nat" Showalter III, a folksy but intellectually ravenous son of a high school principal from Century, Florida (Nat was soon rechristened Buck for his propensity to roam the locker room buck naked—meaning that, yes, two of the most important men in recent Yankee history were named while standing around in the nude).

Almost immediately, the two began what turned into a decades-long conversation about the nuances of a game they both saw with greater clarity than nearly anyone else.

In his own journey toward becoming a four-time Manager of the Year and one of the most respected skippers in the history of the sport, Showalter trained his eye based on a concept learned from scouting with Michael: the importance of "off ball" evaluation.

Watching a baseball game, the viewer is naturally drawn to the ball—the pitcher throwing it, the sound and path of it off a bat, the fielders chasing it. But great scouts like Michael know to look elsewhere and scrutinize other moments.

It goes without saying that a player must be able to handle the baseball when it is hit to him. Michael discovered that what often separates the players you keep from the players you discard is how they behave when the ball is nowhere near them.

Is the right fielder fully engaged on a groundout to second base? Is the pitcher backing up third? And who in the dugout is focused on the game? These questions, passed down from Michael, resonated with Showalter like few notions he encountered.

Once in Paul O'Neill's early years as a Yankee, a teammate hit a ball down the right-field line. O'Neill was seated in a spot in the dugout with an obstructed view, so he jumped up, excited, and craned his neck to see what was happening.

At the time, apathy defined the Yankees' clubhouse culture. Outfielder Mel Hall, for example, never turned his neck on the bench to follow the flight of the ball, and he wasn't the only one.

Feeling subtle peer pressure to disengage, O'Neill quickly sat down. Showalter looked at him, smiled, and said, "I got you now." That was off-ball player evaluation.

"The story of a game is told off ball," Showalter says. "By watching this, Stick sniffed out phonies in a heartbeat."

As Showalter—and later Billy Eppler, who started working for the Yankees in 2004 as a scout and became assistant general manager in 2011—would discover, sitting in the stands with Michael was an education in how to sharpen one's scouting eye.

"That's how I started," Eppler says. "That's how I learned to evaluate at a deeper level, or a more granular level—sitting there with him and watching every pitch come in."

During Yankees spring training games, Eppler would make sure to park himself next to Michael in the scouting section, which was always a few rows behind home plate. Many rival scouts like to sit near one another and gossip; Michael, while friendly, sat off to the side, all the better to concentrate.

As the game began, he would nudge Eppler with a bony elbow.

"Billy Boy," he would say. "What do you see on this kid? What do you think?"

Michael would listen as Eppler developed and articulated his own insights. But he would also occasionally reveal the nuances that he perceived.

"Look at that guy on deck," Michael would say. "He looks like a really good concentrator."

Eppler would home in on the player preparing for his at bat and notice how closely that player was watching the pitcher. *Oh,* he would think. *Stick is talking about the process that leads toward the result we value. The desired outcome is to get on base. And he is talking to me about the process behind that.*

From this level of concentration came an uncanny knack for knowing during spring training when a player was ready for the season. Eppler once watched Andy Pettitte pitch in a late March exhibition in Florida, holding the radar gun while Michael sat with a yellow legal pad on his lap.

On each pitch, Michael would write down the velocity, along with an assortment of other observations: the pitch type, a note that said, "Strike/ball" or "swing and foul." Then he would make a line across the pad and do the same all over again—a total of hundreds of times over the course of the game.

"He knew what was happening on every single pitch," Eppler says. "Then, and I can still remember this as clear as day, Andy was three or four innings in and Stick looked over at me, put his pen down on the pad in his lap, and said, 'He's ready. He's ready for the season. Look at the pitch sequences. Look at the velocities.'

"Same thing with the hitters. He looked at each pitch that came in. Did they swing at it or did they not? He would talk about, 'That was a good swing.' Or, 'That was a little overaggressive.' He was calculating it in his mind. I wasn't at that level, so I had to write it down.

"He could sit there and say, 'Okay, what do I think the concentration or focus level of this player is, based on his decisions to swing or not swing?' Then, as a former player, he would always be able to go right to game situations to make that call. Runner on, score, inning—should he be swinging at that pitch? It's not as simple—it's not binary—as swing or no swing. And so I learned how to evaluate using that approach."

A key in Michael's evaluation of a hitter's ability to draw walks and get on base was a phrase he appears to have invented, and often repeated: "Can he quit on the baseball?"

Eppler explains, "What that meant was when you watch a hitter, and you see him in swing mode as the pitcher enters his delivery and windup—once the ball is in flight, at release, and points after release, do you see the hitter's shoulders or hands relax? Sometimes a hitter puts the bat back on the shoulder. Sometimes his shoulders sink; sometimes his hands drop. Stick would call that 'quitting on the baseball.'"

Eppler himself was a college pitcher and understood how demoralizing it was when a hitter quit on one of his offerings.

"It's really frustrating for pitchers," he says. "I can speak from experience from a much lower level. I did not have overpowering tools. I could not throw my fastball by people, so I had to pitch off the edges [of the strike zone] to that power hitter. When I would see his bat go down on his shoulders, basically acting like the pitch I threw was not even competitive—it's very deflating on the mound."

Michael would look for this quality and become excited when he found it.

"'Oh, man, Jason Giambi [.399 career on-base percentage],' he would say. 'Look at him quit on the baseball.

"'Bobby Abreu [.395 career OBP], look at him quit on the baseball. Look at Gary Sheffield [.393 OBP] quit on the baseball. Look at that bat speed. Look at how he ripped through the zone. Look at how he quit on the baseball.'"

Body language in the batter's box was hardly the only subtlety that Michael noticed.

"He watched the game within the game," Showalter says. "He saw the game from a different prism; for example, he might scout how a guy takes ground balls from the first baseman between innings.

"I remember one time Omar Vizquel [perhaps the greatest defensive shortstop of the 1990s and early 2000s] caught a throw down from the catcher between innings with the back of his glove. Stick got such a big kick out of that. He said that guys like Vizquel can get bored, so they look for different ways to do it.

"He told me, 'Never take the imagination away from an infielder from Latin America. They played on these awful fields. When they catch the ball, they're trying not to get killed. Don't try to turn them into something they're not. Let them have that flow. Let them have that imagination. Let them have that individuality.'"

It wasn't just Showalter and Eppler sitting at Michael's side over the years, soaking up his extreme attention to detail. Brian Cashman himself, while not a scout, spent enough time with Michael to understand what the Yankees should look for in players.

These principles were consistent across eras. Cashman remembers an early-career review that Michael gave Andrew McCutchen, who went on to become the National League MVP for the Pittsburgh Pirates in 2013.

"One April he was watching Andrew McCutchen in the on-deck circle and how focused McCutchen was," Cashman says. "And in the box, he would describe his mannerisms as 'no panic.' He's like, 'This guy is gonna be a great player, because he's got no panic, and he's got focus.'"

In 2018, the year after Michael died, Cashman traded for McCutchen to fortify the Yankee outfield during a playoff race.

Says Brian Sabean, legendary Giants GM, "In order to evaluate, the first thing is, you gotta pay attention. You've got to be in deep thought at games, just zeroed in.

"Gene just had a knack for seeing somebody's body language, along with their baseball tools and their physical abilities. How they play the game, if they were a cut above, or they were more or less going to be in a mediocre category. He also was a big believer in character, and he was a believer that being a Yankee—the press, the pressure from ownership—wasn't for everybody. His evaluations were not fleeting."

Watching a player's shoulders, hands, eyes. His head and face. Subtle signs of enthusiasm or apathy. It was with this uniquely specific style of player evaluation that Michael would oversee the construction of the next Yankee dynasty.

It was an opportunity he likely would never have received if not for a further escalation of Steinbrenner's misbehavior.

How Stick Got the Chance to
Run the Yankees Again

E VER SINCE THE EARLY 1980s, George Steinbrenner had been at war with star outfielder Dave Winfield. The Boss had courted Winfield as a free agent in the 1980–81 offseason, seeing him as a shiny new replacement for Reggie Jackson, who was thirty-four years old and about to enter the final year of his contract.

Days after reeling in his target, Steinbrenner discovered that he had misunderstood cost-of-living escalators in the ten-year agreement, pushing its potential value significantly higher than he had expected. It was the Yankees' mistake, but Steinbrenner fought it.

It didn't help when Winfield went 1-for-22 that year in a World Series loss to the Dodgers. Steinbrenner later nicknamed him Mr. May, a pointed contrast to Jackson's Mr. October moniker. The tone was set for a toxic relationship.

Also in Winfield's contract was a provision calling for Steinbrenner to make an annual contribution of $300,000 to the outfielder's charitable foundation. Steinbrenner, upset about the escalator clauses, refused to make the contributions.

The two spent years in and out of litigation over the issue, which underscored the depth of Steinbrenner's antipathy toward Winfield; he was generally a softy for needy cases, eager to give money to anyone who asked.

"I can't tell you how many times over the years people have stopped me on the street and said, 'I don't know who else to tell this to, but George Steinbrenner secretly paid for my college,'" says

Suzyn Waldman, the longtime Yankee broadcaster. "He could be very generous."

But the Boss's heart remained cold to Winfield and his foundation, and he went to increasingly questionable lengths to undermine Winfield himself.

Toward the end of the 1980s, Yankees beat reporters began to receive late-night phone calls in their hotel rooms from a shadowy figure named Howie Spira, who said he had damning information about "that bastard Winfield."

The writers had seen Spira around Yankee Stadium, where he worked as a freelance radio reporter. Spira claimed to have worked for Winfield and said that the outfielder had made usurious loans to him, threatened him, and misused funds from his foundation. Spira even alleged that Winfield's agent wrote a fake death threat letter addressed to Winfield during the 1981 World Series, to deflect attention from Winfield's poor performance.

"I just had a really icky feeling about this Howie Spira," says Michael Kay, the longtime Yankee broadcaster who in 1990 covered the team for the New York *Daily News*. "I'd had some dealings with him and just didn't feel good about it."

Kay and the other reporters knew that Spira was a heavy gambler, and they did not consider him credible, but, as it turned out, Steinbrenner did. The Boss paid Spira $40,000 in exchange for damning information on Winfield, and to stop Spira's attempts to extort him.

Predictably, this payment led to further, increasingly aggressive attempts at extracting money from Steinbrenner. Spira harassed the Boss and his family and was ultimately arrested and sentenced to two and a half years in federal prison for extortion.

But Steinbrenner had not won. Unbeknownst to him, Spira had been cooperating with Richard Pienciak, an investigative reporter at the New York *Daily News*. On March 18, 1990, the paper ran an exposé about the Yankee owner paying a gambler for dirt on his own star player.

The article shocked assistant farm director Brian Cashman and other Yankee rank and filers into realizing that the franchise was about to change forever.

"I was in such a low level of employment that it wasn't something

I was aware of until all hell broke loose—when that story came out and it became a big issue with Major League Baseball and the commissioner was dealing with it," Cashman says. "Before that it wasn't anything that I was even aware of."

The Spira affair quickly leaped into the forefront of consciousness for every Yankee employee and fan, most of whom were tired of Steinbrenner and rooting for change.

On July 30, the commissioner of Major League Baseball, Fay Vincent, handed down a two-year suspension for Steinbrenner. It was the owner's second such penalty; in 1974, the MLB commissioner, Bowie Kuhn, had suspended Steinbrenner for two years for making illegal contributions to Richard Nixon's presidential campaign (that ban was later reduced to fifteen months).

Bizarrely, Steinbrenner instead asked to resign as Yankees managing general partner and be placed on baseball's permanently ineligible list. At the time, he served as a vice president of the U.S. Olympic Committee and was concerned that having the word "suspension" attached to his name would cost him that position.

"He was essentially bargaining a two-year suspension into a lifetime ban," Vincent later told author Bill Pennington. "And that was a silly deal. I tried to talk him out of it. I said, 'You'll go on the permanently ineligible list.' But I don't think he understood that it was actually a lifetime thing. It was a terrible mistake."

Vincent finally agreed to what he called a "very strange" decision by Steinbrenner. MLB did allow the Boss to remain involved in the Yankees' radio and television contracts, banking matters, concessions contracts, leases, and government dealings. His family was permitted to retain its ownership stake. But the Boss himself was banned from baseball.

In preparing for his exit, Steinbrenner first tried to designate his thirty-three-year-old son, Hank, as the new managing general partner, but Hank declined.

George spoke of his younger son, Harold, a twenty-year-old senior at Williams College and his father's temperamental opposite, as an eventual successor. But Harold, who went by Hal, was too young.

At that time, Hank was better known to Yankees employees than Hal because he worked in baseball operations. Cashman's early memories of both are fuzzy.

"When I was an intern, Hank was involved in amateur scouting, so I definitely knew him [by the time of George's suspension]," Cashman says. "I'm not sure if I had met Hal back then or not. I know I met him after college, because he was working for the Yankees in New York then."

The important Cashman-Hal relationship was still years in the future. But it turns out that Hal did, in fact, become involved in team operations during the suspension, when his family asked him to step in.

"To whom much has been given, much is expected of, right?" Hal Steinbrenner says. "I just wanted to help the family, especially given the fact that he was out of baseball. Did I ever see myself succeeding him [at that time]? I think at twenty-two, with George in his prime—I don't know that anybody ever thought he would retire. So no, I didn't think it then. I just wanted to be there, wanted to help the family and put eyes on the organization with him out of baseball. That was kind of my duty, if you will."

With Hal present but not ready for the top job, his father elevated Robert Nederlander, a Yankees limited partner, to the role of managing general partner.

On the evening of July 30, 1990, Vincent announced the decision at a news conference in midtown Manhattan. The Yankees were playing in the Bronx—losing again, and in possession of the worst record in baseball.

As word of Steinbrenner's ban spread around the stadium via transistor radio, many of the 24,037 fans erupted in cheers and chants of "No more George! No more George!" that drowned out "Take Me Out to the Ballgame" in the seventh-inning stretch. Yankee broadcaster Tony Kubek suggested on air that the team hold a "Howie Spira Day."

Why was the public so happy? After all, Steinbrenner had captured two championships in the 1970s, and the Yankees had posted a cumulative winning record in the 1980s, albeit one that came with no postseason appearances after 1981.

But to most Yankee fans, it had been clear for several years that the franchise was headed in the wrong direction. The team was spiraling toward a ninety-five-loss season in 1990, and after more than a decade of Billy Martin and Dave Winfield drama, not to mention the hiring and firing of more managers and GMs than any other owner, Steinbrenner's behavior had caught up with him. The impatient owner had ordered his GMs to trade away prospects, and he had chased free agents who did not succeed the way Reggie Jackson and Catfish Hunter had earlier.

The team's biggest star of the era, first baseman Don Mattingly, had been in frequent conflict with Steinbrenner and by 1990 was in decline on the field, as was Winfield and All-Star closer Dave Righetti. The Yankees finished that season in last place—their first visit to the basement since 1966, the year that a "dumb broad" in Cleveland had so offended Roger Maris. Steinbrenner had led the team all the way back to the grim place from which he had supposedly rescued it.

However much the public would later lionize Steinbrenner in retrospect, in real time it cast him as a Yankee villain.

"Talk about a narrative that changed over the years," says a Yankee official from that time. "George was hated at the time. Hated. Later, when the team was winning, everyone was paying homage to him and throwing bouquets at him, and it changed the perception. But at the time he was suspended, it was like, 'Ding-dong, the witch is dead.' The team winning later in his life gave him a softer landing, but he was much more controversial at the time."

Steinbrenner's final day in charge was August 20. At 6:00 that evening, he held a news conference at Yankee Stadium and presented himself as at peace with the decision.

"I am not remorseful; I am not in shock," he said.

Then, in his final move as owner of the Yankees—or so it seemed at the time—he announced that Gene Michael would once again serve as general manager, replacing Pete Peterson. The reporters covering the news conference had no idea that Steinbrenner was about to put Michael in charge.

"No one knew," says Michael Kay. "The reason he went to Gene Michael, in retrospect, is that he really trusted Gene to always do the right thing for the organization and never do anything for Gene. He knew how honorable Gene Michael was."

Michael, who had been working as a Yankees scout at the time, inherited a mess comparable to what CBS ownership faced when it took over the team in the mid-1960s. Although the Yankees were already making headway in drafting and player development at the minor-league level, the organization under Steinbrenner lacked an overarching direction.

Just as he did during his first term as GM a decade earlier, Michael had an immediate effect. He stood by as Righetti signed as a free agent with the San Francisco Giants, because he had been scouting the pitcher closely enough to see signs of aging. Sure enough, Righetti struggled as a Giant. Michael then acquired closer Steve Howe and starter Scott Sanderson, both of whom pitched well for the Yanks.

Buck Showalter, who became a Yankees coach in 1990 and manager in 1992, was at Michael's side during these Steinbrenner-free years.

"Stick had four or five guys in the farm system he identified as keepers," Showalter says. "Mariano Rivera, Andy Pettitte, Jorge Posada, Bernie Williams, even Gerald Williams, who we thought would be a great fourth outfielder. If Mr. Steinbrenner hadn't been suspended, I doubt we would've been able to keep those guys. I remember him telling Stick to trade Bernie: 'He's overrated, da da da.' Stick just maneuvered around behind the scenes to keep it from happening."

To Showalter, Michael proved a wily executive, able to con rivals into trades that proved favorable to the Yankees. At the 1991 Winter Meetings, Michael and Showalter hosted in their hotel suite Chicago White Sox general manager Ron Schueler, and Eddie Brinkman, one of his top scouts. After engaging in the standard chatter about potential trades, Schueler and Brinkman stood to say their goodbyes.

"Oh, by the way, before you guys leave," Michael said in a casual, almost tossed-off way. "We would probably think about moving Sax if we had to."

In fact, the Yankees were extremely eager to dump Steve Sax, a onetime All-Star second baseman who was set to make $3.6 million the following season. Sax had batted .304 for the Yankees in 1991, but Michael's sharp scouting eye saw impending decline.

To hear him tell it to the White Sox, Michael was barely inclined to consider a deal.

"We don't want to move Sax," he said. "But anyway, just chew on that if you have any interest. Just want to throw that out there before you leave."

Schueler continued toward the door, then turned back.

"If we did have any interest in a guy like Sax, what would you be looking for in return?" he asked.

Michael shrugged.

"I don't know," he said. "We'll kick it around. I doubt we're going to move the guy. He's too good a player. But I'll look at it."

Schueler and Brinkman left, and the door closed. Michael turned to Showalter with a Cheshire grin.

"I got a fucking nibble!" he said, giddy. "I got a nibble!"

More than thirty years later, Showalter still marvels at the performance. "He threw that fucking hook out there and I was like, 'Jesus Christ, that's good,'" he says.

The month after planting that seed, Michael traded Sax to Chicago for pitchers Mélido Pérez, Bob Wickman, and Domingo Jean. Pérez pitched four seasons for the Yankees, and Wickman five. Sax's batting average dropped to .236 in his first season with the White Sox, and he was out of the game two years later.

"Stick used to keep a list in his back pocket called 'Other People's Problems,'" Showalter says. "His point to me was you could trade anybody if you didn't care what you were getting back. Because there's some people that have problems as bad, if not worse, than yours."

Later in his GM tenure, one of Michael's (and Showalter's) problems was Danny Tartabull, an outfielder who had signed a big contract with the Yankees, then gone on to frustrate team brass by what they perceived as an unwillingness to play.

Michael told Showalter that he was going to move Tartabull. Showalter was highly skeptical that Michael could find a taker.

"If you can trade Tartabull, I will kiss your butt at home plate," Showalter said.

Michael proceeded to find another person's problem in Rubén Sierra, a talented outfielder who was clashing with Oakland's manager, Tony La Russa. He swung a Tartabull-for-Sierra trade.

As he walked into the manager's office at Yankee Stadium to inform Showalter that Tartabull was no longer a Yankee, Michael started to unbuckle his pants. It was time for Showalter to deliver on that kiss; apparently, Michael couldn't even wait to get to home plate.

"Wait a minute," Showalter said. "What did you get for him?"

"No, no, no, no," Michael said, undoing the button. "That wasn't part of the deal."

But if there was a single trade that embodied Michael's evaluative genius, his savvy negotiating skills, and his vision for the dynasty to come, it wasn't the Sax or Tartabull deals.

It was the move that reverberated around the organization for decades to come—the one about which young up-and-comers in the front office would quiz Michael for the rest of his life.

7

Billy Eppler Asks the Right Question

BILLY EPPLER'S FIRST GOAL was to make sure that Gene Michael felt comfortable during the long flight from Los Angeles to Tokyo, but there was also a question he'd been holding on to for quite a while. Now was the time to ask it.

This was 2011, and Eppler was a thirty-five-year-old executive on the ascent, about to be promoted to assistant general manager. Michael was by then a baseball guru emeritus for the Yankees. The pair had traveled together before, but typically on shorter trips to see the team's minor-league affiliates in the eastern United States.

Now the two met from separate locations at LAX airport to make a connection to Japan and scout one of the highest-profile players to ever become available on the international market, pitcher Yu Darvish.

This long flight presented an opportunity for Eppler to even better understand Michael's methods. One particular inquiry burned in his mind.

As the plane took off, Eppler turned to Michael.

"Hey, I've got a question for you," he said.

"Yeah, Billy Boy?" Michael said, his white hair mussed as usual, and his baritone, which he was forever unable to modulate, filling the entire cabin.

"How," Eppler asked, "did you have the guts to trade Roberto Kelly for Paul O'Neill?"

If Eppler was looking to unlock a deeper understanding of

what made the Yankees the Yankees, he was asking about the right transaction.

The Yanks finished the 1992 season with a 76–86 record. To the casual observer, it seemed that Kelly was one of their few promising players, a homegrown center fielder who, at twenty-seven years old, had made the American League All-Star team that year.

But Michael's sharp eye saw beyond that surface. Kelly was not selective enough at the plate to fit Michael's preferred approach. He was a right-handed batter, and Michael wanted more lefties, who were more likely to hit home runs over Yankee Stadium's short porch in right field. And the Yankees had an outfield prospect in Bernie Williams (.394 on-base percentage in the minor leagues) ready to take over in center.

"The poor guy just really wasn't a fit," Showalter says of Kelly. "And Stick knew it. He saw Kelly as probably a fourth outfielder on a championship team."

Mulling his ever-present list of Other People's Problems, Michael identified O'Neill, the intense Cincinnati Reds right fielder who was clashing with his manager, the equally intense Lou Piniella. Michael had known Piniella for decades and suspected that the two were simply too much alike.

"Stick loved Piniella, but he knew that he and O'Neill weren't a good match," Showalter says.

O'Neill would beat up watercoolers after striking out and scream at umpires; once, he even kicked a ball in anger after bobbling it in the outfield. Those traits typically marked a player as selfish and rendered him unpopular among teammates, but Michael thought that O'Neill's intensity could be corralled. He believed that the Yankees could use a player who cared as much as O'Neill did. Michael also understood—from scouting, if not from this exact stat—that Kelly's 6.7 percent career walk rate at the time was significantly lower than O'Neill's 10.3 percent.

Kelly was popular with fans, or at least as popular as a player on a losing team could be, but he wasn't a Gene Michael Yankee. O'Neill was. Williams was.

In a meeting at the Tampa hotel owned by George Steinbrenner, Michael convened his front office to debate the potential move. Brian

Cashman had a seat at that table. Throughout intense discussion, Michael held firm to his conviction that Kelly was overrated and O'Neill undervalued. Some in the room didn't want O'Neill because of the possibility he would clash with coaches. Others weren't sure if Williams was ready to take over in center.

Michael made the deal. With a single transaction, he had created roster space for both O'Neill and Williams. The Yankees were starting to look more like the team they would become. At the time, fans and media did not see it that way.

"That one was really ballsy," Showalter says. "Roberto Kelly at the time was the center fielder of the New York Yankees. This was not a popular trade."

By the time he acquired O'Neill, Gene Michael was not long for the GM job. Within a few years, his days leading a team on or off the field would be over forever. But he was already conveying his ideas about how to do the job to the man who would assume control for decades to come.

Let's say modern Yankees history began with a flying hot dog in 1973. Or with Michael trailing a hobbling Mickey Mantle down the steps of the visitors' dugout in Fenway Park in 1968. Choose which transitional moment from the old Yanks to the current Yanks you prefer, as long as it centers on Michael.

The next big Yankee entrance, the one that enabled those traditions to stretch deep into the next century? That had long since happened by the time Stick traded Kelly for O'Neill.

That came when Brian Cashman, summer intern, walked in the door in 1986.

PART TWO

Brian Cashman and the Yankee Way

8

Brian Breaks a Horse

O N A HOT SUMMER day in Kentucky in the mid-1980s, Brian
Cashman watched a veterinarian stick his hand all the way up
a horse's ass. It was gross.

Brian's father, John Cashman Jr., was general manager and executive director of one of the top breeding operations in the country,
Castleton Farm in Lexington. Brian was in high school, unwittingly
preparing for life with George Steinbrenner by working a summer
job that required calming angry, hormonal equines.

"You've got a pregnant mare," Cashman recalls. "And you've got a
vet with a glove on that stretches like—you ever pick up dog poop
with a little dog poop bag? Well, it's like that type of material: see-
through, so you can see your hand. It's a glove that goes from your
hand all the way up to your shoulder."

While the veterinarian donned that glove, Cashman's job was to
pull a device called a twitch—this was a round piece of rope attached
to a stick—through the mare's top lip and then twist it.

"So the mare is focusing on, 'What the fuck are they doing to my
lip? They've got my lip caught,'" Cashman says. "While somebody
else is holding the tail of the mare up so the vet can check on the
pregnancy by sticking his hand through that nasty glove that goes all
the way up. So his hand would go all the way deep into the mare's ass.

"Obviously, he has to make a pathway to pull the shit out and
dump it on some poor bastard, typically myself, holding the tail up.
It was fucking gross."

Gross, yes, but the experience also left Cashman with two takeaways, both of which imparted lessons for the future. "I got a work ethic through the process," he says. "And a check."

The Cashman family's immersion (literally, in this case) in horses and harness racing came as a result of John Cashman Jr.'s headstrong pursuit of his dream. Brian's dad grew up on Long Island, with a father who worked on Wall Street and served as a judge for harness racing at Roosevelt Raceway in Westbury. As a young boy, John Jr. would accompany his father to the track, deciding early that it was where he wanted to spend his life.

John Sr. did not approve, and John Jr. ran away from home to Florida at age sixteen to work in harness racing. Three years later, after a rapid ascent in the industry, John Jr. became racing director at Roosevelt Raceway.

Brian Cashman, named general manager of the Yankees at age thirty, draws pride from the parallel. The two shared a striking physical resemblance, even for a father and son, via common traits like thinning hair and a pointed nose, but it was their fast career trajectories and total immersion in work that stood as deeper similarities.

"In terms of a mirror image of some stuff, I became the second-youngest GM in baseball history at the time," Brian Cashman says. "My dad was, in his time, the youngest race director in the country at Roosevelt Raceway. It's like history repeats itself."

John Jr. married his fellow Long Islander Nancy Pratt in 1963. Brian, the third of five children, was born in 1967. When Brian was a baby, John left his position at Roosevelt to pursue a more lucrative wing of the horse business, breeding and selling. He did well.

In 1980, when Brian was thirteen, John got a job at Castleton Farm, and the family relocated south. In the horse-breeding world, this was not dissimilar in status to taking a job running the New York Yankees. Castleton was, according to the website for the Harness Racing Hall of Fame, the "premier Standardbred nursery."

Owned by Frederick Van Lennep, whose late wife, Frances Dodge Van Lennep, was a Dodge Motor Company heiress, Castleton Farm sat on fourteen hundred pastoral acres. One could stroll through rows of thick-trunked, drooping buttonwood trees, past green-shingled barns, and into the stone chapel that sat on the grounds.

Van Lennep ran the place like a character from another era; a 1973

Sports Illustrated profile described him as "a trim, well-tailored man of 61 with chiseled Barrymore features and lacquered hair that suggests the wet look is not dead everywhere[.] Van Lennep might have stepped at such moments from the pages of *Vanity Fair*."

Such was the well-heeled, historic sporting environment in which Brian Cashman spent his teenage years.

In Kentucky, as on Long Island, the Cashman family was loving but reserved. Nancy served as a traditional homemaker, chauffeuring her children to school and sports. John fought a battle with alcoholism, which Brian learned about only when he stumbled upon literature on sobriety in a desk drawer. John didn't take a drink for the final forty years of his life, but he and Brian never discussed it.

Nor did they talk much about John's highly successful career, which at Castleton included the breeding of several prominent horses and a key role in designing the Breeders Crown series for harness racing. Most of what Brian knew about his father's origin story, at least during his childhood, came from what he read in newspapers.

"I was the first in my family to graduate college," Brian Cashman says. "My dad definitely wanted us to go to college. So [John Jr. running away from home to pursue the sporting life] was kind of like something that wasn't spoken about. You heard about it, you read the articles, [but] he wouldn't really talk about that."

Strong traces of the family reticence remain in Brian Cashman today. If he has a problem with someone, he will confront them—he learned from his dad and Gene Michael the necessity of screaming back at George Steinbrenner—but he's not generally one for long, emotional heart-to-hearts, at least with colleagues.

John spent endless days and nights on the job, consumed by it to the exclusion of other interests—just as Brian would later do with baseball. John's status in that sport was at least equal to that which Brian would later attain in baseball; in 1992, John was inducted into the Harness Racing Hall of Fame.

On summer vacations, Brian and his siblings worked—hard. "I always joke that my dad broke every child labor law in the country, putting his underage kids to work on the farm," Brian Cashman says.

His many jobs included the aforementioned duty holding the tail of a pregnant mare. But his father offered more fulfilling tasks, too.

The summer before Brian started at Georgetown Preparatory School, the Maryland boarding school to which the family sent him as a high school junior and senior, John acquired a new quarter horse.

"You want to break him?" he asked Brian.

"Sure," Brian answered.

That horse's name was Nifty, and Cashman still remembers all the details. He began with no idea how to break a horse, but when that horse is bucking and angry, one has to learn quickly.

"You start in the stall and get him strapped up with a shank [a cheek piece that adds leverage to a rider's hands]," he says. "You lay a blanket on his back, and do that again and again over the course of time. At first, he doesn't like anything on his back. He's never been used to having a thing on his back.

"So the blanket is on his back and you're in a locked stall. You're walking in circles for a while so he's getting used to it over the course of days. After a week or so with the blanket you add more weight. Then you add a strap. He doesn't like that. He's kicking and bucking. As he's getting used to that, you add a saddle, which he's going fucking crazy over in the course of a week or so, and then he gets used to it.

"Then, over that week or so, you lay on your belly over the saddle. And he's going fucking crazy again, and you're in a stall and you don't like it until he gets used to it. You have that experience with him; then all of a sudden you sit on top of him with all that other stuff on top of him, too. He's going fucking crazy again, trying to knock you off.

"So he gets used to it; then you take him outside of the stall and do it in a paddock. Once that's no longer an issue, he's considered broke."

Bonding with the horse during those intense weeks left the young Cashman with a deep sense of satisfaction. Apparently, Nifty felt it, too.

"The cool thing was, I was sent to a boarding school my junior year, and I heard that somebody else tried to drive and ride Nifty," Cashman says. "But the horse was having none of it. He was used to me alone and would throw the others off."

Once Cashman departed for Georgetown Prep, he excelled in

baseball as a speedy second baseman who hit for a high batting average. Senior year, the football coach persuaded Cashman to join his squad too, even though Cashman had never played at any level.

There, Cashman displayed a feistiness that recalled a young Gene Michael barking at managers and umpires as a minor leaguer in the Pittsburgh Pirates system.

One day in the locker room, Cashman walked past a pair of hulking starters. One of them pulled the towel off Cashman's waist, then snapped another towel on his ass.

"Don't do that again," Cashman said, replacing the towel.

The big guy did it again.

"Motherfucker, I told you to stop," Cashman said, clenching his fists, ready to fight.

"I chased him, stark naked, out of the gym and onto the quad," Cashman recalls. "My temper was gone."

By then Cashman had attracted the attention of Division I baseball programs. He committed to Tulane University in New Orleans, one of the top baseball schools in the South. Before reporting, Cashman listened to an impassioned pitch from the head baseball coach at Division III Catholic University in Washington, D.C.

"You'll never play there," the coach, Bob Talbot, told Cashman. "You're going to be miserable down there. You can come here and play as a freshman."

That logic resonated with Cashman, who made the switch. At Catholic University, he batted leadoff. Knowing that he was vulnerable to striking out if he found himself behind in the count, Cashman frequently swung at the first pitch of an at bat.

The strategy worked to the extent that it allowed him to record fifty-two hits in thirty-eight games in 1988, which stood for eleven years as a school record—but it would not mark him as a prospect in the Yankee mold. Cashman was not one to work a walk or, in the Gene Michael parlance, "quit on the baseball." He was up there to hack.

By this time, Cashman's father had been working with George Steinbrenner for several years. The Yankee owner was also a passionate devotee of the track and owner of horses. John Cashman's portfolio with Frederick Van Lennep's equestrian empire had grown by the early 1980s to include a role as president of Pompano Park in Pompano Beach, Florida.

Pompano Park was a mere half-hour drive north from the Yankees' spring training facility in Fort Lauderdale, and John got to know Steinbrenner, Whitey Ford, and the former Dodgers pitcher Ralph Branca, among others who shared his dual enthusiasms for baseball and harness racing.

The Cashmans were a passionate Yankee family—except for Brian. During the 1978 World Series, when Brian was eleven years old, he rooted hard for the Dodgers, a modest act of rebellion. In 1982, John secured through Branca a gig for Brian as spring training batboy for the Dodgers in Vero Beach, Florida.

"I hated the Yankees," Brian Cashman says. His explanation is about as detailed as most of his family stories: "I went my own way."

As Steinbrenner bought horses from John Cashman, he behaved in a manner consistent with his temperament as a baseball executive: charming and charismatic at times, angry and bombastic at others.

When Cashman sold Steinbrenner a horse that lost, Steinbrenner would blame Cashman, and the two would go months without speaking. Once, Steinbrenner wanted Cashman to fix the draw for the Red Mile, a celebrity race in which he was participating, by guaranteeing him the inside rail.

Like Gene Michael contemporaneously and his own son in later decades, John Cashman knew how to stand up to the Boss. He refused to do it. For a time, his relationship with Steinbrenner soured, but the two seemed always to find their way back to each other. At one point, Steinbrenner even hired Brian's older brother, John Cashman III, as a horse trainer.

In 1986, Brian was on a baseball trip to South Florida with the Catholic University team when he lost all his money in a card game. He called his father, who told him to go to Pompano Park and ask for a meal and a loan from Allen Finkelson, the track publicist.

When Cashman walked into Finkelson's office, he felt as if he had entered a Yankees museum. Pictures of Mickey Mantle, Billy Martin, Mickey Rivers, and other players adorned the walls. And was that . . . a Yankee World Series ring on Finkelson's finger?

"Where'd you get that ring?" Cashman asked.

"I'm best friends with George Steinbrenner," Finkelson said.

He asked Cashman about his plans after the school year, and Cashman said he planned to play in a summer league.

Finkelson offered another suggestion—one that, as it happened, would set the course for the rest of Cashman's life.

"What if I get you an internship with the New York Yankees?" Finkelson asked.

9

The Internship Begins

*K*EEP OUT OF THE *way and do your job the best you can.*
That was John Cashman's advice as his nineteen-year-old son Brian's summer internship with the Yankees began in 1986. Taciturn as usual, John omitted the grisly details of his own experience with George Steinbrenner. No need to tell all: Brian would spend the next two-plus decades learning firsthand what it was like to work for the Boss.

Cashman rented an apartment on 192nd Street, in the Kingsbridge neighborhood in the Bronx. There he first became acquainted with the challenges of New York City in the summertime and on a budget: stifling heat, no air-conditioning, a fifth-story walk-up, and crime on the streets below.

"Washington Heights, Harlem, the Bronx—it was a war zone back then," Cashman recalls. "I lived in the belly of the beast."

In a different way—more cloistered and privileged, but hardly less frightening to a young man entering for the first time—the Yankee offices also felt like a battleground, especially when Steinbrenner came to visit.

"George didn't live in New York, so when he came up from Tampa to New York, it certainly was a scene," Cashman says. "He made his presence felt every single time. The atmosphere was that everybody was always on edge, because nothing was ever running well enough for the Boss. He would whip up the troops."

Those troops, especially the ones in uniform, would sometimes rebel. One such moment involving a veteran pitcher left an indelible mark on the young Cashman.

"Tommy John tore up George Steinbrenner once," Cashman says. "If the team wasn't playing well, George would move the families' tickets to the upper deck to give them shitty seats. If the Yankees were struggling, next thing you know George would visit the team and be like, 'All right, if you guys want to shit the bed on me, I'm gonna fucking screw your families.'

"I remember Tommy John coming up from the basement. I guess his wife, Sally, was pissed. She called Tommy on the clubhouse phone and fucking aired him out because she and her family were sitting in the upper deck. Right at game time, Tommy John goes up through the lobby, on the elevator—in uniform!—up into the owners' box and tells George that this ain't fucking acceptable.

"He was hot. He was like a heat-seeking missile. I'm like, 'Oh my God, there's a game about ready to start and there's this guy right in the middle of fans coming through our lobby.' The elevator went right to the club-suites level, where the suites were, and then to the owners' box. Tommy John is furious, and he's on his way to track the Boss down, because his family is sitting in the upper deck."

Explosions like these enlivened workdays that seemed never to end. Cashman reported to the assistant general manager Peter Jameson. "He was a brilliant guy," Cashman says, "who taught me everything I needed to know about the administrative side of the game: the American League rules, the Basic Agreement, contract stuff." But in his role as an intern, Cashman was exposed to most aspects of the organization.

"Before intern laws, we were just working around the clock," Cashman says. "It was nonstop, working our asses off. But I was on the front lines. Whether it was driving [first baseman] Orestes Destrade to a doctor's appointment or picking up [general manager] Clyde King at the airport or having a seat at the table."

That last phrase—"a seat at the table"—is what any baseball intern or young staffer dreams about: being in the room during discussions about trades, signings, and game strategy. Almost from the start, Cashman found himself invited.

"They would have tryouts at the stadium," Cashman says. "Hank

Steinbrenner would call me in with [director of scouting] Brian Sabean when they were looking at tapes."

Cashman cannot recall the first time he met his future mentor Gene Michael. But Bill Livesey, who at different times ran player development and the amateur draft for the Yankees, says that Michael was drawn early on to Cashman's combination of playing experience, intellect, and drive.

"Brian was a bright kid, but he had a baseball background," Livesey says. "Today we have a lot of bright people with no baseball background. He knew the game. His college coach at Catholic University was a good friend of mine. Brian had a feel for the game right off: very intelligent, picked things up quickly. Eager to learn, and he was always in the right spot trying to find out what was going on. He was a rapid learner, and I think Stick saw that in him quickly."

Michael wasn't the only Yankee official who took notice.

"I laugh when I think about him back then," says Sabean. "I don't know how much I want to put this out there, but it is what it is, and it's not common knowledge. I just laugh because when I think about what he has done—he's the best general manager of all time, in any organization—but how back then he was just a wide-eyed person in the office who would do anything during that summer internship.

"The one thing I always saw in him, even then: He was a 'look, listen, think, speak' person. This is very unique, and I think it's one of the reasons his career grew the way it did and he became so successful. He took it all in. He was from a family of means, but he never came across that way. Very diligent and dependable."

To hear Cashman himself describe his duties as an intern is to board a time machine to baseball's low-tech days—a view of how the Yankees, and every other organization, operated in the century before rapid advancements in technology and analytics changed the game forever.

"Today, everything that happens is filed on the internet," Cashman says. "There was obviously no internet back then. We had like seven minor-league affiliates, and they would call in the game report on an answering machine. I would have to transcribe it first thing in the morning, then print it out on paper and make photocopies to distribute throughout the important people.

"For instance, Wally Moon was the manager at Prince William. He would call in and be like, 'This is Wally Moon, calling in the game against whoever on June 17. First pitch, 7:06, game time temperature was eighty-four degrees. Batting first and playing second base was Andy Stankiewicz. He was 1-for-4 with a double, a stolen base, and a walk and a strikeout. Batting second was . . .'

"And you'd have to write all that stuff in. On both sides, the pitching line, then any comments.

"Scouting reports were the same way. The advance scouting reports. I remember Billy Martin was the manager one year and the advance scouting report was called in. Billy Martin did not trust that Peter Jameson copied it properly. He was so paranoid that he thought Peter fucked it up. So he made Peter bring the tape down and play it to prove to him that this is what a scout said about the player."

In the 2020s, nearly every minor-league park is equipped with high-speed cameras that capture advanced data on each pitch. Game video is easily available, and a prospect's every at bat is chronicled online.

"I worked in the caveman world," Cashman says. "There were no cell phones. There was no internet. It was all so tedious."

Less tedious was the time Cashman spent working with the security team.

"I worked at the front desk, which was like mission control," Cashman says. "Players' families came there for tickets. I had the radio. Lou Piniella, he was in the dugout managing and you couldn't get him, but he'd always forget to leave tickets for his wife. That was something I would never forget, when his wife would come in and not have her tickets waiting for her."

Cashman got off the desk to serve as a night security guard at Yankee Stadium, which led to a highly uncomfortable moment a few years later.

In 1989, Steinbrenner hired the veteran executive Syd Thrift to run baseball operations. Thrift had most recently worked for the Pittsburgh Pirates, who accused him and a young assistant, Jim Bowden, of stealing scouting reports on their way out.

A Major League Baseball investigation cleared Thrift and Bowden, but Cashman and everyone else in the Yankee offices took it as a given that the pair had in fact made away with the reports. Thrift chafed under Steinbrenner's tyranny and lasted less than a year. Soon after Thrift left, Steinbrenner wanted Bowden fired.

"I was in my office," Cashman recalls. "I shared an office with Jim Bowden; he was the assistant GM and Bob Quinn was, like, director of baseball operations. Syd Thrift got fired by George or Quinn, I can't remember which.

"Syd's right-hand man was Jim Bowden and so now he was left for prey. Dallas Green—he was the manager—got whacked around that time, too. No one knew what was gonna happen next."

In Cashman and Bowden's office, Cashman's desk was to the right of the door, and Bowden's behind it, next to a window that overlooked the field.

"Bob Quinn walks in and he starts to shut the door, and I could just feel something wasn't good," Cashman says. "And he starts to fire Jim right in front of me."

Cashman got up and tried to excuse himself.

"Mr. Quinn said, 'No, no, no, you stay right there, Cash,' " Cashman says. "And he whacked Jim right in front of me. And I guess he had it on order from George. He said, 'You're terminated.'

"It was very well reported back then, and when Jim and Syd came over, they took boxes and boxes of Pirates scouting reports. So, like, we were making trades based on the Pirate stuff, not based on Syd.

"George thought Bowden might be taking Yankee stuff. So if Jim was taking a box with him, I had to approve it. Then, because I did work security at night back then, I had to walk him out to his car. It was very uncomfortable."

(Bowden responds, "Any reports or allegations of us taking scouting reports from the Pirates or making any trades based on scouting reports from anyone except Yankees scouts at that time are false and untrue. The commissioner's office investigated those false reports at the time and cleared us of any wrongdoing.

"Cash has always been a friend of mine, and I was glad that George wanted him to check my boxes and walk me out because that would eradicate any future false claims. Later that year I was hired by Bob Quinn and Lou Piniella with the Reds, and we went on to win a world championship with the Reds in 1990.")

Such were the duties of the lowest-level Yankee official. The organizational drama, which was peaking by the late 1980s, spared no one—not even the interns.

10

From Billy to Buck

D URING THE EARLY YEARS that Cashman spent learning the
business, the Yankees remained in decline on the field and
in frequent turmoil off it. As had been the case since the 1970s,
Steinbrenner and Billy Martin's complex relationship caused much
of the instability.

Cashman was too low ranking through the 1980s to know the
intricacies of that dynamic, but those who were better placed at the
time recall Martin as a troubled person, though one who left a strong
imprint on the field—one that would last at least through Buck
Showalter's tenure as manager.

"The Billy days, I wouldn't say it was Wild Wild West, but it kinda
was," recalls longtime Yankee broadcaster Michael Kay, who started
covering the team full time for the *New York Post* in 1987. "The war-
ring factions—and a front office against the manager and the owner.
I think that one of the strengths of George was that he liked the division that inspired people to do better."

Prior to the 1988 season, Steinbrenner decided to bring Martin
back for his fifth stint as Yankees manager. Just before spring training,
Mickey Mantle was holding a grand opening for his new restaurant
on Central Park South. Kay's editor at the *Post* told him to go to the
event to introduce himself to Martin.

"The line was down Central Park South," Kay recalls. "You just
couldn't get in. There was an apartment building connected to it,
so I walked into that building and gave the doorman twenty bucks,
which was a lot of money back then. I said, 'Is there a side door?' He

said yeah. I worked my way from the back, walked up to Billy Martin, and introduced myself."

"Let me ask you a question, kid," Martin said. "What do you think of me?"

"What do I think of you?" Kay said. "I don't even know you."

"Okay," Martin said. "But what have you heard about me?"

"Well," Kay said. "What I've heard isn't good. But what I will tell you is this: I promise you I'll give you a chance. How you treat me is how I will deal with you."

Martin put his hands up, palms facing out.

"That's all I wanted to hear," he said.

Soon after, spring training began in Fort Lauderdale. On one of the first days, Martin stepped out of his office in the clubhouse and gestured to Kay.

"Kid," he said, in full view of Kay's competitors. "Come here."

"Let me ask you a question," Martin said, once Kay was in the office. "If I give you stories before anybody else, does that hurt Bill Madden?"

Madden was a longtime baseball reporter at the rival New York *Daily News* who would one day earn a spot in the writers' wing of the Baseball Hall of Fame. But he was known to be close with Steinbrenner, and as Kay puts it, "Bill and Billy hated each other."

Kay said that if Martin gave him a scoop, it would indeed hurt Madden. With that, in an effort to exact vengeance for slights either real or perceived from Steinbrenner and the writer associated with him, Martin handed the *Post* one back-page scoop after another.

A story that Kay didn't write turned out to be Martin's final act in an iconic managerial career. Following a loss in June to the Tigers in Detroit, Martin summoned Kay to his office.

"I'm out," he said.

"Aren't you being a little paranoid?" Kay asked.

"Kid," Martin answered. "I know the signs when I'm being fired. I've been here before."

Kay figured that Martin was just imagining his imminent dismissal—the Yankees were 40–26, after all—but he was wrong. Two days later, Steinbrenner fired Martin.

Martin remained involved in the organization and attended the

1989 Winter Meetings in Nashville as a member of the front office. One night, drinking at the bar, he again confided in Kay.

"Don't write it yet," Martin said. "But I'm next. I've got all my coaches lined up. They're going to bang Bucky right at the beginning of the year if he gets off to a bad start, and I'm next."

Since Martin's firing in 1988, Steinbrenner had been on his typical managerial merry-go-round. Lou Piniella, who had preceded Martin on the job, returned to complete the year. Then Steinbrenner went outside the organization for his next hire, wooing Dallas Green, a World Series–winning skipper with the Philadelphia Phillies in 1980.

Green lasted all of 121 games before Steinbrenner replaced him with former Yankees shortstop Bucky Dent. The Yankees finished the year 18–22 under Dent, and Martin saw his opportunity to return—and, as it turns out, to shape the future.

"He was going to put Buck [Showalter] on his coaching staff and train him to one day take over the job," says broadcaster Suzyn Waldman, who spoke to Martin about the plan at those Winter Meetings.

Showalter, thirty-three at the time, had emerged as an up-and-comer in the organization, known for clever in-game managing and attention to detail that bordered on obsessive. Starting in the early 1980s, he and his wife, Angela, had been making homemade spray charts of opponents' hits, which helped to position his fielders more precisely. He was skilled at picking up opponents' signs and at determining, by observing the tiniest subtleties of body language, if one of his own players was fully engaged in the game.

During spring training workouts in the 1980s, Martin noticed Showalter as a fellow baseball obsessive. Showalter, in turn, saw a seasoned manager whose sharpness belied his reputation as a drunken brawler.

"The Yankees used to bring every minor-league manager to spring training," Showalter says. "The seven of us would walk behind Billy. Between every drill, he said what we were trying to accomplish and how he wanted it taught. 'If I get a player from you guys,' he would say, 'they had better be able to fucking do this.' He was way ahead of his time on that, to have that kind of cohesiveness up and down the organization.

"People thought he was some drunken cartoon character, but this guy at ten o'clock in the morning on the back field in Fort Lauderdale? He was nails. He was articulate about the game, passionate, knew the game like the back of his hand, and by God he wanted to talk about it to the players."

One of Martin's favorite back-field drills, which he would use to evaluate players in a way that resembled Gene Michael's off-ball scouting, involved catching pop-ups.

"He loved a good pop-up drill," Showalter says. "We had this bazooka, this gun you could pump up the air pressure and shoot the ball up. We could take planes out of the sky with this thing. Billy loved using it when it was windy with no clouds and sunny on the back field. He learned something from that: Don Mattingly would call for the ball. Others would run from it, and that was telling him something."

One day, the bazooka broke. Martin still wanted to run the drill.

"He was so pissed," Showalter says. "He yelled, 'Who can hit a fungo?' I kept my mouth shut, but he said, 'Buck boy!' I hit fungoes for twenty minutes, jerking up in the air. The next day I couldn't get out of bed. My fucking back."

Before long, Martin and Showalter began taking long drives around Florida at night, discussing the finer points of the game. "I think he just wanted someone to talk to," Showalter says.

Those sessions recalled the conversations that helped mold Martin's own baseball mentor, Casey Stengel. While playing for the New York Giants in the early 1920s, Stengel, an outfielder whose career was winding down, would sit up late at night at the home of future Hall of Fame manager John McGraw and talk baseball strategy and philosophy.

In the 1950s, when Stengel was the Yankee manager, he connected deeply with Martin, a scrappy infielder whose knowledge of the game exceeded his athletic ability. Their bond was so tight that Martin became known as Casey's boy.

McGraw had broken into the big leagues as a player for the Baltimore Orioles in 1891. In 2022 and 2023, Showalter managed the New York Mets—meaning that the McGraw-to-Stengel-to-Martin-to-Showalter chain represented more than 130 years of baseball experience and oral tradition passed through just four men.

Martin's aggressive managerial style was a mix of the Stengel-

McGraw influences, blending with his own instincts and personality. Showalter describes it this way: "Billy—well, I think now we are too predictable, which sometimes becomes non-entertaining. You want to think about games that make you go, 'Wow, did you see that? Did you see this?' Billy, he was unpredictable in lots of ways. Not everybody could be that because they were afraid. There's some managers, I know everything they're gonna do. I just know because I know the way they look at things. Billy was the opposite.

"Billy threw caution to the wind. He didn't give a fuck what somebody might say, or what he was going to have to answer for with the writers after the game. When Stick managed, he had some caution to him. He thought about repercussions—not necessarily with the media or the fan base, but with the players. He just thought about the arteries of his decisions. Billy would just do it. He would knee-jerk and just go for it.

"He didn't play bad defenders. He was drawn to those athletic, speedy, defensive-minded players. So in the spring, whether it be from our system, whether it be from another team, Billy knew the type of players he wanted. And Casey wanted the platoon thing, which Billy liked, too."

Martin was also decades ahead of his time in how he would instruct relief pitchers to utilize their repertoire. For most of baseball history, pitchers were supposed to use an arsenal of pitches—three or four for a starter, two or three for a reliever—to set up hitters and play an intellectual chess game.

In the 2010s, modern analytics changed all that, determining that relievers should throw mostly, if not entirely, their best pitch. Cutting-edge teams like the Tampa Bay Rays would summon pitchers from the bullpen and call for a dozen or more consecutive sliders or curveballs.

According to Showalter, Martin was doing this as far back as the 1970s.

"He would bring in a guy and tell him to throw twenty-eight curveballs in a row," Showalter says. "With [relief ace and 1977 American League Cy Young Award winner] Sparky Lyle, it was the slider."

Showalter could have spent even more time marinating in Martin's knowledge, if only he had been able to serve as a coach for Martin in 1990. Though Martin told Suzyn Waldman and a few others of his plan to promote Showalter, he hadn't yet gotten around to looping in Showalter himself.

"I have heard that story from multiple people, and not just Suzyn, but Billy didn't tell it to me directly," Showalter says. "The last time I talked to him was in 1989. He was supposed to turn in scouting reports for my Double-A team, and for whatever reason he wasn't able to get it done. He called and asked me to send my evaluations, and he put his name to them. It meant a lot that he trusted my judgment on players to that extent."

Less than a month after telling Kay and Waldman about his imminent return, Martin was dead. Following a Christmas Day spent drinking at a bar near his home in Broome County, New York, Martin either drove or was in the passenger seat of his truck, which skidded on ice and tumbled three hundred feet into a gully. There would be no sixth managerial term.

"When Billy was sober, he was unbelievable," says Kay. "To this day, he's the greatest manager I have ever seen, though I later went to Buck Showalter University, and that was incredible, too. Billy managed a game well ahead of everybody else. He could suck the last ounce of what a team could do out of them. He was so good. He would see things three innings ahead of everyone else, and I think that included the opposing manager. His demons off the field sunk him."

Even with Martin gone, Showalter received his first big-league opportunity in 1990, though not initially on the field or in the dugout, as Martin had planned. Steinbrenner made him the "eye in the sky" coach, a clever position that stemmed from the Boss's long-standing passion for another sport.

"George was a big football guy," says Doug Melvin, the first eye in the sky, who would go on to serve as general manager of the Texas Rangers and Milwaukee Brewers. "And he could not figure out why in football they have coaches upstairs and in baseball we didn't."

First pursuing this idea for the 1979 season, Steinbrenner looked for a person athletic enough to throw batting practice and perceptive enough to provide insights from the press box once the game began, especially regarding defensive positioning.

Melvin, a sinkerball pitcher and minor-league teammate of Showalter's in the Yankees' system, was ready to retire. One of his minor-league managers, Stump Merrill, recommended him for the new position.

From his seat in the press box, Melvin communicated his information via walkie-talkie to coach Yogi Berra in the dugout. He later left for a front-office position in Baltimore; in 1990, Showalter took over the role, which provided his first chance to direct his unusually sharp insights toward affecting major-league games.

"One of the problems at old Yankee Stadium was that if you were in the dugout, you could only see maybe the top half of the left fielder," Showalter says. "There was a big drop-off from the infield. And even down the right-field line, if you got too far in the dugout, you couldn't see him. The sight lines were obviously a lot better [in the press box]. And some guys would drift around, like Mel Hall would play where the shadow was of the lights, just to stay cool. So I would call down [and have him moved into position]."

As the season progressed, other patterns revealed themselves. Showalter noticed that Mike Greenwell, the All-Star outfielder for the Boston Red Sox, had a habit uncommon for a left-handed batter: he would hook the ball down the first base line against lefty pitchers.

One day before a game against Boston, Showalter mentioned this to first baseman Don Mattingly and suggested that Mattingly play on the line against Greenwell.

"I don't know . . ." Mattingly said. "Left on left?"

"Donnie, I'm telling you," Showalter said. "I've seen him hit about six balls there. It's just way too much of a tendency."

Mattingly decided to follow Showalter's advice, and sure enough, in a key situation, Greenwell hooked a ball right at Mattingly.

In the clubhouse after the game, Mattingly looked at Showalter, smiled, and shook his head. Buck had been right.

On the morning of June 6, 1990, after a loss the night before to the Red Sox in Boston, Steinbrenner fired Dent and replaced him with Merrill. It was the Yankees' nineteenth managerial change in sixteen years.

When word reached Showalter in his hotel that morning, he had no idea if he was still employed. All he could do was report to Fenway Park to find out.

"I'm sitting at my locker at twelve thirty for a seven o'clock game," Showalter says. "George came in, took me into the shower, and said,

'We want you to be the hitting coach for three days before Darrell Evans gets here, and then we want you to be the third-base coach. You think you can handle that?' "

Showalter said that he could, and a long career on big-league fields began. Gene Michael took over as the eye in the sky coach, giving Showalter a friend and mentor on the road.

Michael and Cashman were becoming closer during those years, too, but as Cashman came to know the entire organization, he realized that Stick was hardly the only strong influence.

In fact, working at the same time on the sunburned fields of Florida, far from the big-league team and front office in New York, was a hard-driving baseball man from the University of Maine—which, of all places and through sheer coincidence, proved central to the development of the philosophy that would drive a dynasty.

The man's name was Bill Livesey; the philosophy was becoming known, at least informally, as the Yankee Way.

11

The Yankees' Secret Sauce

Brian Cashman started every game at second base for Catholic University during his four years there before graduating in 1989. He then stepped immediately into a full-time position as an assistant in the Yankees' baseball operations department.

The following year, Cashman earned his first promotion, to assistant farm director, which required a move to the team's new player development complex in Tampa. There he found a fertile learning environment, deepened key relationships formed during his internship, and developed the contrarian take on Yankee history to which he still subscribes.

In Cashman's view—the view, in other words, of the franchise's longest-tenured general manager—a true account of the franchise in recent decades has never been put forth.

"The story that is always told about the Yankees is wrong," Cashman says (this same quote, used in the introduction of this book, was from a different interview; Cashman believes it so deeply that he unconsciously repeats it, or perhaps consciously repeats it). "Even Gene Michael used to say, 'I get too much credit.'"

Most tellings center Michael alone as the Yankee architect. Cashman does not think that any credit should be subtracted from Michael's record—after all, it was Stick who was there the longest, even before Steinbrenner.

It was Stick who brought on-base percentage, the Yankees' foundational offensive principle, into the organization. It was Stick whose eye for talent defined countless aspects of the way the Yankees chose and retained players. And it was Stick who served as a mentor to Cashman, Showalter, Billy Eppler, and other key figures over five decades.

It is Cashman's belief, however, that the story should expand to include former scouting director Brian Sabean, former farm director Mitch Lukevics, former player development executive Mark Newman, and—perhaps above all others—Bill Livesey, a sharp and cantankerous New Englander who became a Yankee through sheer coincidence and who developed the innovative methods for choosing and training players that persist into the present day.

"They built the greatest farm system in the history of the sport," Cashman says. "It resulted in the dynasty."

To explain this, we must rewind to an even more distant figure, longtime University of Maine baseball coach Jack Butterfield.

Butterfield, born in 1929, was a Massachusetts native who played for Maine in the early 1950s and took over as head coach in 1957. During his eighteen seasons in that job, Butterfield's players included future Yankee fixtures Livesey, Stump Merrill, and Brian Butterfield, Jack's son who would go on to become an important defensive mentor to a young Derek Jeter.

In 1974, Jack Butterfield took a job at the University of South Florida. It was there that a chance encounter with Steinbrenner changed the trajectory of how the Yankees developed players.

"It all really does begin with Jack," Buck Showalter says.

Adds Merrill, Butterfield's first hire with the Yankees, "A lot of people don't know how this whole thing originated. Jack had left the University of Maine and gone to South Florida. And that happened to be in Tampa, where George lived. George was there for a fundraiser and met Jack and was impressed by what he saw and what he heard.

"For whatever reason, Jack was on a nine-months-a-year contract at South Florida. So George said, 'Hell, that's easy enough. I'll hire you for the summer months.' He hired him as an advance scout."

An advance scout's job is to watch an upcoming opponent and provide the manager and coaching staff with up-to-date intel on how to beat them.

"As a stroke of fate, Jack's first scouting assignment was the Red

Sox," Merrill says. "And what organization did he know better, coming from the University of Maine and witnessing the Red Sox over a period of time? Then the Yankees went into Boston, and the story goes that they swept the Red Sox [with help from Butterfield's advance scouting].

"Billy Martin was managing, and even though Billy was not particularly high on college people or college coaches, he said that Jack's was the best scouting report he had ever seen. And so George said, 'Hell, why don't we hire him?'"

In 1977, Steinbrenner named Butterfield director of player development and scouting. The two were in lockstep not only about baseball ideas but on how Yankees should act.

"Dad was organized and detailed," says Brian Butterfield. "He was in perfect line with what Mr. Steinbrenner represented. Mr. Steinbrenner was extremely disciplined—the short hair and playing the game the right way. He had a football background, and Dad had also been the football coach at Maine. Mr. Steinbrenner valued toughness, and Dad believed in all the same things. He was fearless."

Steinbrenner and Butterfield began to collaborate on ways to ensure that Yankee prospects stood out for their professionalism.

At the time, most minor leaguers wore hand-me-down uniforms; the Yankees began a tradition of purchasing new ones for each affiliate every season and paying for dry cleaning. Steinbrenner bought every player a nylon jacket and Yankee-branded travel bag.

He paid generous bonuses to prospects who made All-Star teams and achieved other benchmarks of success. At a time when most minor-league teams had a manager and no full-time coaches, Steinbrenner sprang for an extra coach at every level.

The Boss's financial commitment to the minors—which belied his reputation as an owner who cared only about winning at the MLB level—extended well beyond matters of style. At a time when few if any organizations provided strength and conditioning services, Steinbrenner hired Ohio State football legend Howard "Hopalong" Cassady to design a weight training program. Cassady traveled to each affiliate and showed players how to use a Nautilus machine.

On all these matters, and on rules regarding hair length, facial hair, and uniform regulations, Steinbrenner and Butterfield were a perfect match. And while the Boss knew less about player development than he did about his preferences for personal style, he entrusted Butter-field to teach baseball fundamentals across the system.

Just as that partnership was gaining momentum, tragedy struck. On November 16, 1979, the team held a party at Yankee Stadium for Cedric Tallis, who was stepping down as general manager to make room for Michael's first stint on the job. Butterfield attended, then drove home to New Jersey.

"I still can remember when I got the phone call from his wife," Merrill says. "Jack was coming home from the party for Cedric Tal-lis, driving on Route 17. He ran into a parked street sweeper. It was parked at the crest of a hill, in the passing lane, with no lights on. Being in the passing lane, Jack was going at a high rate of speed.

"The only way they could identify him was with his teeth."

Butterfield was dead at fifty, leaving behind not only a family but an organization that had quickly deemed him essential and was only just beginning to benefit from his work.

"The magnitude of our loss cannot be expressed in words," Stein-brenner said at the time. "He was the epitome of what you would look for in a teacher of young men. I doubt we will ever be able to replace Jack Butterfield. He was that great."

Needing to fill Butterfield's now-vacant position, Steinbrenner summoned Livesey, then forty, to New York for an interview.

Livesey had played for Butterfield at the University of Maine, then served as head baseball coach at Brown University and Eckerd College in Florida. When Butterfield began working for the Yankees, he brought Livesey with him, initially making him an amateur scout in Florida, Georgia, and South Carolina in 1977.

In 1979, Livesey switched to managing and guided the Appalachian League Paintsville (Kentucky) Yankees to a championship. That club's 52–13 record set a mark for minor-league winning percentage that would stand for three decades.

Steinbrenner loved this. So often the focus in the minor leagues was on player development alone, but didn't the Yankees want to develop winners, too? The Paintsville championship was right up the Boss's alley.

"What's your background before you came to us?" Steinbrenner asked Livesey in the job interview.

Livesey said that he had been a college coach before following Butterfield to the Yankees.

"Good," Steinbrenner said. "I want teaching in this organization."

Steinbrenner promoted Livesey, and the Yankees continued to pursue the investments in minor-league infrastructure that began under
Butterfield. These included early forays into technology.

In 1980, Livesey and his assistant Bobby Hoffman went to the
Sony store in Times Square and purchased seven massive video cameras, then lugged them uptown to the office so they could send them
out to each affiliate. The idea was for players to watch themselves and
make adjustments based on what they and the coaches saw.

Empowered to hire player development staffers, Livesey sought
a blend of former college coaches—the teachers—and former big-
league players, who had the expertise that came from lived experience
at the highest levels.

In dealing with those employees, Livesey operated with a personal
style that matched Butterfield's and, perhaps even more important,
the Boss's: he was loud and intimidating.

"One of the only men I've ever been terrified of," Buck Showalter
says of Livesey. "To call him rough around the edges would be kind."

Once, when Showalter was managing in the minor leagues, he sent
Livesey a report that said outfield prospect Gerald Williams had trouble hitting a curveball and did not know how to take a lead off bases.

The phone rang in his office.

"What the fuck are you there for?" Livesey screamed in his thick
Massachusetts accent, dispensing even with a quick hello. "Maybe
I've got the wrong fucking guy!"

"Hey, Mr. Livesey," Showalter said, rattled.

"I just got your fucking report," Livesey said. "Let me ask you a
question. Can Gerald Williams run?"

"Yeah," Showalter said. "He's a fucking 80 runner [on a 20–80
scouting scale], top of the chart."

"Can he throw?"

"Yeah, borderline 80 arm, as good as there is."

"Can he go get the ball in the outfield?"

"Oh yeah."

"Then why don't you teach him how to hit a fucking curveball?"

Livesey screamed. "Why don't you teach him how to hold the fucking bat? Why don't you teach him how to take a fucking lead?"

At this, Showalter summoned the nerve to cut Livesey off.

"I got it," he said.

As soon as he hung up the phone, Showalter found Williams in the clubhouse.

"Come on, Gerald," he said. "We're going out on the field."

As Livesey explained in 2023, "Nobody was more conscientious than Buck, but we did not want scouting reports from our player development people. We have scouts. Don't tell me what he can't do. Call me back in September when you've worked with him all year."

Though Livesey spoke with the authority of a drill sergeant, colleagues noted an important distinction from the similarly bombastic Steinbrenner: he was a baseball genius.

"He was on a different level as far as how active his mind was, his brilliance," says Brian Sabean, who played for Livesey at Eckerd College and followed him into the Yankees organization in 1985. "He didn't waste a day; he was constantly learning and teaching. Being around him, we were all recipients of that."

Livesey stayed in Butterfield's old job for three seasons, but hated front-office life in New York. He was a field guy. In 1982 he begged Steinbrenner to let him move back to Florida so he could resume teaching and scouting.

"Those three years with Jack in that job, followed by my three years in his role, gave us six consecutive years of continuity in scouting and development philosophy and procedure," Livesey says.

That extended to Yankee style, a matter on which Livesey agreed with Butterfield and Steinbrenner, although sometimes even he couldn't match the Boss's intensity on that front.

One spring training in the early 1980s, several squads of Yankee minor leaguers were playing Baltimore prospects on a back field. Steinbrenner was sitting between the Double-A and the Triple-A fields.

"Livesey, come here!" he barked.

Livesey ran over.

"You see those uniforms?" Steinbrenner asked.

"Our uniforms?"

"No!" Steinbrenner answered. "The Baltimore uniforms!"

Sure enough, the name patches on the back of the Orioles' jerseys were sloppily applied and peeling off.

"If I ever see a Yankee uniform like that, you're gone!" Steinbrenner said.

Recalling that, Livesey laughs and says, "He can't find anything we're doing wrong, so he warns me about the other team's uniforms!"

Unlike many Yankee employees over the decades, Livesey did not mind Steinbrenner's intensity. In fact, he appreciated it.

"Mr. Steinbrenner cared," Livesey says. "And he backed it up by spending the money. He could be tough, but some people have said the same about me."

By the early 1980s, Livesey had both scouted and coached in the Yankee system, and a pattern was established for his usefulness in the years to come. While some people were evaluators and some were teachers, Livesey shifted between both, with one hand in player development and the other in scouting.

Throughout that decade, he continued to hone his beliefs—which, due to their later influence on Cashman, came to determine which players the Yankees would acquire for the next forty-plus years and counting.

"Mr. Livesey is the architect of it all," says Mitch Lukevics, the farm director to whom Cashman reported while working for the Yankees in Tampa from 1990 to 1992. "He is the generator. He is the engine master."

Livesey's first and perhaps most important innovation was called the player profile, which he—in close collaboration with his protégé Brian Sabean, who took over the amateur draft in 1986—utilized to scout, select, and develop future Yankees.

These ideas had their deepest roots in 1960s championship basketball.

"I was a great Celtics fan," Livesey says. "Red Auerbach put the same teams together every year. By that I mean there were different guys but they played the same positions. If you followed the Celtics, you knew there would be a certain type of point guard. There was a shooting guard.

"There was usually a slender, rebounding center, and there was a sixth man who was second to none. And somewhere on the team he would have a hatchet man. So when he looked for people, he didn't look for the same guys everyone else looked for. He looked for people who fit his mode. He took guys who he knew exactly how to use, and what it took to be successful in their roles."

Livesey translated this concept to baseball, ranking a player's "tools" in order of importance to each position. This was designed to create a team with the consistency and stability of Auerbach's Celtics, no matter who was on the roster in a given year.

Traditionally, scouts identify five tools for every position player: hit, power, run, field, and arm. They rate each tool on a scale of 20–80, with 80 representing an elite, Hall of Fame–level skill, then add up the tools and divide the number by 5. A player is thus defined as a 65 or a 50 or a 40, and so on.

Livesey's player profile method takes that approach, scrambles it, and provides a map for how to find the players best suited to each position.

"Scouts would add up the tools for a player and divide them by five," Livesey says. "I thought, what is that really telling me? So I developed a profile for every position, and what it took to play those positions—the tools required to play those positions.

"Why should the catcher's running tool be equal to his arm? Why should I care if a catcher could run? It made no sense. Left field— look at most of the left fielders we had. Most of them were not good fielders. But it was an offensive position, so it didn't matter. We developed a profile of every position and what tools were required to play those positions."

Livesey's position-based player profiles, which have been the Yankee secret sauce since the 1980s, are as follows, with the tools ranked in order of importance:

Catcher: (1) field (2) arm (3) hit (4) power (5) run

First base: (1) power (2) hit (3) field (4) arm (5) run

Second base: (1) hit (2) field (3) power (4) run (5) arm

Shortstop: (1) field (2) arm (3) hit (4) run (5) power

Third base: (1) hit (2) power (3) field (4) arm (5) run

Right field: (1) power (2) hit (3) arm (4) field (5) run

Center field: (1) field (2) run (3) hit (4) arm (5) power

Left field: (1) hit (2) power (3) field (4) run (5) arm

Per Livesey, the top two tools on that list for any player had to add up to a number, typically 110, in order to indicate a championship-caliber talent.

For example, Yankees scout Dick Groch in 1992 graded high school shortstop Derek Jeter as a 60 arm and 65 field—meaning that the top two shortstop tools added up to 125 in Jeter's profile. That was a Hall of Fame–level score for a player who ended up in the Hall of Fame.

When Livesey arrived as a Yankee employee in the 1970s, the center fielder Mickey Rivers struck him as a model for the player profile system that he was still developing.

"Mickey Rivers is the perfect example," Livesey says. "He was a 70 hitter. He had 25 power. He was a 70 fielder with a 35 arm and 70 speed. Now, if you add all those tools up and divide by 5 [as teams typically do], it's not a very good player. But he doesn't need those other tools. Why penalize him? Therefore, we can go after people who don't appeal to other teams."

In other words, Rivers couldn't throw or hit for power, but a center fielder didn't have to do either particularly well. The average of his five tools was 54, indicating a player who was only slightly above average. But his top two center-field tools added up to a whopping 140.

In 1976, Rivers finished third in American League MVP voting and helped the Yankees reach the World Series—results far more indicative of the 140 than the 54.

Livesey noted this and continued to develop his player profile system. When he and Sabean prepared for the Yankees' amateur drafts in the 1980s and 1990s—those crucial moments when the team selected a core for its coming dynasty—they would evaluate players through this lens.

"When we put all the candidates that we were thinking about taking in the draft on the board, we would just list the profile—the tools in order of importance," Livesey says. "When you do that, it jumps out at you who you want to take."

The tool rankings were not totally fixed. As Livesey used to tell his scouts, "This is a profile, not a portrait"; a team could adjust its priorities to take into account an individual's skill set.

First baseman Jason Giambi, for example, was a well-below-average defender—not ideal for the player profile system. But Cashman and his department signed Giambi after the 2001 season because they believed that his power, on-base percentage, and leadership outweighed the glove deficiency. Livesey had created a road map, not a dogma.

When a roster was full of players who fit Livesey's profile, team defense flowed perfectly, with strengths matched with weaknesses.

"When it comes time to play defense in a game, let's say you've got an extra base hit," Livesey says. "You've got your strongest arm in right field matched up on cutoffs and relays with your weakest arm at second base. And in center field you have maybe your weakest arm, and in left field is a weaker arm—and you line up with the shortstop, who has the best arm. So on all the cutoffs, relays, extra base hits, you're taking these into consideration."

This played out on both sides of the field during the 1990s, when right fielder Paul O'Neill and shortstop Jeter had strong arms and were able to strengthen plays by providing the power half of any relay play. Even as Jeter's range declined later in his career, he maintained what scouts called a "plus" arm.

When Livesey first presented his player profile idea to the Yankees, Reggie Jackson asked if it was "some kind of college thing."

"No, Reggie, it isn't," Livesey said. "This is something we're developing."

"So it's basically guys who play up the middle, bring your glove, and drag your bat?" Jackson said.

"That's right," Livesey said, chuckling. "Now what would you say about the corners?"

"Bring your bat, drag your glove," Jackson said, glib but basically correct in his summary.

In the decades since, the Yankees have stuck with the profile system, both in drafting amateurs and in identifying MLB free agents and trade targets.

"We talk about the player profile internally every day," Yankees' vice president of baseball operations, Tim Naehring, said in 2023.

As Livesey sees it from his perch in retirement, Cashman and his staff occasionally drift too far from the system. The profile for a first baseman holds that he should have the hit tool and the power tool at one and two, in any order, and that the glove tool has to be third. The position calls for a fielder who is average or better.

Tino Martinez (1996–2001; 2005) and Mark Teixeira (2009–16) were excellent fielders who fit Livesey's profile; Giambi (2002–8), as previously detailed, was not.

Later, the Yankees neglected the portfolio at two infield positions. In 2020 and 2021, the Yankees assigned Gleyber Torres to shortstop, a position at which he was a below-average defender due to limited range and arm accuracy. Luke Voit, the first baseman, was also a poor defender. Between the two of them, plenty of routine groundouts became base hits or errors.

"[Cashman] got away from it there," Livesey says. "Oh, yes he did."

Late in the 2021 season, the Yankees moved Torres to second base, a position for which his tools were better suited. That winter, Cashman acquired shortstop Isiah Kiner-Falefa, a better defender, while waiting for slick-fielding prospects Anthony Volpe and Oswald Peraza to emerge from the minor leagues.

At first base, Cashman replaced Voit at the 2021 trade deadline with Anthony Rizzo, an excellent defensive first baseman. Once again, the player profile system served as the Yankees' North Star.

"We made a conscious effort to get back to it in '21 and '22," says a high-ranking member of the Yankees' front office.

That effort continued during the 2022 season, when Cashman made the difficult decision to trade a left-handed starting pitcher, Jordan Montgomery, to the St. Louis Cardinals for center fielder Harrison Bader. It was not Bader's bat that attracted the Yankees, but his elite defense.

"The Harrison Bader trade was like an homage to Bill Livesey," Cashman says. "He always said that championship teams were strong [defensively] up the middle."

According to Sabean, Livesey's ideas were innovative and original, not just for the Yankees, but for the sport.

"There is a certain amount of common sense in there," Sabean says. "But I don't believe anyone else simplified it to this degree [before Livesey]. I know it has been copied since. I know other people took note of it."

Future Philadelphia Phillies manager Rob Thomson came to the Yankees as a minor-league coach in 1990. "I was a young coach, but I had never talked about baseball in that way," says Thomson, who led the Phillies to the World Series in 2022. "It just made perfect sense. I would sit there and listen to Bill talk about the player profile and how the individual should look, and then how it looks as a team. He was just an incredible mind."

The profile applied not only to scouting and drafting players. Livesey and the Yankees staff could also use it to find hidden value already in their system. Positional changes in the team's minor leagues became common.

"I count at least six players who wouldn't have made it to the major leagues without the position change, the most famous being Jorge Posada," Livesey says.

"Posada came to us as a shortstop. He had good hands, a good arm. He could hit, and we thought he would hit with power. He didn't run real well. I told him, 'If you can't get to the ball, I've got a place where the ball comes to you.'"

Just like that, a great Yankee career was born, and a shortstop flameout averted. In fact, finding catchers hidden at other positions was a Livesey specialty. Quality backstops were hard to find, so it made sense to look for them at, say, shortstop. Before Posada, Livesey had done the same with Jim Leyritz.

As Cashman arrived on the scene, he internalized all of this, and he would never forget the force with which Livesey implemented his principles.

"I still remember him blowing up on one of our area scouts for cross-checking a player who was not physically big in stature," Cashman says. "He was like a drill sergeant; people were in fear of him. This player was not big enough, and Livesey screamed, 'I want battleships, not U-boats! If you want to work here, you'll never make this mistake again!'"

Years later as GM, Cashman would coin the phrase "Big Hairy

Monsters" to describe the type of slugger he liked. Under his leadership, the Yankees often sought tall or brawny players, from pitchers like Dellin Betances to sluggers like Giambi, Alex Rodriguez, Aaron Judge, and Giancarlo Stanton.

"That's probably why I've gravitated to size as much as I have," Cashman says. "Because always in my mind, it's 'We want battleships, not U-boats!'"

That metaphor was yet another element that informed the way Sabean ran Yankee drafts in the late 1980s and early 1990s.

"Our scouting motto was size, strength, and athletic ability," Sabean says. "And we preferred the college player to the high school player because they were further advanced mentally, physically, and emotionally."

In the contemporary era, the Yankees continue to draft with the Livesey-Sabean approach in mind.

"Still today, in each guy that we evaluate, we're considering the profile for their position," says Damon Oppenheimer, who has been in charge of the Yankee drafts since 2005.

"The five tools have a certain ranking. The most important thing for a shortstop is not going to be power. It's nice if he has that, but he's got to be able to field, he's got to be able to throw. For us, he has to have the hit [tool]. We pay attention to it a lot. It's a big deal. It also creates questions of, 'Hey, this guy is catching right now, but his tools are hit, power, run; maybe he's better off in center field.' You can create other applicants for spots based on their tool profile."

Oppenheimer adds that because the industry has placed an increased emphasis on offense and home runs since the 1980s, the Yankees have had to update some of the tool rankings—if not in writing, at least in their minds as they evaluate potential draft picks.

"One of the things we have probably had to adapt to a little bit more in this era is that even some of the positions that were considered defensive positions—catcher, shortstop, and at one point center field—you have to really take a deep dive nowadays to see if the bat tool has climbed. Has the bat tool climbed higher in the profile than it used to be? It probably has."

Livesey concedes that his system should be tweaked to fit different eras—though not too much. Neither he nor the Yankees have drifted far from the initial principles developed on those back fields when Reggie Jackson and Billy Martin were still with the organization.

It wasn't long after that time, when Livesey honed his ideas, that he began to organize them into what became a foundational—and mostly secret—book.

12

The Yankee Way

B Y LATE 1981, WHEN Bob Lemon was managing the Yankees, George Steinbrenner had noticed that Bill Livesey's work with minor leaguers included innovative ideas and drills. Impressed, the Boss issued a command that made Livesey uncomfortable.

"I want the big leaguers to do what you guys are doing," Steinbrenner said.

Livesey had been in the game long enough to know what most major-league skippers would say if some guy from player development marched in with big ideas.

"George, I'm not telling Lemon that," Livesey said. "But if you want to, go ahead."

Steinbrenner did indeed force Livesey on Lemon. But the manager had a kind temperament and did not resist.

"Bob Lemon was as good a man as God put on earth," Livesey says. "He said, 'Yeah, no problem.' So my assistant Bobby Hoffman and I wrote this thing up and got it off to Bob in the big leagues. It lasted maybe a day. Bob said, 'Do we have to hold to this?' I said, 'Of course not.'"

Although the experiment didn't take, it did force Livesey to organize his thoughts in writing. From there, he continued to tinker, scribbling down theories, drills, and diagrams detailing the proper ways to execute plays.

Throughout the 1980s, Livesey would print up copies of his latest ideas and distribute them among colleagues, typically near the beginning of every season.

"At first it was crude, but over the years we got more organized, probably because of [advances in] computers," Livesey says.

In 1989, the Yankees hired Mark Newman, a player development executive with a law degree and a background in college coaching. A well-organized administrator, Newman began to collaborate with Livesey on a more formal treatise.

In preparing this document, Livesey and Newman wanted to collect the knowledge and oral traditions developed over the years at the Yankee facilities. Rather than just composing a document themselves, they convened long discussions with coaches.

Included in those meetings was Glenn Sherlock, a minor-league catcher who in 1989 transitioned into a player-coach role with the Double-A Albany-Colonie Yankees, a team managed by Buck Showalter.

Sherlock was a quintessential example of yet another Livesey profile: the organizational player, or a non-prospect who had the skills and personality to help the team in other ways.

"Toward the end of the draft, we would get players who we would call organizational players," Livesey says. "They would be support players; they would support our prospects at the various levels. They might have been outstanding players in big college programs, but maybe they didn't quite have the tools to be prospects.

"It gave us maturity, because the profile of the organizational player was that he had to have passion for the game, he had to be a good kid, and he had to know how to play the game. When you put them in the mix, it really helped our learning environment. And as it turned out, when their careers were over, they became our scouts and coaches."

Brian Butterfield was another of the team's notable organizational players who transitioned to coaching. In the late 1980s, he and Sherlock were asked to lend their voices to the development of what became known as the Yankee Way book.

"That whole group came up with this manual," Rob Thomson recalls. "It talked about every facet of how we were going to develop players."

"I remember sitting in a room with all the coaches, along with Mark Newman and Bill Livesey, when Bill and Mark were putting this together," Sherlock says. "They would ask questions that drew from everybody's expertise in that room. We had a lot of young coaches, but we had a lot of experienced coaches in there, too.

"It was interesting, the attention to detail. When Mark Newman was asking about outfield play, I can remember sitting in that room and listening to [former major leaguers] Ted Uhlaender and Clete Boyer getting into this discussion: whether you should catch the ball on the left side of your body or the right side of your body or over your head. This was going on for hours. At some point it was like, man—it was on and on and it was just a small thing. But I'll just never forget how much time we spent talking about it. People gave their opinions, explained them, and Mark and Bill put it all together."

After many sessions like that, the book took shape. Officially called "The Yankee System Developmental Manual," it ended up as a five-hundred-some-page tome (the pages were not numbered).

Bound in a white spiral notebook with the Yankees' "top hat" logo in the center of the cover and the recipient's name in computer-generated calligraphy in the lower-right corner, its sections were printed on white paper and divided by blue tabs.

As it was passed around, read, and discussed, the book became known informally as "The Yankee Way." Thirty years later, its principles have remained deep in the Yankee DNA. By 2023, Sherlock was in possession of one of the few known copies of the 1989 version.

"I've had people who I don't even know call and email me, asking if they can get a copy," Sherlock says.

His answer is always a polite no. This was an internal, proprietary document, and through more than twenty years of coaching for the Arizona Diamondbacks, Pittsburgh Pirates, and New York Mets, Sherlock has remained loyal to that principle—though he described it in detail in an interview for this book so its flame could be kept alive.

Leafing through the manual during a telephone conversation, Sherlock says that it does not begin with a table of contents. The book jumps right into a section that formalizes many of the regulations for how a Yankee must present himself that dated back to Jack Butterfield's tenure in the 1970s.

"It starts by talking about Yankee traditions—a bunch of rules," Sherlock says. "It was the first time I had ever seen anybody talk about how to wear the uniform properly. That was important to the

Yankees, along with being clean shaven, having a reasonable haircut, and not wearing jewelry with the Yankee uniform. Blousing your pants. Showing four inches of blue on your stirrups."

These militaristic standards were as controversial in the 1980s as they are now. The Yankee policy on facial hair has long annoyed players required to conform immediately upon joining the team.

"Players sometimes didn't like it," Sherlock says. "But I do know that when we were playing other teams and you looked in that other dugout, you could just see how everybody was so different. Everyone in the Yankees was the same. Most of us understood why and were pretty happy to be in the Yankee dugout."

After that first section on uniform standards, the rest of the book concerns actual baseball techniques.

There is a chapter on first base, one on second base, one on shortstop, and so on. "It talks about the fundamentals of playing each position, whether it's throwing or fielding or how to get yourself into an athletic position," Sherlock says.

The book goes on to include sections on pregame preparation, practice drills, and in-game defensive strategy. Those chapters feature diagrams with directional arrows indicating where players should move during specific drills and plays.

"It goes into team defenses," Sherlock says. "It's where an outfielder should be throwing the ball with a runner on second, ball hit in the gap. There are sections on bunt defenses, pickoff moves to first and third, and double cuts [when a ball is hit deep enough to necessitate that two infielders serve as cutoff men].

"It talks about how to take infield [practice]," Sherlock says. "How to take pregame. How many throws the outfielder should make to the bases. That's the preparation part of it. It's the practice. It's the drills."

The Yankees would implement the drills diagrammed in the manual during spring training, organizing the day around position-specific and full team practices.

"You would split up the day," Sherlock says. "First you split into individual defensive groups where the infielders would practice with the infielders, the outfielders would go practice with the outfielders, the catchers would be with catchers, and so on. Then you would all come together and work on team defense. That involved everyone—

the catchers, the infielders, the outfielders, the pitchers would be there, putting it all together."

During those team defense drills, a coach or manager—often Buck Showalter—would hit grounders all around the diamond, barking out a game situation and expecting all the defenders to know what to do, based on the Yankee Way manual.

The reach of this document is long enough to stretch all the way to a February morning in Port St. Lucie, Florida, in 2023. Showalter, sixty-six, is manager of the New York Mets; Sherlock, sixty-two, is a trusted lieutenant on his coaching staff.

The players begin the day by heading off to the back fields in positional groups. After about an hour, they convene on the field of the main stadium.

Showalter is standing near home plate, bat and ball in hand, calling out game situations.

"Nobody out, man on first!" Showalter shouts, his bark echoing off the back rows of the empty ballpark.

He hits the ball to left field, and the Mets are in motion. Shortstop Francisco Lindor hurries to shallow left to receive the relay throw, while first baseman Pete Alonso runs to the third-base side of the pitcher's mound.

Left fielder Mark Canha's throw misses Lindor, and the ball skips toward catcher Tomas Nido. Showalter grabs a ball and runs it again.

Billy Eppler, the Mets' general manager and a Gene Michael and Bill Livesey acolyte, is standing in foul territory near third base.

"I'm sure Buck is adapting some of these to his own needs, but I guarantee that most of this is straight out of the Bill Livesey playbook," Eppler says. The 2023 Mets players are the directional arrows from the 1989 "Yankee System Developmental Manual" incarnate. The tradition extended into 2024 and beyond, after Carlos Mendoza, a longtime Yankees player development staffer and Mark Newman's protégé, replaced Showalter as the Mets' skipper.

It isn't just the Mets who are following the Yankee Way in the 2020s. Up in Clearwater, Florida, where the 2022 National League champions, the Phillies, train, the manager, Rob Thomson, is talking his pitchers and catchers through ideas that sprang from Livesey's mind in the 1980s.

"The last time I referred to [the Yankee Way], we were talking about how to call a game for different pitchers," Thomson says. "Some pitchers are playing full plate, meaning they want the catcher to set up right down the middle. If you can't command the baseball, we fill the zone up with strikes. Then, once we get to two strikes, we have a quarter plate. There are full-plate guys, half-plate guys, and quarter-plate guys. Not many quarter-plate guys, especially in the minor leagues."

If that sounds like jargon to the casual baseball fan, it makes perfect sense to players and coaches and helps them improve in ways that the general public will never detect but will lead to wins. In this way, Livesey's ideas are scattered around Major League Baseball like dandelion fluffs, or torn pieces of paper floating in the wind.

Back in the early 1990s, after Livesey and Newman completed the book, they reinforced its concepts with hands-on mentorship of young coaches. In 1990, Sherlock managed the Yankees' rookie-league team, which included future big leaguers Mariano Rivera, Ricky Ledée, Shane Spencer, Russ Springer, and Carl Everett. After games, he would bump into Livesey on their way back to the main complex.

"He always seemed to time it perfectly so I ended up walking back with him," Sherlock says. "He would talk about the game, and talk about things I should do, things I should remember. I learned a lot just listening to him on his observations of those games."

Similarly, Newman would sit on the bench with Sherlock, Thomson, Trey Hillman, and other young managers during instructional-league games, talking them through situations and making sure that their techniques were consistent with the Yankee Way.

"The organization was so cohesive then," Sherlock says. "We were all learning, and it was a great time to be a Yankee."

Adding to that cohesion in the early 1990s was the fact that Livesey and his player development staff bought into that most important of Yankee values, Gene Michael's emphasis on on-base percentage. Livesey established benchmarks for on base and power at each minor-league level.

"We used a .360 on-base percentage as the standard in the minor leagues to be a successful big leaguer," Livesey says. "The thought behind that was that they'd lose 25 points when they went to the big leagues. They'd still be at .335, which in those days used to be the league average.

"For power, we used a .420 slugging percentage as a cutoff. If a young kid showed that, we went, 'Oh, boy, we've got something here,' because they get bigger and stronger. Those doubles are going to become home runs. So those were the numbers we used."

Once assembled, the Yankee Way remained subject to frequent updating and revision.

"That manual is a living manual," says Thomson, who worked in the Yankees organization until 2017. "There were all kinds of adjustments and additions and subtractions as time went on, and when I became the field coordinator [in 1998], Mark Newman was my boss. We were still continually just adjusting the manual."

The document's format evolved over the years, keeping pace with a time of dizzying technological change.

"It was a book when I got it," says Pat Roessler, the Yankees' director of player development who arrived in 2004 and was put in charge of updating the manual. "Then it was on a disk. Then we had it on flash drives. We gave it to each of our minor-league managers on flash drives. In spring training, you'd come in for the morning meeting, and guys would have a flash drive, looking at pivots in the outfield, bunt defense. And you review it so everyone is on the same page."

Thomson keeps the CD, which somehow still works, in his Phillies travel bag.

In the 2020s, the Yankees uploaded many of these materials onto the team-issued iPad Pro distributed to every player, coach, and member of the front office.

"The biggest thing we wanted to do was to stay current," Livesey says. "So everything we did, we reviewed. Once the season was over, we brought in all the managers and talked to them. We got all the pluses and minuses of the season—what we could do better as a front office to help them. What they could do better. We added the good stuff and subtracted that bad stuff.

"That was our attempt to stay on the cutting edge. During the winter, if anything developed as far as new technological equipment, we put it in if we thought it would help. We constantly reviewed it."

The constant updates continued into the twenty-first century under Newman.

"Thomson, Liv, Butter, Newman, and all these guys who came before me put this together," says Roessler, who remained with the Yankees through the 2014 season and returned as a big-league coach in 2024. "And then we had a philosophy that said, 'This is the way we're going to do it. But if you have a better way of doing something, or something emerges as a better way, all right, then we'll adjust. We'll keep updating.' It was great. Guys would bring up ideas and we would update. It was a lot of fucking work.

"Over the years, we made sure we had what Joe Torre wanted. Then we made sure we had what Joe Girardi wanted. There were multiple times when somebody in the organization would come in and say, 'Well, I always thought that a double cut on a ball to left center should go like this . . . ' And I'd go, 'Yeah, I understand, but this is how Joe Torre wants it, so this is the way we're gonna fucking do it.' And Girardi had a little bit of baserunning stuff, a little bit of catching stuff."

Roessler is telling these stories while standing in the visitors' dugout in New York's Citi Field one evening in May 2023. He's in town as the hitting coach for the visiting Washington Nationals before a game against the Mets. When I mention that only Glenn Sherlock seems to have kept a hard copy of the original book, Roessler lowers his voice, looks around, and says, "I still have mine, too."

In a separate document, Livesey also chronicled the organization's scouting and draft philosophy and made sure to keep it just as current as the Yankee Way manual.

"After every draft, we reviewed with the [scouts] what we did right, what we did wrong, what we could do better," he says. "We did it right after the draft because if you don't do it right away, there's a time when things become less important than how they seemed in the bar that night.

"At the bar, when you're talking over how it went, there is great information, but nobody is there to collect it. We got them up the next morning and said, 'Okay, get the bar talk out right now.' As an organization, we benefited from the attempts to review constantly and stay current."

Livesey called that document "The Yankee Scouting Manual." Along with the Yankee Way, its core concepts live on within the organization.

How unique was any of this to the Yankees? After all, plenty of other organizations have employed innovative coaches and put into writing their beliefs on specifics of the game. Most famously, the St. Louis Cardinals formalized decades of their own ideas and traditions in the Cardinal Way, a 117-page proprietary document created in 2011.

But a key difference between the Yankees and nearly everyone else in this regard is the continuity in the front office since Livesey and Newman wrote the Yankee Way. From then into the future, Cashman functioned as a human through line across four decades.

By contrast, most teams have overhauled their baseball operations departments many times since Cashman became a Yankee. The norm in the industry is for owners to become impatient with their front offices and seek an overhaul every few years. Or for the owners themselves to sell and give way to entirely new organizations, as the New York Mets did when passing from the Wilpon family to the hedge fund billionaire Steve Cohen in 2020.

George Steinbrenner, in the decades prior to his 1990 suspension, embodied as much as anyone the impulse for constant change, but the team itself has remained in his family for more than fifty years. And Livesey and Michael, for all the turnover below them, were there long enough to leave their mark on Cashman.

The Oakland Athletics and Cleveland Indians/Guardians are the only other teams that can claim front-office continuity to rival the Yankees. In Oakland, Sandy Alderson took over as GM in the early 1980s and mentored Billy Beane in the 1990s, which enabled Beane to pass the same torch to his successor, David Forst. In Cleveland, Hank Peters ran the team beginning in 1987 and was succeeded by John Hart, who was succeeded by Mark Shapiro, who was succeeded by Chris Antonetti. Each of the executives in that chain worked for his predecessor—a lineage that runs deep, but more than a decade short of the one Cashman inherited.

The Yankee Way manual and the people who taught it were not the only manifestations of organizational cohesion. During the Yankees' pre-dynasty years of the late 1980s, the physical space to which the Yankees moved helped Livesey and his staffers to implement their ideas in a more holistic way.

For years, the team's player development operation was spread out over a few disconnected fields in South Florida. Then, in the 1980s, the team took over what had once been the Cincinnati Reds' complex in Tampa; there, they began to create the sprawling, connected space that was still growing more than thirty years later.

Nicknamed Himes because of its address at 3102 North Himes Avenue, the complex holds Yankee offices, minor-league fields, and, in recent years, increasingly advanced biomechanical and sports science labs.

Players, from Derek Jeter as a young prospect in the 1990s all the way up to star outfielder Aaron Judge and infielder DJ LeMahieu in the 2020s, settled in Tampa and utilized the complex year-round. Yankees staffers were now able to work with both major- and minor-league players year-round, which rendered their teaching that much more holistic.

Cashman, along with Sabean, Lukevics, Newman, and Livesey, was part of a small group that helped to develop the Himes complex. Lukevics, who was Cashman's immediate boss, remembers Cashman as a young man who would "arrive early and stay late" and was part of a hardworking, hard-partying group.

"It was a really unique staff," Sabean says. "We had a very diligent work ethic, but we had fun that was off the wall, too. We enjoyed each other. It was a lot of give-and-take.

"Moving our operation to Tampa, we built a year-round facility. It was a major factor in our later success that we all got ourselves under one roof. There was no separation now, because our scouts would be coming in year-round to evaluate our players, and it became almost seamless. This was ahead of its time, and it's one of the reasons the Yankees have such a strong scouting system."

It was here that the Tampa staff, and the Yankees scouts, made a mark on the organization in ways that Michael could not.

"Gene Michael was rarely able to go out and look at players at that time," Cashman says. "George had this idea that a GM should be in the office."

Looking back, Sabean praises Steinbrenner for investing in the infrastructure that helped them to improve scouting and player development.

"Steinbrenner doesn't get enough credit for being innovative,"

Sabean says. "He was the first one to add coaches. He was one of the first to expand minor-league coaching staffs and training staffs. He just saw the forest for the trees: If you're investing money in amateur talent, you need the facilities. You need the expert people around them, and they need to take great care in how you're dealing with them and developing them."

By the end of the 1980s, prior to Steinbrenner's entanglement with the gambler Howie Spira over Dave Winfield and subsequent expulsion from the game, the Yankees' player development apparatus was ahead of its time. It had multiple instructional-league teams rather than the standard one team; it had extra coaches at every level and paid them above-market salaries; it had a big-budget facility; and it had its own internal book.

The whole system was clicking: Sabean and his scouts were identifying good players, and Lukevics, Livesey, Cashman, and others were turning them into prospects.

There was just one problem.

"We traded them all away," Livesey says with a rueful laugh. "With the exception of [Don] Mattingly, we traded them all away. And I mean all of them."

Soon, though, that would change. Soon Steinbrenner would be temporarily gone, Michael would be empowered, and the prospects developed in Tampa would be safe to actually become New York Yankees.

"We finally did learn to hold on to our core guys," Livesey says. "Stick was the GM [in the early 1980s] when we were trading all our core guys. He stepped aside but came back in '90, and I think we were all better prepared because of that experience.

"This time it was, get a nucleus, and don't trade it off. We traded for Tino, David Cone, and others. But this time we tried to have enough prospects where we could say no to trading the core guys— the Jeters, the Posadas, the Bernies, the Marianos, Pettittes. And we did say no to trading those guys.

"This time, we knew better."

13

The Boss Returns, Tells Showalter
and the Other Assholes That They
Better Make the World Series

I T WAS MARCH 1, 1993, and the stage was set for George Steinbrenner's return—save for one detail: Don Mattingly, Yankee captain, did not want any part of it.

The year before, Steinbrenner had negotiated an end to his "lifetime" ban with Commissioner Fay Vincent, one of Vincent's last
decisions before Major League Baseball owners forced him out of
office in favor of one of their own, the Milwaukee Brewers owner,
Allan H. "Bud" Selig.

The Boss's reentry was not a subtle production. The issue of *Sports
Illustrated* that hit newsstands on March 1 featured a cover image of
Steinbrenner sitting atop a white horse, dressed as Napoleon. The
article, written by Jill Lieber, reported that he had been walking
around his Tampa home in a black bathrobe with "The Boss Is Back"
embroidered on the back in white.

"This is the most ballyhooed return since the Resurrection," the
Chicago White Sox owner, Jerry Reinsdorf, told *SI.* "Originally I
thought it was going to be like a coronation in New York, but it's
become too massive for that. It's a resurrection. Vincent nailed him to
the cross. This is the biggest thing to happen in 2,000 years."

The Toronto Blue Jays president, Paul Beeston, offered a contrasting but only slightly less dramatic analogy. "It's like Sherman storm-
ing Atlanta," Beeston said.

In advance of the big day in spring training the Yankees' public
relations staff passed out hundreds of "The Boss Is Back" buttons,
and the team planned a show that included skydivers, trained dogs

jumping through hoops, and a Marilyn Monroe look-alike descending on the complex in a helicopter, then stepping out of the aircraft holding a sign that said, "Welcome Back, George."

While the crowd was watching this spectacle, a man in a long wig and a denim jacket would emerge from the stands, strip off the accessories, and reveal himself to be George Steinbrenner. A terrorist bombing of the World Trade Center in late February necessitated that the Yankees tone down those plans, but Steinbrenner still wanted to make an entrance of some kind.

"They were going through all these scenarios about helicopters coming in," says Buck Showalter, who was the manager in 1993. "But I remember we ended up getting Mattingly to come over and shake his hand on the field. Donnie didn't want to do it. And I said to Donnie, 'I don't think we have a choice here.'"

Tensions between Steinbrenner and Mattingly stretched back at least to 1987, after Mattingly won a salary arbitration hearing. Following that decision, Steinbrenner said, "He's like all the rest of them now. He can't play little Jack Armstrong of Evansville, Indiana, anymore. He goes into the category of the modern-player-with-agent looking for bucks."

Mattingly did not respond, and Steinbrenner continued to needle him in the press. After a loss to Seattle at Yankee Stadium on August 21, 1988, Mattingly finally fired back.

"You come here, you play and you get no respect," he told a group of reporters in the locker room. "You get money and that's it. They think money is respect. Call us babies, call us whatever you want—if you don't treat me with respect, I don't want to play with you. They treat you like shit. They belittle your performance, make you look bad in the media. After they give you the money, they can do whatever they want to. They can beat you over the head and you just take it."

Mattingly knew that the bad old days of Steinbrenner's reign—the ugly underbelly that would soon be whitewashed during the brighter years of the late 1990s and beyond—had created an unsustainable culture. To some extent, those days were soon to return.

But there was one significant difference: after nearly three years in which Gene Michael, Bill Livesey, Mitch Lukevics, Brian Sabean, Mark Newman, and Brian Cashman were left to their own devices, the organization was much stronger.

Not that the owner immediately felt that way. As Michael later recounted to the author Bill Pennington, Steinbrenner said upon returning, "While I was away, you guys really messed things up."

"Oh really?" Michael answered. "So things were going well when you left in 1990?"

Steinbrenner said Michael was being a wise guy, but he backed down. On some level, he must have seen the improvement that was evident on both the major- and the minor-league sides.

The Yanks had lost ninety-one games in 1991 and eighty-six in 1992, but were projected to improve in 1993. Michael had acquired two top-shelf left-handed starting pitchers, Jim Abbott and Jimmy Key, and snagged the righty Bob Wickman in that slick Steve Sax deal with Chicago. Abbott and Key in particular were known as fierce competitors and popular teammates and helped to reinforce the positive clubhouse culture that Showalter was working to establish.

On the position player side, Steinbrenner returned to find Paul O'Neill in right field, the popular Mike Stanley catching, and future Hall of Famer Wade Boggs—who had led the league in on-base percentage six times—at third. In an even stronger sign of better days ahead, Bernie Williams stood in center field as the tip of a farm system iceberg.

Other homegrown Yankees who made appearances that year— a season in which the team took a dramatic leap forward, winning eighty-eight games—were outfielder Gerald Williams, second baseman Pat Kelly, and starting pitcher Scott Kamieniecki.

Layered under them in the minors were future Hall of Fame closer Mariano Rivera, lefty Andy Pettitte, and Jorge Posada, the former stocky shortstop whom Livesey had converted to a catcher.

By 1993, Derek Jeter had also arrived in the system.

Jeter was a highly touted high school shortstop in Kalamazoo, Michigan, projected to be one of the top picks in the 1992 amateur draft. When Sabean, who ran the draft for the Yankees, went to look at him, he saw a young man with advanced instincts for the game— uncommon for a cold-weather state, where players do not have the advantage of staying on the field for twelve months a year. In scouting terms, Jeter seemed like a West Coast prospect.

"He used his athletic ability," Sabean says. "But it was his awareness on the field where you could tell he was so advanced, which is rare being from the Great Lakes."

Livesey, who at that time was working alongside Sabean evaluating amateur players for the draft, also traveled to Michigan to take a look at Jeter and came away impressed. Both he and Sabean understood why area scout Dick Groch, who had spent the better part of two years watching Jeter, had become a fierce advocate for him.

"The behind-the-scenes guru of all this was Dick Groch, who had fallen in love with Jeter the summer before, and really got on the soapbox for him," Sabean said.

In part because of Groch's emphatic advocacy, Sabean brought to Michigan Don Lindeberg, an area scout from the West Coast with a particularly interesting résumé. Lindeberg was born in 1915, played minor-league ball in the 1930s and 1940s, and served as a pilot in World War II, when he was shot down on three separate occasions.

He then became one of the top scouts for the Brooklyn Dodgers under Branch Rickey, the Hall of Fame executive who had invented the very concept of a farm system. Because of his dual skills in baseball and aviation, Lindeberg would fly Rickey to tryout camps. As Rickey evaluated players, it was Lindeberg's job to write down his boss's comments.

"Rickey would tell Lindy what to keep an eye on, and they would bounce ideas off one another," Sabean says.

With a lifetime of experience stretching back almost to the very creation of player development, Lindeberg watched Jeter.

"Lindy never put a comp on Jeter, but he had an ability for comparative analysis like no other. In scouting, a lot of what people define as gut instinct or gut decision making—that couldn't be farther from the truth," Sabean says. "Good scouts are looking at something based on their experiences and making a comparative analysis. And as Lindy watched Jeter, he saw potential star quality."

The Yankees had the sixth pick in the 1992 draft. Livesey wanted Jeter, but did not know if Jeter would sign, because he had committed to the University of Michigan. He looked to Groch for guidance on that point.

"He's not going to Michigan," Groch said. "The only place he's going is to Cooperstown."

The Houston Astros had the first pick. On the morning of the draft, Livesey was elated to learn in a phone call from Astros' scouting director Dan O'Brien that the team was planning to select the Cal State–Fullerton star Phil Nevin.

Of the next four teams, the Yankees viewed Baltimore at four and Cincinnati at five as the biggest threats. In both cases they caught lucky breaks.

"Frank Robinson [the Hall of Fame player and former Orioles manager who was still working for Baltimore in 1992] went to Tallahassee for a regional NCAA tournament where Jeffrey Hammonds from Stanford went completely off," Sabean says. "He was the best player there and shot up everyone's board. As luck would have it, I think Frank's recommendation came from being there and watching this firsthand."

Baltimore selected Hammonds, and Cincinnati was next up. The Reds were seriously considering Jeter, even though future Hall of Famer Barry Larkin was established at shortstop. Ultimately, Larkin's presence proved a strong factor in dissuading the Reds from taking Jeter.

When Cincinnati instead chose Chad Mottola, an outfielder from the University of Central Florida, the Yankees' draft room at the Steinbrenner-owned Radisson Bay Harbor Inn in Tampa erupted in cheers. Somehow Jeter had fallen to them.

Over the next few years, Jeter's development hit rocky patches, most notably when he made fifty-six errors in 1993 while playing for the Class-A Greensboro Hornets. Gene Michael flew to Tampa to see for himself what the problem was; using his elite scouting eye, which worked especially well on fellow infielders, Michael saw correctable issues with Jeter's footwork.

The Yankees sent Jeter to the instructional league that fall and assigned coach Brian Butterfield—son of Jack Butterfield, the man who started their player development tradition—to work with Jeter for thirty-five straight days.

Jeter bore down and made dramatic improvements. The following season he would reach Triple-A; the year after that, on May 30, 1995, in Seattle, he slapped a single to left field for his first of 3,465 big-league hits. Rivera and Pettitte also debuted that year.

Organizational progress had been steady throughout the early

1990s. In 1993 the Yankees posted a winning record for the first time since 1988, finishing 88–74. And the following year was shaping up as special before labor unrest brought it to an abrupt conclusion.

On August 12, 1994, the Yanks sat in first place in the American League East when the Major League Baseball Players Association declared a strike. A month later, MLB canceled the World Series.

For a Yankees organization that had worked hard for years to reemerge as contenders, the developments of 1994 were both heartbreaking and encouraging. It hurt to see a promising year spoiled, but the team entered 1995 with high hopes.

Bolstering an already strong team, Michael traded for Montreal Expos closer John Wetteland and Chicago White Sox All-Star Jack McDowell, a former Cy Young Award winner. As the strike ended and a delayed spring training began, many around the game considered the Yankees World Series favorites in 1995.

Despite that sense of momentum, Steinbrenner declined to extend the expiring contracts of both Michael and Showalter, leaving both as lame ducks. The initial weeks of the season, which did not begin until April 26 because of the strike, served only to increase the owner's impatience.

The Yankees were 10–16 in May and 13–14 in June. At various junctures during those two months, Mattingly, McDowell, Paul O'Neill, Wade Boggs, and Jimmy Key suffered injuries.

The team did not appear able to recapture the halted magic of 1994. In August, Mickey Mantle died at just sixty-three of liver cancer. The beloved broadcaster Phil Rizzuto missed Mantle's funeral because of work obligations, a disappointment that led him to announce his retirement. The vibe in Yankeeland, defined the year before by a buzz about the future, had become downright somber.

Within the front office, employees saw troubling signs that Steinbrenner was returning to his old, mercurial ways. He and Michael had always fought, but as the 1995 season unfolded unevenly, the pair began to tangle more often, and more viciously, than usual. The Boss began to muse openly about why he paid Michael just to argue with him.

Steinbrenner could also be overheard questioning Showalter's in-game moves and wondering if the thirty-nine-year-old had enough experience to lead the Yankees to their next championship.

After a losing August, the Yankees finally began to click in September, winning twenty-one of twenty-seven games to finish in second place in the American League East and capture the AL Wild Card under a newly established expanded playoff format.

Key to that turnaround was Mattingly, who had suffered for years with back trouble and was a severely diminished player; as it turned out, he was just weeks from playing his final game. Home run swings were too painful, so he had learned to shorten up and try to dunk singles into left field.

In September, Mattingly approached Showalter and said, "I'm just gonna let it rip the rest of the way. No more going the other way. If I blow out my back, I blow out my back."

Showalter found himself worrying that every Mattingly swing would be the last. But Mattingly survived, pushing through pain to hit .321 with two home runs in the final month of the season.

On October 1, after 1,785 career games, the much-loved but least decorated Yankee captain finally reached the postseason. After the Yankees defeated the Blue Jays in Toronto to clinch the Wild Card berth, Mattingly stopped on his way off the field and pounded his fist into the artificial turf, as if to confirm that the moment were real.

The Yankees had made the playoffs for the first time since 1981, and did it in part by utilizing the principle that Gene Michael valued most, getting on base. In 1990, when Michael took over as GM, the Yankees' collective OBP was .300. In 1995 it was .357, tied for second best in all of baseball.

After the clincher, Steinbrenner walked into Showalter's office, where the manager sat with his coaches. "You assholes better get to the World Series," Steinbrenner said.

It wasn't the only moment that predicted dysfunction to come. In fact, Steinbrenner had already engineered a significant setback for the organization.

In August, Bill Livesey had begun to get calls from Steinbrenner about specific scouts.

"What's this guy do?" the Boss would ask. "Do we really need this guy?"

"I'm thinking, 'Here we go,'" Livesey says. "'He must be thinking about cutting down.' I just didn't know it involved me."

During his time with the Yankees, Livesey had noticed a pattern:

Steinbrenner would provide resources for improvements, then grow impatient roughly six years later. He had felt it in the mid- to late 1980s, but then was allowed to develop the Yankee Way in 1989. Six years after that—1995—the Yankees still hadn't won a championship, and the Boss was restless again.

"I think the strike really killed us," Livesey says. "We were in first place. If we had won that year, maybe he would have been in a different mood in '95.

"But we got to '95 and the big-league club got off to a slow start. Now all of a sudden [Steinbrenner] is thinking, 'Dammit, I've got to make some things happen.' He set the wheels in motion for a change, and the wheels were too far down the road by the time we turned it around."

On September 19, Livesey, Mitch Lukevics, and scouting coordinator Kevin Elfering were in Scottsdale, Arizona, for the annual meetings for MLB's scouting and player development directors. The trio thought it strange that Joe Molloy, a general partner with the Yankees and Steinbrenner's son-in-law at the time, had traveled with them.

Yankees scout Bill Geivett, another Livesey disciple, was walking from his car to the hotel when he saw Livesey leaving the building. This confused Geivett, because the meeting was just beginning. Once inside he would learn that an entire era had ended.

"We spent the night at the hotel, and the next morning Joe Molloy called us into his room and he fired us," Lukevics says. "So we left."

Livesey, Lukevics, and Elfering, not knowing what else to do with themselves, went to a nearby shopping mall, where they tried to figure out how to get home.

This was a seismic change, and very much for the worse—and Steinbrenner had executed it just as a dynasty was about to begin.

"It was really, really difficult," Rob Thomson says of the firings and their aftermath. "We tried to go about our business as if Bill and Mitch were still here."

Decades later, Livesey, Lukevics, and Elfering can only speculate about who undermined them with Steinbrenner. Many of those whose names come up in conversations, like longtime Steinbrenner crony and pitching coach Billy Connors, are no longer alive to give their versions of the story. Cashman does not know definitively who poisoned the well with the Boss, either. Molloy carried out the orders and says he does not recall who put the idea in his father-in-law's head. It all unfolded with cold inertia, like a scene from *The Godfather*.

In 2023, a sixty-nine-year-old Lukevics was still trying to process all the interoffice drama.

"It was a shock because Bill [Livesey] had blinders on," Lukevics said. "We were focused on the task at hand. We weren't focused on whoever sunk us. Somebody had to get to Mr. Steinbrenner—somebody for their own greater good."

Livesey freely admits that he was hard-driving and capable of making enemies. "One of our standards was, respect me now, like me later—maybe!" Livesey says. "Those standards were nonnegotiable."

"Some people said Bill was hard," Lukevics says. "You're goddamn right he was hard. But he was fair."

The expansion Tampa Bay Devil Rays immediately scooped up Livesey, Lukevics, and Elfering. Lukevics was still working for the Rays in 2024 (Livesey was in his eighties and retired).

Just like that, most of the men who developed and wrote the Yankee Way were forced to watch in exile as the new Yankee dynasty took off and soared.

"Bill Livesey knew what we had," Lukevics says. "We couldn't predict the future of every player, but it was a really good group. I mean, stellar athletes with stellar character, and I say to this day that I give Bill Livesey and Brian Sabean a lot of credit.

"You can jump off the bridge after you get let go and they play five World Series. There's no single person that has everything to do with success, which is total team effort, and I'd say I had a part. If I had to single out one person that had the most impact, it's Bill Livesey. I don't read everything, but in the little I read, he doesn't get nearly a pat on the back."

Sabean, who had departed in 1993 for the San Francisco Giants, remains wistful about a time when he was working for a mentor and with good friends, united by the common purpose of rebuilding the Yankees from the ground up.

"I learned about what it took to become a man within the business of baseball from Bill Livesey," Sabean says. "Other than my dad, he was the biggest influence on me. On a lot of us. It was a special group."

Says Livesey, "Sabean was in San Francisco, licking his chops at the idea of bringing over six or seven Yankee [officials]. Buck, Sherlock, and Butterfield went to Arizona. Mitch and I went to Tampa Bay. We were all scattered."

Cashman—who by 1995 was back in New York and working as assistant general manager—was suddenly left to proceed without most of his important teachers. He would later regard Livesey's firing as the beginning of the end of the Yankee dynasty, even though it happened before the team won its first championship of the era.

Because of the timing, many of the architects never got to enjoy the finished structure. "You just want to be able to stand off to the side of a [World Series] celebration and say, 'Goddamn. Those guys got it done,'" Livesey says. "And we didn't get to be there for it."

Of Cashman's early mentors, only Gene Michael had retained his power—but his day of reckoning as GM was coming soon.

14

Those Assholes Didn't Make
the World Series

Y OU'RE A STUBBORN GERMAN cocksucker!"
George Steinbrenner, once enamored of Buck Showalter as a managing wunderkind whose attention to detail recalled the vaunted Billy Martin and Jack Butterfield, had of late been growing characteristically impatient with his skipper.

One day in 1995, he stormed into Showalter's office with an unexpected insult. After all, neither Showalter nor his ancestors were in any way German.

Steinbrenner, on the other hand, actually was of German and Irish descent.

"Takes one to know one," Showalter shot back, understanding that the Boss was occasionally looking for a little pushback, provided it happened in private.

As the Yankees began the 1995 postseason, fans remained unaware of the discord boiling under the surface. They were simply enjoying the long-awaited return of playoff baseball to the Bronx.

Showalter was also able to live fully in the moment. On October 3, in the minutes before Game 1 of a division series matchup with Seattle, public address announcer Bob Sheppard began the starting lineups by calling the manager from the dugout.

Sprinting to the first base line, Showalter broke from his typically taciturn character to wave his cap in the air and pump his fist.

Drafted by the Yankees in 1977, Showalter had worked as a player, minor-league manager, and big-league coach to help turn the organization around. He had internalized the principles of the Yankee Way.

The franchise meant the world to him, and now he was manager when the sun finally peeked through the clouds.

With the stadium so loud that it seemed to shake, David Cone started the game. Cone had been a key trade deadline acquisition by Gene Michael that July; on this day, he pitched well enough to win, and the Yankees grabbed a quick lead in the series.

The next night, Mattingly launched a game-tying home run in the bottom of the seventh, inspiring further escalations of drama and joy. As the ball landed in the right-field bleachers, television play-by-play announcer Gary Thorne tried to shout over the raucous fans.

Thorne's call—"hang on to the roof!"—was apt; if there had been a roof on the stadium, it would have blown off at that moment.

In a happy accident of TV choreography, the broadcast then cut to Jeter, the next Yankee captain, standing on the top step of the dugout and cheering.

Up two games to none in the best-of-five series, the Yanks traveled to Seattle—and lost the next two, setting up a win-or-else Game 5.

Throughout those defeats, Steinbrenner stewed in a suite at the Kingdome, the Mariners' home park. Watching with a group that included Michael, Cashman, and Reggie Jackson, the owner repeatedly groused that Showalter was being out-managed by his counterpart, longtime Yankee Lou Piniella.

The events of Game 5 did little to dissuade the owner from his new, more negative opinion of Showalter. The manager left an exhausted Cone in the game to throw 147 pitches, the last of which was ball four in the dirt and allowed the tying run to score in the eighth inning.

When Showalter trotted out to retrieve him, Cone hunched over, hands on his knees. He handed his manager the ball, then walked down the dugout steps and into the clubhouse, where he buried his head in a towel and cried.

Mariano Rivera had been ready in the bullpen, but came in only after Cone surrendered the lead. Rivera proceeded to strike out Mike Blowers on three pitches, an overpowering performance that launched him on the national stage.

Now that Rivera is in the Hall of Fame, it is easy to wonder why Showalter hadn't summoned him sooner. But from the vantage of 1995, the veteran Cone seemed a better bet. That year, moving between the starting rotation and the bullpen, the twenty-five-year-old Rivera had posted a 5.51 earned run average. He had only that year acquired the extra tick of velocity that made his fastball effective.

As recently as that summer, Michael had seriously considered trading Rivera to Detroit for starting pitcher David Wells. The Yankees were just beginning to realize what they had in Rivera, and how to use him. No matter. Steinbrenner was irate, sputtering about his manager.

Knotted at 4–4, the game proceeded into the eleventh inning, when Randy Velarde singled in Pat Kelly to give the Yankees a 5–4 lead. If they had held it for three more outs, Showalter might have remained manager into the future with Michael as GM.

As it turned out, Edgar Martinez's two-run single in the bottom of the inning off Jack McDowell made it a historic day for the Mariners, not the Yankees: Seattle won, 6–5.

While the Mariners collapsed in a heap near home plate, the Yankees sat stunned in the dugout, incapable even of filing down the steps to the clubhouse as players usually do once eliminated.

Paul O'Neill made a zombie march from right field and walked the length of the dugout, all the way past the bat rack, appearing present in body but elsewhere in spirit. On the field, Piniella laughed and waved his cap to the fans. Up in the suite, Steinbrenner stood glowering.

Sensing the end not just of Mattingly's career but of an entire era, grown men wept on the flight back to New York.

Within days, Steinbrenner stripped Michael of one of the key duties of a GM, informing him that he, the owner, would decide Showalter's fate. Later that month, Steinbrenner essentially fired Michael by telling him that he could return as general manager but at a pay cut. It was an offer designed to be refused, and Michael agreed to step down from the top post and return to scouting.

Few veteran executives were willing to even interview with Steinbrenner for the GM vacancy, but the Boss was able to persuade Bob Watson, a mild-mannered former first baseman and GM of the Houston Astros, to take the job.

Way back on November 8, 1979, Watson had signed with the Yankees as one of Michael's first acquisitions during his initial stint as general manager. Now he was coming in cold to lead a baseball operations department he knew nothing about.

Steinbrenner dithered over what to do with Showalter. Cashman recommended keeping the manager, but Steinbrenner did not seem in the mood to listen. The Boss did end up offering Showalter a two-year contract to return, but with the stipulation that he fire four coaches. That was a nonstarter for Showalter, who believed in the principle that a manager should stick up for his lieutenants.

Among those coaches at risk was Brian Butterfield, son of Jack and a link to traditions that had already been severely weakened by recent dismissals. Steinbrenner soon changed his mind on Butterfield, but not on the other coaches.

It was not going to work. Showalter had another offer to essentially design the Arizona Diamondbacks, an expansion franchise set to begin play in 1998. He knew he needed to take it, but in doing so left a piece of himself at Yankee Stadium.

So it came to pass that by the end of 1995 the Yankee Way was at risk of extinction. Showalter was in Arizona, taking Brian Butterfield with him. Jack Butterfield and Billy Martin were long deceased. Brian Sabean was in San Francisco.

Bill Livesey and Mitch Lukevics were across the Sunshine Skyway Bridge from the Yankees' Tampa complex, helping to launch the Devil Rays in St. Petersburg. Gene Michael was still a Yankee, but Steinbrenner had taken his power away.

The team was about to begin one of the great runs in the history of the sport, but would do it largely without the people who got them there. Fortunately for those remaining, the foundation was strong enough to get the Yankees through the next few years, but were the seeds for the end of a dynasty already planted, even before the first championship?

"No doubt," Cashman says. "Because George put in play people who were subpar [compared with the people he fired]. There's a reason that the Giants got really good after they hired Sabean. That alone was a huge loss for us."

Cashman tried to carry the torch for those left behind. For the next three decades, he would watch—and at times seethe—as the world identified the Yankee dynasty with Joe Torre, Jeter, Steinbrenner, even Michael and wonder why no one thought to mention Sabean, Livesey, Lukevics, and the others.

When Cashman says that we've all gotten Yankee history wrong, this is a big part of what he means.

PART THREE

DYNASTY

15

"Are You Ready, Son?"

A RE YOU READY, SON? You better be ready!"
George Steinbrenner sat at his desk at Yankee Stadium, flanked by his burly driver, Eddie Fastook. Before him stood a twenty-nine-year-old Brian Cashman.

"This guy Bob Watson, he's not gonna make it!" the Boss shouted, referring to his own general manager. "Are you ready?"

Ready for *what*? Cashman thought, but he remained silent for the moment.

"I'm thinking of replacing Watson with you," Steinbrenner said. "Are you ready? If I do make a change, are you ready?"

This was September 1996. The Yankees were leading the American League East but in the month of August had lost more games than they'd won. The second-place Baltimore Orioles were closing the gap.

Steinbrenner had been telling his first-year GM, Watson, and first-year manager, Joe Torre, that they were "going to blow it" and were turning the Yankees into a "laughingstock."

"Baltimore was flying high," Cashman recalls. "We were crapping ourselves."

Cashman was not surprised that Steinbrenner had become impatient, but the suggestion that he should take over landed as wholly unexpected. General manager? Cashman had never viewed himself as a candidate for that job. In fact, he didn't expect to remain with the Yankees much longer.

"I thought this was a pit stop," Cashman says. "I thought this was something that I'd be doing for a few years until I got a real job.

"If you turn the clock back to then, former major-league players sat in that [GM] chair. The general managers around the game were Bob Watson, Woody Woodward, Ed Lynch, Ron Schueler, Pat Gillick. Those are former players. These were all former minor-league and major-league players who were hired and went into front offices. Sandy Alderson [in Oakland] was not a former player, but he was a lawyer. I wasn't a lawyer.

"So there wasn't that aspiration of, 'I'm gonna be this,' or 'I can do that.' That wasn't really the makeup of front offices at that time. I was kind of just cutting my teeth as a young professional. In college, I worked at UPS part time and was offered full-time positions there. I took the LSATs and was thinking about going to law school.

"I just didn't know what I was going to do. And that was okay. I had no idea where I would be going in life. I mean, I loved baseball, but I never expected to make a career out of it."

After the Yankees elevated Cashman to the position of assistant general manager in 1992, he continued to assume that he would spend the bulk of his working life in a different industry.

"Even then, I still thought about bouncing," he says. "Trying to apply to Wharton Business School or something like that. Because I never thought I would be going places here."

Now Steinbrenner was suggesting otherwise. Despite that potentially life-altering surprise, though, Cashman's first thought was about chain of command. Without Watson present, this was not an appropriate meeting.

"Listen," Cashman told Steinbrenner. "I work for you, but I report to him. And I am not having this conversation. I'm not comfortable with it."

He left the office. On September 18, the Orioles came to Yankee Stadium for three games and lost two of them. The crisis passed. Cashman remained the assistant, and Steinbrenner temporarily forgave Watson and Torre, a pair of Yankee newcomers with no bank of goodwill or background in the team's traditions.

Watson had played briefly for the Yankees in the early 1980s but lacked the institutional knowledge of his predecessor, Michael, or the trusting relationship with Steinbrenner that Michael enjoyed.

Torre, at least, was a New Yorker and a natural on the big stage. A Brooklyn native and former National League MVP, he was fifty-five years old when Steinbrenner hired him in 1995. Baseball fans identified Torre with the Atlanta Braves, St. Louis Cardinals, and New York Mets, all of whom he had played for and managed.

But Steinbrenner, vulnerable to the grass-is-greener impulse, occasionally liked to go outside his circle for GM and managerial hires, as he had with manager Dallas Green and GM Syd Thrift in 1989 and Watson in his recent GM selection.

Torre represented a complete break from the managerial DNA that preceded him—the Casey Stengel–to–Billy Martin–to–Buck Showalter connection that rooted Yankee managers in the game's deepest traditions and stretched all the way back to New York Giants legend John McGraw. Torre was an outsider with no experience in the Yankee Way.

It certainly wasn't all change for the worse. Unlike Showalter, Torre had a naturally relaxed demeanor; where Showalter obsessed over every detail, Torre didn't tend to sweat the small stuff. That made him—in his first years as a Yankee at least—a fit for the needs of a stormy team.

He also bonded quickly with the young assistant GM who would soon become his boss. "At first," Cashman says, "Joe Torre was like a second father to me."

One of the first significant decisions for the Yankees after Torre took over was whether to begin the 1996 season with Jeter as the starting shortstop. That had been the plan entering spring training, but as Jeter struggled and the season drew closer, some in the organization began to wonder if it was wise for a ballclub with championship aspirations to entrust such an important position to a rookie.

In late March, a group of the highest-ranking Yankee officials gathered in Torre's spring training office to discuss the issue. Present for the meeting were Steinbrenner, Watson, Torre, Cashman, Gene Michael, and Clyde King, a Steinbrenner crony and occasional pitching coach, manager, and GM in the 1980s.

Torre's coaches, including Willie Randolph, were also there, as was Ron Brand, Michael's old friend from the minor leagues in the 1950s and 1960s and now a top Yankees scout.

At Steinbrenner's behest, King spoke first. He said that Jeter was not ready and should begin the season either on the bench or in the minor leagues. In order to address the hole at shortstop, the Yankees could trade Mariano Rivera to Seattle for light-hitting veteran Félix Fermín.

King's opening monologue shocked many in the room. The plan had been to give Jeter a shot. Now, as discussion began, Cashman voted to stick with the rookie.

Torre agreed, but in a soothing, measured way that Yankee officials had rarely experienced.

"If you want to send Jeter out, you can always do it a month from now," the manager said. "You don't have to do it because he had a bad spring. Start the season and see what happens."

Michael, no less feisty in his new role as a scout, struck a different tone.

"Clyde King came in and decided that they were going to send Jeter out," Brand says. "Stick went ballistic. He said, 'Wait a minute, wait a minute, what about all the plans? We knew this guy was going to be our shortstop. Now we're going to shy away from that?'"

Michael argued that he saw in Jeter a player who, even while trying to make the roster, was less concerned about personal performance than he was about the team winning. That, Michael said, was exactly what the Yankees needed.

Randolph, responsible for coaching the team's infielders, also spoke up for Jeter.

"Hey, George," Randolph said. "Give me this kid and don't worry about it. He's gonna be fine. I know he made a lot of errors in the minors, but he's gonna be fine."

Randolph bolstered the case for keeping Jeter by mentioning Bobby Meacham, a young infielder in the 1980s whose confidence and chance at consistency suffered from frequent trips between Triple-A and the Bronx.

"As long as you don't yo-yo him back and forth and play with his head like Meacham, he'll be fine," Randolph said. "We'll deal with some of the errors."

Randolph went on to argue that Jeter's athleticism would make him an asset no matter how else he performed.

"Even if he struggles, we can carry him," Randolph said. "He can run, and we could use his speed."

Momentum in the room was turning away from King and toward the case for Jeter.

"You sure about this, Willie?" Steinbrenner asked.

Randolph said that he was.

"All right, you said it," Steinbrenner said, then repeated: "You said it."

"I'm looking at him like, 'Okay, what are you gonna do?'" Randolph recalls. "You're gonna give me forty lashes or something? Hey, man, my reputation is on the line here, but if it doesn't work, it doesn't work. But I thought the kid had potential. I saw that we needed an infusion of young speed and youthfulness, and I thought he would be an asset to our team. If he starts making errors, pull him and send him back to Triple-A."

The room had turned against King, and Steinbrenner conceded, though not without issuing his oft-repeated dictum on the way out: "You better be right."

On this one, Michael, Randolph, Cashman, Torre, and the other pro-Jeter voices would find immediate validation. Jeter won the American League Rookie of the Year award in 1996 and served as the starting shortstop for the Yankees' first World Series championship since 1978.

During the regular season and then the October run, Torre's calm, empathic leadership proved vital. He and Jeter, who called him Mr. T., connected immediately.

A key moment in that relationship came on August 12, when Jeter made a rookie mistake of overaggression, trying to steal third base with two outs and slugger Cecil Fielder batting. That was a big no-no; he was already in scoring position, and a player is never supposed to make the first or third out of an inning at third.

Torre was so angry that he decided to wait until the next day to speak with Jeter. But when Jeter returned to the dugout, he plopped himself right between Torre and bench coach Don Zimmer. Torre, impressed by the instant accountability, patted Jeter on the head and said, with affection, "Get outta here."

In the World Series that year, Torre served as a balm for Steinbrenner's jangly nerves. The Yankees, facing the defending champions, the Atlanta Braves, sent Andy Pettitte to the mound in Game 1 at Yankee Stadium.

Pettitte had won twenty-one games that year and made the All-Star team, but on this night the Braves knocked him out of the game in the third inning. His opponent was the twenty-four-game winner John Smoltz, who would soon be named the 1996 National League Cy Young Award winner. Smoltz lasted six strong innings, and the Braves won, 12–1.

Before Game 2, Watson addressed the team, saying he was proud of them for the season they'd had. Torre, knowing that Watson had spent the day with a miserable Steinbrenner, thought that the GM sounded too funereal, too past tense. He decided to follow Watson's speech with a few rosier words.

"Listen," Torre told the players. "We've played and beaten better offensive teams than Atlanta. . . . There's no reason why we can't beat this team."

In fact, Torre knew that the night's pitching matchup was not at all favorable: Greg Maddux, probably the pitcher of the decade, against Jimmy Key, an excellent competitor but no Maddux. But the manager also knew it was a long series—a thought that he conveyed to Steinbrenner himself when the anxious Boss charged into Torre's office.

"This is a must [win] game," Steinbrenner said.

Torre, making a point to hardly look up from his desk, said, "You should be prepared for us to lose again tonight. But then we're going to Atlanta. Atlanta's my town [Torre had played for and managed the Braves]. We'll take three games there and win it back here on Saturday."

It played out exactly as Torre predicted. Maddux blanked the Yankees through eight innings that night, and the Braves won, 4–0. Then the Yankees swept the three games in Atlanta.

During that road trip, Torre maintained a heightened awareness of his players' individual psyches. Prior to Game 5, he decided he would start Tim Raines over Paul O'Neill in right field.

Before posting the lineup, Torre called O'Neill into his office that afternoon to explain. Minutes earlier, the manager had done the same for Tino Martinez and Wade Boggs, who were also benched. Boggs took it in stride and Martinez clenched up in anger, leaving the office without saying a word.

But O'Neill, upon hearing the news, walked away with shoulders slumped and head down. Moments later, the bench coach, Don Zimmer, popped his head in.

"O'Neill's down," Zimmer said.

Torre's gut told him he'd made the wrong call. Realizing that he might lose a sensitive player for the rest of the series if not forever, the manager summoned O'Neill back to the office and told him that he'd changed his mind: he was playing.

Hours later, the Yankees led 1–0 in the bottom of the ninth. Atlanta had runners on first and third with two outs when Luis Polonia launched a fly ball to right field that tailed toward center.

O'Neill raced for it, stretched his arm high into the air, and snagged the ball in his glove while heading at full speed toward the wall. He slowed himself in time to avoid a crash, then pounded the wall with his hand and screamed.

That play put the team one win away from a championship and would live forever in Yankee highlight reels. Gene Michael's trade of Roberto Kelly for O'Neill four years earlier had never looked better, and Torre's decision to reverse course and play him proved a masterstroke of intuition.

Two nights later, championship baseball returned to the Bronx. Yankees' closer John Wetteland began the ninth inning with a 3–1 lead and allowed singles to Ryan Klesko, Terry Pendleton, and Marquis Grissom.

With two outs and runners on first and second, it was now a 3–2 ball game. Mark Lemke worked a full count, then lofted a pop-up to foul territory in shallow left field.

Third baseman Charlie Hayes tracked the ball, settled under it, and made the catch a few feet in front of the stands. He leaped in the air. Torre screamed in ecstasy, then poured from the dugout along with the rest of the team. The Yanks had captured their first title in eighteen years.

At about eight o'clock the following morning, after all the champagne was poured, beers chugged, and tears shed, Cashman placed a phone call.

Bill Livesey picked up at home, and Cashman offered two deeply felt words that Livesey would treasure into his eighties: "Thank you."

16

Brian Gets the Job

THE YANKEES CAPTURED THE American League Wild Card in 1997 but lost to Cleveland in the division series. By the end of that season, the stresses of working for "a maniac," as one Yankee executive from that time called Steinbrenner, had begun to overwhelm General Manager Bob Watson.

Once a formidable big-league hitter, Watson was now spending entire days shut in his Yankee Stadium office, ordering take-out food and watching soap operas on TV.

Cashman does not deny those details, but recalls Watson, who died in 2020 at age seventy-four, with affection and defends his malaise.

"George would just beat him down and tell him, 'No, this is what we're doing,'" Cashman says.

"In his heyday George was the GM, the ticket director, the operations guy, the marketing director. He did everybody's job. He was the director of all. I think ultimately Bob Watson got accustomed to waiting for that phone to ring to be told what to do. And then obviously in between there is that time to fill with whatever.

"It got to the point where if you're a laboratory rat and you go straight, you get zapped. You go right, you get zapped. You go left, you get zapped. You go backward, you get zapped. So you learned to condition yourself not to do anything so you don't get zapped.

"It was no different than the other GMs working under George prior to that. Like, Syd Thrift [the veteran baseball executive who arrived in New York in 1989, only to leave five months into a five-year contract] would come in and be like, 'It's gonna be different. I know what he's done to other people. He won't treat me that way.' And Syd was practically carried out on a stretcher. It was all a very hostile working environment."

On February 2, 1998, Watson decided that his days as a lab rat were over. He told Cashman that he had quit. Cashman tried to talk him out of it, but Watson was done.

"I think you're going to be offered the job later today," Watson said. "You've got a lot to think about, buddy."

Because of the conversation in 1996 in which Steinbrenner said he was thinking of naming him GM, Cashman was not surprised. By now he'd had more than a year for the idea to marinate.

Steinbrenner soon called. He summoned Cashman to a meeting that afternoon at the Regency Hotel on Park Avenue in Manhattan, where he was staying.

"I could recycle someone," the owner told him, before repeating the line he had sputtered at Cashman the year before. "But do you think you're ready?"

Some in the organization teasingly referred to Cashman as George Costanza, after the *Seinfeld* character who worked for a time in the Yankees' front office on that show. And Cashman's thinning hair and round eyeglasses did lend him a superficial resemblance to Costanza, as did Steinbrenner's apparent affection for him.

But while the comedian Larry David's portrayal of an impulsive Steinbrenner on *Seinfeld* was uncannily accurate, Cashman was in fact no whiny, insecure Costanza. Still just thirty years old when Steinbrenner offered him the keys to the premier franchise in sports, Cashman met the moment with preternatural confidence. Rather than trying to leverage his employer's interest into a long-term contract, Cashman insisted on a one-year deal; he wanted to prove he could succeed before asking the Boss to commit.

More than a quarter century later, a basic question lingers: Why would Cashman accept a job that he'd seen defeat men with significantly more experience?

"I would say that being born in this environment makes it easier to deal with, rather than if you were nurtured in another environment and dropped into this one," he says. "I have always wondered if I have been able to navigate this environment because I grew up in it."

Thus, the GM job—while it wasn't a gig he sought or desired—was one that Cashman was uniquely prepared to handle. He recognized that and figured he would give it a shot—although the night before the official news conference, in a moment of endearing vulnerability, Cashman had asked a reporter the question that Steinbrenner had posed to him: "Do you think I'm ready?"

Though word had already leaked out overnight, Watson convened a news conference the next day, February 3, to publicly resign and announce Cashman as his replacement.

"I want to say something out front here," Watson said. "This is not about a health issue. This is because I'm changing the focus of my life and my career. I want to take some time off. This is my thirty-third year in professional baseball and I haven't had a vacation."

Watson stood at a lectern, a banner with an oversized Yankees logo affixed to the wall behind him. Cashman, in a dark suit and a wide tie with a loud pattern in beige, red, and blue splotches—a very mid- to late-1990s look—sat in a chair to his right, about to step into his moment.

Watson was twenty-one years Cashman's senior and, at six feet tall and more than two hundred pounds, towered over him physically. The visual effect was not unlike a starting quarterback stepping down and handing his position to the water boy.

As Watson spoke, Cashman folded and unfolded his hands, looked up at Watson, down at the floor, and back up again. Was he nervous? A bit, but he had rehearsed that morning. The preparation helped to steady his adrenaline.

When Watson wrapped his remarks, Cashman hugged the outgoing GM, then stood at the microphone. He spoke with a barely perceptible tremble in his voice; watching the clip now, one is struck more by his firm tone and upright posture than the trace of fear that is indeed evident.

"I think I'm better prepared than other people for this job because my entire pro career has been with the New York Yankees," Cashman told the press that day.

Asked about working for Steinbrenner, he said, "Can I deal with it? I'm going into this with my eyes open. I fully understand it's one of the most difficult jobs in sports, if not the most difficult. It's a tense situation. I've made that decision."

Cashman had just become the second-youngest general manager in baseball history.

17

Inside the Early Deals

Four days after Brian Cashman became general manager of the Yankees, he executed his first transaction, and it was a big one.

By early 1998, the roster of the mid-dynasty Yankees was mostly set. Gene Michael, Bill Livesey, Brian Sabean, Cashman, Watson, and the others in the front office from the late 1980s to the mid-1990s had drafted, developed, and signed a championship team.

The Yankees were more than just formidable; they were a loaded, powerful behemoth. By the end of the year, the team would take its place among the very best in the history of the game.

But there was a remaining hole at second base, and in early November 1997 the Minnesota Twins called Watson with a suggestion: How about a trade for Chuck Knoblauch?

Knoblauch was a dynamic leadoff hitter, just twenty-nine years old, and had asked the Twins to be dealt. Though he had a no-trade clause in his contract, Knoblauch submitted a list of teams to which he would agree to move: the Yankees, Los Angeles Dodgers, Cleveland Indians, Atlanta Braves, and a few others.

The low-budget Twins knew that the Yanks would be able to pay the final four years of Knoblauch's five-year, $30 million deal, and they began talks by asking for Andy Pettitte. The Yanks were not interested and suggested Bernie Williams instead.

Williams was already an important Yankee—not only a graceful center fielder who reached base at a clip that Stick Michael and his acolytes could appreciate (a .408 OBP in 1997), but a mainstay on the roster since the team's lean and formative years. He debuted as a twenty-two-year-old way back in 1991.

Williams's personal quirks—he was so shy and wide-eyed as a young player that teammates called him Bambi; he was a skilled musician who would sometimes play air guitar while standing in center field; he was absentminded enough to have left his wife and son at Yankee Stadium after games on separate occasions, and had to sheepishly ask his Westchester County neighbor Pettitte to drive them home—had endeared him to Torre.

Michael had resisted Steinbrenner's many efforts, over many years, to trade Williams. But now Williams was a year away from free agency, and the Yankees were trying to negotiate a new contract with his agent, Scott Boras.

The Williams-Boras ask—at that point, seven years and $70 million—struck the Yankees as unreasonable.

"We're not on the same page to feel Bernie is in that stratosphere of dollars," Watson told Jack Curry of *The New York Times* on November 7. "We're nowhere. We'll continue to talk. But you can't just keep beating your head against the wall."

The Yankees, at that point, did not think they would re-sign Williams after the season, and were ready to move on. But the Twins couldn't afford Williams's 1998 salary, so talks for Knoblauch failed to progress.

Still, when Cashman took over as GM in February, a deal for Knoblauch remained a live possibility. Cashman kept at it, and on February 6, he completed his first trade.

Cashman had managed to hold on to both Williams and Pettitte, but paid a steep price nonetheless. The Yanks sent a boatload of prospects—pitchers Eric Milton, Brian Buchanan, and Danny Mota and shortstop Cristian Guzmán—along with $3 million to Minnesota in exchange for Knoblauch.

Milton and Guzmán in particular were promising youngsters and would go on to have productive careers in the big leagues. But Knoblauch was already a four-time All-Star. He had stolen sixty-two bases in 1997 while getting on base at a nearly .400 clip and flashing better-than-average power for a middle infielder.

"It was an obvious need and an obvious fit," Cashman says. "This guy was a stud. Chuck Knoblauch was exactly what we needed. The player that he was in Minnesota, you're talking impact. Oh my God. He did it all—with fire. I thought he would be a perfect addition to that '98 team to help us push through once again. He had all the characteristics that we would gravitate toward. He had plate discipline, power, defense, speed, toughness, grit, all the above."

Cashman was confident enough in Knoblauch's skills—and, by that time in his career, in his own baseball judgment—that the transition from assistant GM to decider for that first deal did not feel like a dramatic one.

"Bob Watson was an incredible mentor, and he included me," he says. "I was in the front row with Bob every step of the way. And so the one thing I know about my first year of experience doing this job—I didn't realize how well Bob had prepared me. Although I was now making final recommendations to George Steinbrenner, I had always been in the room with Stick, when he was GM, and then Bob, as an assistant GM for both. Because of that, nothing felt different.

"The pressure—I'm sure it was different, but I felt more pressure having to call a rain delay. That was harder than getting everybody together, getting all their information and recommendations, and trying to address our team needs. Then going all in and saying, 'All right, I would do this, how about everybody else?' And then talking through it with the Boss.

"So I want to say no, I didn't feel different, because I had been a part of those iterations so many times. And the Boss, the way he ran things, he wanted everybody's opinion regardless. So I just presented everybody's opinion as well as my own and put my name to it."

At the time of the Knoblauch trade, Bill Livesey was working for the Tampa Bay Devil Rays and was discouraged to see a player of that caliber join an American League East rival.

"He was such a good player," Livesey says. "Him and Jeter up at the top of that lineup, with their on-base percentages? My God. With Tampa Bay, I hated to see him come to town. I had been stressing on-base percentage because that's what we had with the Yankees. And now they had those two."

In his first two seasons with the Yankees, Knoblauch maintained his career norms for both on-base and slugging percentages. He later developed a strange inability to execute routine throws to first base—a mental block that baseball people refer to as the thing or the yips—which the team believed stemmed from the pressure of being a Yankee.

That issue hastened Knoblauch's exit from town after the 2001 season. But he contributed to three championships first.

"Obviously, he wasn't the same player here that he was in Minnesota," Cashman says. "Obviously, New York was overwhelming. But he helped us, no doubt about it."

Cashman's next move completing the 1998 team would turn out to be among the best signings of his career: the acquisition of pitcher Orlando "El Duque" Hernández.

Hernández had long been a star for the vaunted Cuban national team, putting him out of reach for American ballclubs. The opportunity to acquire him arrived almost literally out of nowhere—or more specifically out of a small boat that washed up in the Caribbean.

By 1998, Hernández had been banned from the Cuban team for more than a year, mostly because the government suspected he had helped his half brother Livan defect to the United States, and that he was soon to follow. Livan had just been named World Series MVP for his efforts guiding the Florida Marlins to a championship, and Cuba was punishing Orlando for the embarrassment.

Suddenly an unemployed pariah at home, El Duque decided to leave behind two daughters and sail for the United States. At one point in the journey, his boat sprang a leak. Hernández and his crew found themselves stranded for four days on a narrow strip of land, surviving on their supply of Spam and crabs from the sea.

Rescued by the U.S. Coast Guard and granted a visa on humanitarian grounds, Hernández held a showcase for MLB scouts on February 9 in Costa Rica.

"A lot of [scouts] said they didn't like him," the Yankees' scouting director, Lin Garrett, told *Sports Illustrated* later that year.

"They said he didn't throw hard—he was 88 to 92 mph—they worried about his ability to get lefthanded hitters out, and they weren't sure how old he was. But there was more to this guy. He was taking ground balls at shortstop when a ball was hit foul into a parking lot, and he sprinted after it and ran back with it. Who does that? No, this was a special type of person. The radar gun wasn't going to tell you his story. That night I called up Mark Newman [then the Yankees' vice president of player development] and said, 'We've got to be in it. I don't care if he's 28 or 32 or whatever.'"

The Yankees offered Hernández $6.6 million, and he chose them over the New York Mets, Cincinnati Reds, Seattle Mariners, and Detroit Tigers. The volume of production he contributed relative to that price made him an all-time free agent bargain.

The Yankees' plan for Hernández was to keep him in Triple-A throughout 1998, but he began dynamically enough to provoke an early promotion. After striking out seventy-four batters in fifty-three and a half innings, El Duque was a Yankee by early June.

He went 12–4 the rest of the way, with a 3.13 ERA and a fighting spirit that contributed to the edge that those late-1990s Yankee teams displayed (sometimes that fighting spirit was literal, as when Hernández brawled with Jorge Posada in the trainers' room).

Entering that 1998 season with new acquisitions Knoblauch and Hernández, Cashman considered the rest of his roster set, the result of years of collaborative work.

At first base, Tino Martinez had been in place since 1996, when the front office faced the challenging task of replacing an icon in Don Mattingly. In 1995, with Steinbrenner watching every pitch, Martinez batted .409 for Seattle in their division series win over the Yankees.

Once that offseason began, the Yanks targeted Martinez, who at twenty-seven years old in 1995 hit thirty-one home runs and made the All-Star team. He played with a smoldering intensity that the Yanks saw as a fit for their culture.

As the Yankees tried to swing a trade with the Mariners, they also considered the free agent first basemen B. J. Surhoff, Mark Grace, and Mickey Tettleton as Mattingly replacements, but always preferred Martinez.

On December 7, 1995, the Yanks sent pitcher Sterling Hitchcock and third base prospect Russ Davis to Seattle for Martinez, pitcher Jim Mecir, and Jeff Nelson, a reliever who would become a key piece of several World Series teams. They immediately signed Martinez to a five-year, $20 million contract.

The move left Seattle's ace Randy Johnson irate. He knew what his team had in Martinez.

"I'm disappointed," Johnson said on the day of the trade. "You work so hard to build chemistry and get everyone together and playing well. We finally started winning, and then they started dismantling the team. That stuff gets frustrating."

Both the Yankees and Johnson had evaluated Martinez correctly, as proven by his response to early adversity. On April 13, 1996, Martinez went 0-for-5 in a loss to Texas, which dropped him to 0-for-16 in a home uniform at Yankee Stadium. All through that game, he heard vicious and escalating boos, and he did not wilt. After hitting .244 in April and .284 in May, Martinez batted .314 or better in June, July, and August.

By season's end, Martinez had established himself as a productive cornerstone of the team's first championship since 1978. In 1997, he found an even higher plateau, bashing forty-four home runs and earning a Silver Slugger Award, given annually to the best hitter at each position.

At shortstop, Jeter was long established by the time Cashman took over as GM. In the outfield, O'Neill was in right, where he'd been since the famous Roberto Kelly trade, and Bernie Williams was an All-Star in center. Chad Curtis, a June 1997 trade acquisition, was set to take most of the at bats in left.

David Cone, David Wells, and Andy Pettitte sat at the top of the starting rotation, and Mariano Rivera had taken over as closer in 1997 after the departure of John Wetteland in free agency.

Rivera had dominated throughout that regular season, though the team did have some concerns about how his confidence would recover from a blown save that essentially cost the Yanks the division series in 1997. Still, he would return at the back end of the bullpen, providing stability there. And as it turned out, memories of the Cleveland loss did not hamper him at all.

At catcher, Jorge Posada—the former shortstop who had switched jobs based on Bill Livesey's innovative position profile—seemed ready to capture more playing time from veteran Joe Girardi.

After that 1997 season, second and third base were two of the only areas in need of addressing, and second eventually went to Knoblauch.

At third, Wade Boggs had departed as a free agent, and the Yankees decided they wanted to move on from Charlie Hayes. On November 11, they traded Hayes to San Francisco.

In seeking a replacement for both Hayes and Boggs, Gene Michael's longtime friend and former minor-league teammate Ron Brand, a Yankees scout in 1997, made a case for an under-the-radar choice.

"When we decided to get rid of Charlie Hayes, we needed a third baseman," Brand says. "I said, 'Get Brosius.'"

That player, Scott Brosius of the Oakland Athletics, was coming off a year in which he batted just .203 with eleven home runs. On the surface, he wasn't a Stick Michael Yankee; his on-base percentage in 1997 was a paltry .259.

Sure, Brosius had been much better in 1996, hitting twenty-two homers and batting .304, with a .393 OBP, but by the end of the 1997 season he was generally considered a utility man, not the starting third baseman for a championship-caliber team.

It took sharp and persistent scouting to see otherwise. Brand did much of his work out of the A's ballpark that year and was able to see what Brosius did "off ball," to use one of Michael's favorite phrases.

"He couldn't do anything at the plate [in 1997], but his work ethic, his defense, everything else was great," Brand says.

Beyond that, Brand thought he saw a simple answer for Brosius's down season: after the strong 1996 campaign, the A's had moved him up in the lineup, frequently batting him third in front of slugger Mark McGwire.

Hitting third, especially back then, was a status symbol—a job often reserved for a team's best offensive player. Brand thought that the pressure of that assignment had weighed on Brosius and affected his production.

"He'd hit .300 the year before, and he was a quality guy," Brand says. "I said, if we stick him down low in the lineup, put him at third base, and just let him play, he'll be fine."

The two were able to convince Watson that acquiring Brosius could solve two problems: it would answer the third base question, and it could rid the Yankees of starting pitcher Kenny Rogers.

Steinbrenner, up to his old tricks by late 1995, had lavished on Rogers a four-year, $20 million contract after the pitcher made his first All-Star team. That was in Texas, however, and Rogers always seemed ill at ease in New York. In two seasons with the Yankees, Rogers had pitched to a 5.11 ERA and never earned Torre's trust as a reliable performer under pressure.

After the 1997 season, the Yanks were looking to dump him. Oakland expressed interest, provided that New York absorbed $5 million of Rogers's contract. For that, the team received Brosius, too.

"I got calls from others in the game saying, 'What the heck are you doing?'" Brand says.

Brand responded by citing Brosius's previous success, and the details of his game that were not evident in box scores or on stat sheets.

"I said, 'If you can do it once, you can do it again,'" Brand recalls. "Well, he was there for four years, and we were in the World Series every year. He played great. Because he had the qualities that scouts see in a player, we thought he would be a winner."

For all those quality acquisitions, the vaunted 1998 Yankees might have had one more icon, had Cashman been able to pull off a trade that he was working on in the fall of 1997, while still assistant GM.

"I tried to acquire Pedro [Martínez] from Montreal," Cashman says. "I didn't realize until I read Pedro's book that I never had a chance to acquire Pedro. They took a crap deal from Boston—[Carl] Pavano and Tony Armas Jr. for Pedro. It wasn't even close to what I offered.

"But years later I found out that the Bronfman family [who owned the Expos]—Dan Duquette used to be their general manager, and he was in Boston now. The Bronfman family hated George Steinbrenner. There was no way they were ever trading with George, and they had a great relationship with the owner of the Red Sox at the time. They were like, you know what, we're going to work it out with the Red Sox. The Yankees never had a chance, but I didn't know that."

It is wild to imagine Martínez at the top of the Yankees rotation in 1998 and in the seasons to come, rather than launching a historic run of dominance in Boston. But even without him, the Yanks were ready to make history of their own.

Their Opening Day roster was loaded, and El Duque lurked in the minors. After two excellent seasons, expectations on the ballclub and its first-year GM were high, and understandably so.

Then the Yanks lost their first three games, beat Oakland to break that mini-streak, and lost to Seattle the next day. They were 1–4.

Any guesses to what George Steinbrenner told Gene Michael that day?

"Stick, you're going to have to go back in and take over," the Boss said. "I don't know if Brian can do this."

"Give him some time," Michael said.

The Cashman era did not end there, though it might have had the team's poor play continued. There is an alternate universe in which Cashman was Yankees' GM for two-plus months rather than two-plus decades.

But as it happened, the team won the day after Steinbrenner made that comment to Michael. They won again the day after that. And the day after that. And so on. The Yankees didn't lose again until they were 9–4, and then didn't lose much at all for the rest of the year.

This peak version of a team designed on Tampa back fields years earlier ended the regular season with 114 wins, which at the time was the second most in baseball history.

The Yankees cruised through an 11–2 postseason, making it 125 wins in all, and swept San Diego in the World Series. El Duque started and won Game 2. And the series MVP? Scott Brosius, Ron Brand's clever scouting find from the previous winter.

The first order of business after that historic triumph was to see if the team could retain free agent center fielder Bernie Williams, a player whom Cashman considers as central as anyone to the dynasty.

"People say the Core Four with the Yankees," Cashman says, referring to the nickname later affixed to Derek Jeter, Andy Pettitte, Jorge Posada, and Mariano Rivera. "But that's bullshit if it leaves out Bernie."

In the fall of 1998, the Yankees believed that Williams would follow the money to the highest bidder. New York's five-year, $60 million offer was not nearly enough to satisfy Williams and his agent, Scott Boras, so in November Cashman pivoted to Albert Belle, offering the gifted but perennially malcontent outfielder a four-year, $52 million contract.

"We were trying to retain Bernie, but we were just unable to do so," Cashman recalls. "So then we got tired of this negotiation. At a certain point you want players who want you just as much as you want them, and we weren't really feeling that during negotiations. We pivoted to Albert Belle and actually had an agreement.

"I think that certainly shook Bernie, because he wanted to come back," Cashman says. "But in our negotiations, it was more like we were no different than anybody else. He was going to the highest bidder. We put what we were willing to do on the table, and it still wasn't good enough, so we got frustrated and went in a different direction."

As the Yankees were finalizing the deal with Belle, Williams met with the Boston Red Sox general manager, Dan Duquette, and received a seven-year, $90 million offer. At that point, Cashman believed that Williams was signing with Boston.

Immediately after, a pair of developments converged to change the course of Williams's career: First, the Baltimore Orioles swooped in with a higher bid for Belle. Then Williams asked for a meeting with George Steinbrenner, during which he expressed his desire to remain a Yankee.

Steinbrenner upped his offer to Williams by nearly 50 percent, to $87.5 million. Williams quickly agreed, and the Yankees were able to keep their core together.

"When the Albert Belle thing blew up, Bernie made a call to George," Cashman says. "He obviously was staring at a contract with the Red Sox and he wanted to be a Yankee. I think Bernie got involved and realized that the negotiation was pushed to the brink, to the point where we were walking away from the table. He got back involved and took control of his negotiation, and got a deal done directly with George. That was good because ultimately that's all we wanted, was for Bernie to be a Yankee."

Had the Yankees lost Williams, they would have been without a viable replacement in center field; their primary target, Brian Jordan, had already signed with Atlanta. They would have been markedly worse in 1999 and beyond.

With Williams back, the 1998 team remained intact. Cashman could have kept it that way, and nearly did. Then, with players already in spring training, the GM executed as seismic a trade as he has ever made, sending shock waves through the clubhouse.

18

A "Massive Shake-Up," and More Winning

WHAT IS A YOUNG general manager to do with a team that is already among the best in history? Does he leave it untouched for a few years and let it roll, or does he remain proactive in an effort to maintain the impossibly high standard?

As Brian Cashman entered his first full offseason in charge of the Yankees' baseball operations department, that was the dilemma he faced. The team had won two championships in the previous three years, but a GM's job is to keep it going.

In attacking the challenge, Cashman gathered intel from players and staff on the state of the team and its clubhouse culture. He came away with an unsettling conclusion: the Yankees were already losing some of their edge.

This was a predictable malaise, really, after the group experienced so much success so quickly. In the past three years, the Yankees had not only emerged from a dark period but become the toast of New York and a traveling circus around the country.

They rode up the Canyon of Heroes in ticker-tape parades. They appeared on *Seinfeld, David Letterman,* and *Saturday Night Live.* Derek Jeter dated Mariah Carey and hung out with Puff Daddy. For perhaps the final time, a baseball team was in the center of the pop culture zeitgeist.

How on earth could the people experiencing all this be expected to maintain the same level of hunger they had felt in, say, 1995 and 1996? As it turned out, they couldn't.

"We were a playoff team in '95," Cashman said. "World champions in '96. A playoff team in '97. World champions with the greatest record in the history of the game in '98.

"That winter, I remember, there was a concern by me or a feeling that there was some complacency starting to set in and that it could bleed into our year."

Looking around the league and brainstorming potential solutions to this problem, Cashman landed on a player who was every bit as hungry for a championship as the Yankees had been back in 1995: Roger Clemens, the two-time reigning American League Cy Young Award winner for the Toronto Blue Jays.

Says Cashman, "Roger Clemens, his reputation was the hardest worker in the game, the most dedicated, and he had accomplished everything: Cy Youngs, All-Stars, everything you can imagine— except for a championship, which was still driving him. I thought he would be the perfect fit for our roster if we could make it work."

The Yankees had tried to woo Clemens before. When the pitcher was a free agent after the 1996 season and preparing to leave the Boston Red Sox, George Steinbrenner visited his home in Houston, and even lifted weights with him.

But Clemens ultimately decided to sign with Toronto, where he dominated the league for two seasons. At the end of the 1998 campaign, he exercised a verbal agreement he had with the Blue Jays by requesting a trade to a team that was in a better position to win.

In the weeks leading up to spring training in 1999, Toronto's GM, Gord Ash, called Cashman frequently, but the two could not find a match for a trade.

On Wednesday, February 17, Ash left a voice mail for Cashman. Fatigued by all the talking, Cashman did not listen to the message until the following day. When he did, he heard a new urgency: It was time to trade Clemens, Ash said. He asked the Yankees to make an offer that could get it done.

"No, Gord," Cashman said when he called back. "If you've got something in mind, then make me an offer."

What Ash said next was so bold that it froze Cashman: he proposed a swap of Clemens for pitcher David "Boomer" Wells, along with outfielder Homer Bush and reliever Graeme Lloyd.

Wells was not only the best lefty starter in the league in 1998, going 18–4 with a 3.49 ERA and pitching a perfect game; he was hugely popular with the fans, who saw him as a beer-drinking, big-bellied everyman.

Wells wore his Yankee fandom like one of the "bleacher creatures" who populated the rowdy section of metal benches beyond the right-field wall. He sealed his bond with the public in 1997, when he took the mound in a game-worn Babe Ruth cap.

Wells had purchased the hat for $35,000, snuck it onto the field, and earned a $2,500 fine from Joe Torre. True to his rebellious nature, Wells paid it with twenty-five hundred singles.

But if antics like that endeared Wells to the public, they did not win him favor with Torre or his pitching coach, Mel Stottlemyre. Team leadership found Wells difficult to manage and insufficiently attentive to conditioning.

"I know people had concerns about Boomer bouncing around," Cashman says. "I think he was partying a lot with [actor] Tom Arnold, flying all over the country. There were concerns about what kind of shape he would be in, and he wasn't really popular [internally].

"I loved him. I loved David Wells and still love David Wells. But I know Torre and Mel Stottlemyre didn't like him. And the opportunity to bring somebody in like Clemens, who was hungry and thirsty, with the leadership he also provided, I just couldn't pass it up."

The deal that Ash proposed made baseball sense to Cashman, but he knew it would be an earthquake with the public, far more so than his first trade, the one that brought Chuck Knoblauch to New York. This one felt like a bold, controversial risk.

Adding a layer to that was Clemens's reputation as a headhunter. A competitor who lived right on the line between appropriately fierce and overly dirty, he was loathed by Yankee players and fans alike for throwing at their guys.

"That was a huge trade after the '98 year, especially for a young, inexperienced general manager; oh my God, that was a massive shake-up," Cashman says. "I could see myself easily doing something like that now—going against the grain and trading a popular player off our roster to get a player that your fan base wasn't really a fan of because he always hunted our guys. But to do that one year in?"

Cashman told Ash he would call him back, then called Steinbrenner and shared the proposal.

"Run that by me again," Steinbrenner said, just as taken aback as his GM had been.

At 4:00 that afternoon, the Yankees convened a meeting at their Tampa complex. Three hours later, the group retreated to Malio's, an area restaurant that was popular among team brass.

Over food and wine, the front office voted unanimously to make the deal. Eighteen minutes before midnight, Cashman and Ash made it official.

Cashman and Torre suspected that the news would devastate Wells, so they decided to keep it a secret until they could tell him in person.

When Wells reported to spring training the following day around 8:00 a.m., Cashman approached him at his locker.

"Boomer, I need to talk to you," he said.

"What about?" Wells said, and not in a friendly way. He then made a comment about being sent to the principal's office on his first day at camp.

Once in Torre's office, Cashman told Wells about the trade. Wells's grin turned quickly into a blank, shocked expression.

"Wow," he said, looking down.

Recalls Cashman, "Again, how do you bring back a team that was that successful and keep people motivated? I was obviously not willing to take a sledgehammer to the roster in any way, shape, or form. But there was this one outlier opportunity that existed, and that was Roger Clemens. Him, you would move mountains for. And in doing so, I feel that he helped propel us moving forward over the coming years and championships."

That first year with the Yankees, Clemens struggled to adapt more than Cashman expected. Battling a nagging hamstring injury and adjustment to life as a highly scrutinized Yankee star, he posted a 14–10 record and a 4.60 ERA—nearly two runs higher than the previous season.

But the 1999 team was deep enough to withstand Clemens's Yankee growing pains. Not as dominant as the 1998 version, the Yankees still mowed through the league all spring and summer, finishing with ninety-eight wins, good enough to win the American League East by four games over Boston.

Jeter contributed one of his best seasons, batting .349 with twenty-four home runs. And by season's end Clemens found himself in position to complete the World Series victory that he craved. In Game 4 of a businesslike sweep of the Braves, he pitched like the ace that Cashman believed he was acquiring back in February, offering seven and two-thirds dominant innings and besting Atlanta's John Smoltz.

Relievers Jeff Nelson and Mariano Rivera finished the job, and Clemens, at thirty-seven years old, was able to satisfy his own "hunger and thirst" for a title, as Cashman put it. Giddy at the ticker-tape parade two days later, Clemens brought a video camera and, as he rode up Broadway, smiled and waved while filming the fans who cheered back at him.

The dynasty marched on in 2000, though the season brought precipitous declines in many areas of the roster built during the late 1980s and early 1990s. Tino Martinez, Scott Brosius, David Cone, and Orlando Hernández were among the stars who began suddenly to show their ages, and Chuck Knoblauch, caught in his own head, could hardly make the throw to first base anymore.

A mid-season trade helped to shore up the offense just enough to hold on. For years, Cashman had listened to Gene Michael praise the Atlanta Braves and Cleveland Indians star David Justice for his ability to "quit on the baseball," that favorite phrase of his that indicates a player's deep-seated confidence in his judgment of the strike zone.

"Stick would say, 'Look at David Justice, how he picks up the baseball out of the [pitcher's] hand really well,'" Cashman says. "'This guy's got great plate discipline because of how he quits on the baseball.'"

On June 29, 2000, Cashman sent three players, including the highly regarded prospects Ricky Ledée and Jake Westbrook, to Cleveland for Justice. In the remaining seventy-eight games of the season, Justice hit twenty home runs for the Yankees, got on base at a .391 clip, and batted .305.

Meanwhile, Clemens was finding his old level of dominance. In 2000, he went 13–8, with a 3.70 ERA, and in 2001 he was 20–3, with a 3.51 ERA, winning the sixth of his seven Cy Young Awards. Across six seasons with the Yankees, he won eighty-three games, two championships, and that Cy Young. Much later, the world would learn that Clemens was one of many major-league players credibly accused of using performance-enhancing drugs during those years (allegations he would always deny). But in real time that did not detract from his importance on the mound and popularity among teammates.

"If I had to name my top ten Yankees in my time, he would easily be on the list, if not near the top of it," Cashman says. "Roger Clemens was one of the best teammates, competitors—George would use the word 'warrior'—that I have ever come across."

That competitive nature, which at times ignited into a fire that Clemens could not control, ended up defining the final championship of the dynasty era.

In September 2000, the team lost fifteen of its final eighteen games, including the final seven in a row, and finished with just eighty-seven wins. Though the Yankees somehow held off Boston to capture another division title, they began the postseason in the unfamiliar position of having the worst winning percentage among the entrants.

After squeaking by Oakland in the first round, the Yankees faced Seattle in the American League Championship Series and staked a two-games-to-one lead. Then they took irrevocable command of the series because of a historic gem by Clemens.

Starting Game 4 on the road, Clemens struck out fifteen of the thirty batters he faced and issued just two walks. In the complete-game shutout, he allowed only one hit, and that was a single by Al Martin that glanced off Tino Martinez's glove.

Jeter and Justice homered to seal the 5–0 Yankee victory; Justice would later be named MVP of that series.

"That was the best postseason game I ever saw anyone pitch," Cashman says. "If Tino were three inches taller, it's a no-hitter. That game, and then the game against the Mets, really stick in my mind."

The game against the Mets is a classic Cashman understatement. What he's referring to is perhaps the strangest moment to ever occur in New York baseball.

To understand the events of October 22, 2000, one must rewind to July 8 of that same year. During the perennially hyped regular-season Subway Series, Clemens hit Mets star Mike Piazza on the head with a fastball, knocking him onto the dirt and leaving him concussed.

Clemens said that he had just been trying to throw inside and the pitch got away from him. But his history as a headhunter, combined with Piazza's track record of success against him, left the Mets highly skeptical.

"I don't want to say he intentionally hit me in the head, but I think he intentionally threw at my head," Piazza said the next day, still woozy from the beaning. "I have no respect or appreciation for his comments. Roger Clemens is a great pitcher, but I don't have respect for him now at all."

Those words were more than enough to feed back-page drama in what was still a tabloid-driven baseball town. In the glory days of the *Post* and *Daily News* and the turbocharged talk radio duo Mike and the Mad Dog, Clemens versus Piazza received attention befitting an international incident.

In October, the Mets and the Yankees captured their league's respective pennants, clinching the first all–New York City World Series since 1956.

The Yankees won Game 1 on a twelfth-inning single by José Vizcaíno. From the moment Game 2 began in the Bronx, the energy—both from Clemens himself and from the rabid crowd—seemed more ferocious than usual. The pitcher, rumored to fire himself up before games by rubbing Icy Hot on his testicles, emerged from the dugout like a snorting bull, and the crowd responded in kind.

Clemens began the top of the first by striking out Timo Pérez with a ninety-seven-mile-per-hour fastball, then Edgardo Alfonzo on a ninety-four-mile-per-hour split-fingered fastball. Both velocities were noticeably above the norm for Clemens at that stage of his career; the cheers that followed each were well above typical Yankee Stadium decibel levels.

Next came Piazza, with everyone—including the two principals—wondering how all those months of buildup would affect the moment about to occur. Clemens worked Piazza to a 1-2 count, then fired a fastball inside. Piazza swung and hit a foul ball that shattered his bat.

As the ball bounced into the Yankee dugout, one shard of wood flew to the left side of the infield, one remained in Piazza's hand, and one propelled itself toward Clemens.

Clemens lifted that shard from the ground and flung it, sidearm, toward the first base line. It hit the grass and continued to splinter toward Piazza, who was finishing up his brief trot after the foul ball.

Piazza, gripping the bat handle like a Billy club, stepped toward Clemens.

"What's your problem?" he yelled.

Both benches emptied, and Clemens stammered that he thought he had been throwing the baseball.

From their seats down the third base line, Mets executives Omar Minaya and Jim Duquette were yelling for one of their bench players to go after Clemens to provoke an ejection.

"We were saying that someone—[pinch hitter] Lenny Harris could have been a guy—should just start a fight with Clemens," Minaya recalls. "Clemens would have fought back, and then you've taken him out of the game."

That did not happen. The moment was too deeply weird for anyone to quite know what to do.

Said another Mets official in the ballpark that night, "We just thought Roger came out amped up. The matchup was so hyped."

Clemens has never discussed the incident in detail, but told reporters after the game that he had no idea Piazza was even running.

After that inning, Clemens retreated to the Yankee clubhouse, where he found Mel Stottlemyre. The pitching coach was on leave from the club while undergoing cancer treatments, but on that night was watching from the locker room.

"I didn't mean to do that!" Clemens said, according to Torre's 2009 memoir, *The Yankee Years,* written with Tom Verducci. Then the Rocket started to cry.

Clemens, whatever one thought of him, had provided what was easily the most memorable New York versus New York baseball event since Don Larsen threw a perfect game against the Brooklyn Dodgers forty-four years earlier. And the kicker was that he ended up dominating the game, allowing just two hits and no runs in eight innings, and causing tension within the Mets' own clubhouse.

The general feeling within the Mets was that Piazza had shown admirable restraint for not going after Clemens. But one player was quoted anonymously in news stories saying that Piazza should have fought the pitcher.

"This is coming from my own clubhouse?" Piazza said to a Mets official. "That's fucked up."

The Mets believed that the quotation came from ace pitcher Mike

Hampton. While no one could prove it, the incident disrupted the relationship between two stars.

From his vantage in a suite upstairs, Cashman did not think that Clemens meant to throw the bat at Piazza.

"Piazza was a guy that basically had Roger's number," Cashman recalls. "And Roger was trying to figure out a way to get him out. There was so much noise about Mike Piazza and how Roger couldn't get him out. I kind of took it as he was so amped: 'This guy has my number, and somehow, some way, I gotta get him out. I'm gonna change this narrative.'

"And I'm sure—this is just how I read it—that he was so tired of the noise wrapped around it. Sound bites on the talk shows, ESPN, everything, it was Piazza owns Roger. And Roger was out to change that narrative. He just threw the bat toward the dugout. It wasn't, in my opinion, thrown on purpose at Piazza. I think he was just, like, chucking it. I think he was like a boxer just ready to go. And he was. It was WWE. No, it was UFC."

After all that, the Yankees led the series two games to none by the end of the night. They would go on to win in five games, their third championship in a row, fourth in five years, and last until 2009.

The seasons between those triumphs would be marked by interpersonal drama, innovation, and major changes in Yankee leadership.

PART FOUR

DEREK, ALEX, AND JOE

19

"Okay," Jeter Finally Said

Brian Cashman was driving on I-95, between his home in Connecticut and Yankee Stadium, when he called Derek Jeter with the news.

"We got Alex Rodriguez," Cashman said.

This was February 2004. For the past three seasons, Cashman and his team had been battling the impossible Steinbrenner standard, attempting to recapture the magic that drove a dynasty in the late 1990s.

The Yankees had dropped the 2001 World Series in seven games, lost in the first round in 2002, and lost the 2003 World Series in six games. For any other franchise, this would have been a run of continued success. Relative to George Steinbrenner's expectations, it was a fallow period, a failure.

When Alex Rodriguez, one of the most productive players in the history of the sport, became available in a trade from the Texas Rangers, Cashman saw a chance to inject new life into the roster.

Cashman had a vague sense of Jeter and A-Rod's relationship. He knew the two were once close and that their dynamic had apparently soured when Alex spoke critically of Jeter in a magazine interview a few years earlier.

Only later would Cashman be forced to grapple with the depth of the dysfunction between the pair. He didn't yet know the extent of it, but he did know Jeter well enough to foresee the need to reassure him, even though George Steinbrenner had already alerted the captain to the possibility of an A-Rod trade.

"This won't affect you," the GM told his shortstop once the deal was done. "He's moving to third."

In the silence that followed, Cashman continued to drive, wondering for a moment if Jeter would become angry. Would he question why the Yankees were making the move? Weigh in with his thoughts? Anything?

"Okay," Jeter finally said, in his standard flat monotone.

Whatever Jeter truly felt—and Cashman, always adept at gathering intel from reporters, agents, players, and team employees, would later hear that the captain was deeply unhappy about the acquisition—he wasn't going to share it.

Cashman would also later learn that Jeter wanted no part of the news conference a few days later at which the Yankees introduced Rodriguez. Most of the organization had already reported to the team's spring training facility in Tampa by then, but Steinbrenner insisted on a lavish affair at Yankee Stadium. He wanted Jeter and Joe Torre onstage next to A-Rod, and the pair agreed.

But as the new Yankee buttoned his pinstripe jersey and smiled, team officials in the room noticed that Jeter, standing to the right of A-Rod, could not bring himself to fake it. His flat expression served as a visual complement to the "okay" he'd offered to Cashman on the phone.

"Everything you need to know about the way Derek treated Alex you can find by just looking at those pictures of Alex's press conference, when Torre is helping Alex slip on his jersey," says one long-time employee of A-Rod's. "Most guys will have that fake smile, and Derek didn't even bother."

Still, in their public comments that day, Alex and Jeter remained on message.

"Derek, being the leader of the team, he does it with elegance and class and grace," Alex said. "I'm here to assist him, be one of the guys."

Added Jeter, "Everyone wants us to not get along, but that's not the case. Our relationship is fine."

It wasn't. In fact, it was to become Cashman's primary management challenge for the next decade.

This dynamic was hardly unprecedented in Yankeeland; indeed, the history of the franchise is rich with superstar feuds, all of which helped define key eras.

Before Jeter and A-Rod, there was Reggie Jackson and Thurman Munson. Decades earlier, it was Babe Ruth and Lou Gehrig. Each case presented a similar dynamic: a larger-than-life celebrity failed to mix easily with a quieter team captain.

Ruth and Gehrig were friends throughout the 1920s, socializing and barnstorming together to make extra money in the offseasons. Their relationship started to fray after the 1929 season, when Ruth proposed a joint holdout from spring training and Gehrig demurred.

A few years later, they split for good over a family disagreement. Ruth brought his daughter Dorothy and stepdaughter, Julia, to visit Gehrig's mother at her home in New Rochelle, New York. Julia arrived dressed in the flashy style of the Jazz Age, while Dorothy's clothing was more modest and conservative.

After the visit, Lou's mom was overheard gossiping about Babe's wife, Claire. "It's a shame she doesn't dress Dorothy as nicely as she dresses her own daughter," Mrs. Gehrig said.

The remark got back to the Ruths, and the two icons barely spoke again. They mended their friendship only at Gehrig's retirement ceremony in 1939, when the onset of a deadly disease that would come to bear Gehrig's name moved Ruth to throw an arm around his old teammate.

Four decades later, the Yankees lured Jackson to the Bronx with a five-year, $2.9 million contract, making him the A-Rod of the 1970s, at least in these ways: Jackson was a well-paid, polarizing star prone to media gaffes that hurt his standing with teammates.

Steinbrenner, in a move that predicted his similar request to Jeter in 2004, asked the surly Munson to attend Jackson's introductory news conference in the Bronx. Like Jeter, Munson agreed, and like Jeter he barely endured it.

At Jackson's first spring training, Munson, the manager, Billy Martin, and other old-guard Yanks froze the new star out of their inner circle. Frustrated, Jackson granted an interview that would forever define his image.

Sitting with a *Sport* magazine reporter in a Fort Lauderdale bar, Reggie ordered a piña colada and stirred it with a straw while contemplating his place on the Yankees.

"This team . . . it all flows from me," he said. "I'm the straw that stirs the drink. It all comes back to me. Maybe I should say me and

Munson . . . but he doesn't really enter into it. . . . I've overheard him talking about me. . . . I'll hear him telling some other writer that he wants it to be known that he's captain of the team. . . . Munson can't intimidate me."

Once published, those words hit the clubhouse hard, then simmered through the season. But unlike with Jeter and A-Rod, Munson and Jackson captured a World Series title in their first year together. Winning is the best cure for all clubhouse tensions, and by the time Munson died in a plane crash in 1979, he and Jackson had managed a truce.

Almost forty years later, on a chilly afternoon in September 2018, the Yankees were taking batting practice before a home game. Jackson, trim at seventy-two years old and wearing glasses with trendy blue frames, stood behind the cage, offering feedback to the current generation of stars, Aaron Judge and Giancarlo Stanton (who, breaking precedent, actually got along).

When BP ended, I asked Jackson if his experience with Munson was as close a parallel to Jeter and A-Rod's as it seemed.

He blinked a few times, before saying, "It's similar."

Then he stopped for a beat, made eye contact, and added, "To a point."

"How do you mean?" I asked.

"Thurman and I made amends after a couple of years," Jackson said. "We got past it. The things that I said in an article, I ended up coming off like a jerk. It wasn't my intention."

Jackson paused again.

"Alex and Derek have never made peace," he finally said. "If you cross Derek, you just don't exist."

Jack Butterfield (1929–1979) is the unsung originator of the Yankee Way, a path that Brian Cashman continued to follow into the 2020s. "It really all does begin with Jack," says Buck Showalter.

When Brian Cashman says that the story always told about the Yankees is wrong, he is referring largely to the lack of credit given to Bill Livesey and his lieutenants. Livesey created the Yankees' player profile, which the team has used for four decades and counting.

Beginning in 1968, Gene "Stick" Michael served as a player, coach, manager, scout, and general manager for the Yankees—and later became a key mentor to a young Brian Cashman.

Brian Sabean was another unsung hero in the Yankees' front office in the 1980s and 1990s who helped to build a dynasty. He went on to win three championships as general manager of the San Francisco Giants before returning to the Yankees in 2023.

Gene Michael and Buck Showalter served as Yankees general manager and manager, respectively, in the early 1990s and were instrumental in shepherding the team from its lean years to the cusp of dynasty.

George Steinbrenner (*center*), pictured here with Joe Torre (*left*) and Brian Cashman (*right*), was an extremely difficult boss but managed to foster loyalty in longtime employees like Cashman and Gene Michael.

Brian Cashman (*left*) and Joe Torre (*right*) worked together from 1996 to 2007. At first, they shared an almost familial closeness, but they later had, as Torre put it, a "falling out."

Assistant general manager Jean Afterman joined the Yankees in 2001 and quickly became one of Brian Cashman's most trusted lieutenants, a key member of his inner circle.

Third baseman Charlie Hayes catches a pop-up to clinch the 1996 World Series, kicking off a dynasty and validating years of scouting, drafting, and player development work from the likes of Bill Livesey, Brian Sabean, Gene Michael, and Brian Cashman.

Derek Jeter and Alex Rodriguez endured a rocky relationship as Yankee teammates. This dropped pop-up on August 17, 2006, came to symbolize their disconnect.

The emotional distance between Alex Rodriguez (*left*) and Derek Jeter (*right*) left many teammates sensing tension in the dugout and clubhouse. This became a significant management challenge for Brian Cashman.

All seemed temporarily forgiven when Jeter and A-Rod won their first and only championship together in 2009. Here they are seen celebrating an important step along the way—winning the American League East.

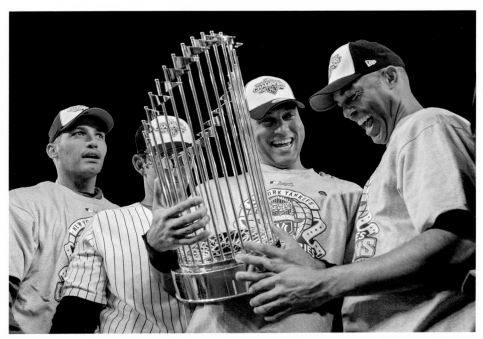

The "Core Four" (*from left*: Andy Pettitte, Jorge Posada, Derek Jeter, and Mariano Rivera) celebrate around the World Series trophy in 2009. All were remnants of the Gene Michael / Bill Livesey days in the early 1990s.

Giancarlo Stanton (*left*) and Aaron Judge (*right*) became superstar teammates in 2018. Unlike Babe Ruth and Lou Gehrig, Reggie Jackson and Thurman Munson, and Derek Jeter and Alex Rodriguez, Stanton and Judge created a fast and enduring friendship.

After moving on from manager Joe Girardi following the 2017 season, Brian Cashman and his front office were blown away by Aaron Boone during the interview process. Boone (*right*) became the thirty-fifth Yankee skipper.

Hal Steinbrenner (*left*), Brian Cashman (*center*), and Aaron Boone (*right*) are as aligned a leadership team as the Yankees have had in decades—maybe ever.

When frustrated fans called for Aaron Boone's job during losing streaks or after playoff losses, Brian Cashman always stuck by him.

Manager Aaron Boone (*left*) welcomes ace Gerrit Cole (*right*) to the Yankees after Cole signed a then-record nine-year, $324 million free agent contract with the Yankees in December 2019.

Gerrit Cole became a Cy Young winner for the Yankees—and a key figure in the team's transition in a data-driven age.

Relief pitcher Zack Britton was a Yankee from 2018 to 2022 and served as an important conduit between the front office and clubhouse as the team ventured further into the analytics age.

Brian Cashman's relationship with superstar Aaron Judge was not without friction, but Cashman appreciated Judge as a highly effective clubhouse leader.

Hal Steinbrenner (*left*) and the Yankees nearly lost Aaron Judge (*right*) during free agency in 2022, but instead re-signed him in dramatic fashion and named him Yankee captain.

20

Origins

ON THE MORNING OF March 3, 2001, three years before the
trade that brought A-Rod to the Yankees, a pack of Yankee
beat reporters advanced on Derek Jeter before he could even reach
his locker.

It should have been a lazy day in Tampa, just one of many at spring
training, but as would happen many times, Alex Rodriguez had created a news cycle. This one involved Jeter, but when the shortstop
reported to camp that day, he seemed the last to know about it.

"I remember Derek saying, 'What's up, fellas?' with a little smile
on his face,'" says Sweeny Murti, who covered the team for the radio
station WFAN. "One of the guys had all the quotes written out in his
notebook and read them to him."

The quotes in question were from a hot-off-the-presses issue of
Esquire magazine that featured a photo of A-Rod on the cover and a
profile of him within.

"Jeter's been blessed with great talent around him," Rodriguez
said in the article. "He's never had to lead. He can just go and play
and have fun. And he hits second—that's totally different than
third and fourth in a lineup. You go into New York, you wanna stop
Bernie and O'Neill. You never say, Don't let Derek beat you. He's
never your concern."

Jeter was forced to absorb those words not in private but with
the media watching. For a celebrity who prided himself on creating
boundaries with reporters and the public, the timing could hardly
have been worse.

"As this was being read to him, the smile disappeared from his face," Murti says. "There was a lot of, 'Well, I'm going to have to talk to him first.' But it was clear he was pissed. There was no hiding that expression on his face."

Instantly, A-Rod's quotes became the talk of Yankee camp—indeed, the talk of the entire sport. When asked that morning to comment, Brian Cashman deflected with a wisecrack. "I can't get involved in a spat between millionaires," the GM said.

Rodriguez called Jeter, then drove ninety-five miles to Jeter's house from Port Charlotte, Florida, where his Texas Rangers were training. As the two sat on the living room couch, Jeter heard Rodriguez out, but he was aware that A-Rod's comments actually represented the second time in less than four months he committed the same offense.

The first came in December 2000, when Rodriguez signed a ten-year, $252 million contract with the Texas Rangers, making him the highest-paid player in baseball history. Shortly after, he appeared on ESPN radio's *Dan Patrick Show.*

"Even a guy like Derek, it's going to be hard for him to break that [record contract] because he just doesn't do the power numbers and defensively he doesn't do all those things," Rodriguez said on the program. "So he might not break the 252. He might get 180. I don't know what he's going to get. 150? I'm not sure."

As Reggie Jackson said, if you crossed Jeter once, you didn't exist. And now, between ESPN and *Esquire,* A-Rod had crossed him twice.

"He hated Jeter, like, next level," says Tony Bosch, head of the Coral Gables, Florida–based Biogenesis clinic that supplied A-Rod with performance-enhancing drugs (A-Rod would admit to federal agents in 2014 that he obtained PEDs from Bosch, and he was suspended by MLB for the entire season; the following year, Bosch pleaded guilty to conspiracy to distribute testosterone). During the 2010 season, Bosch would often meet A-Rod on the road.

"One time we're at the team hotel," Bosch says. "Alex [tells me], 'You go downstairs, wait for me in the bar. I'm gonna go to the bar, and I'm going to call you when I'm ready. And then you'll see me; I'll wave. You come over.'"

"So I was down there at the bar with Yuri [Sucart, A-Rod's cousin] and in comes Jeter. He waves, whatever. He waves to Yuri. I was sitting next to Yuri. Jeter gets a table. He gets two tables. Francisco Cervelli and Curtis Granderson join.

"Cervelli sees me [Cervelli, a Yankees catcher, was also a Bosch client]. 'Hey, Tony.' I go over there. It was like two round tables. Of course there were girls there, and people coming up. And, dude, when Alex comes down and he sees that we were at that table with Jeter—Yuri and I—he gets his table at the other end. And he sends me a text in Spanish, saying, 'What the fuck are you doing with that guy?' or 'What the fuck are you doing with that asshole?' Something to that effect."

It hadn't always been that way between Jeter and Rodriguez. Nearly two decades earlier they had started as friends. The two met in 1993, as spectators at a University of Miami versus University of Michigan baseball game in Miami. Jeter had already been a first-round draft pick, and A-Rod was soon to become one.

"Alex was starry-eyed," recalls Steve Caruso, who was Jeter's first agent and at the time was bidding to represent Rodriguez. "He kind of viewed Derek as being on some other level."

Caruso failed to land A-Rod as a client, and soon lost Jeter to the agent Casey Close. But he did walk away with a unique ability to compare the two at the moment before their professional careers began.

"Alex is easily the best high school player I have ever seen, and I saw Jeter," Caruso says. "Jeter was good. When you saw Jeter, within about five minutes you were like, 'Okay, I get the hype.' With Alex it took five seconds."

Home visits with the two also provided a contrast. Jeter was the product of a strict, loving household; his parents were married and attentive. Alex's father had abandoned the family when Alex was ten years old, sending the boy on a decades-long search for replacements to fill that void.

The strongest of those surrogate dads was Juan Diego Arteaga, a Miami baseball coach and father to Alex's childhood best friend, J. D. Arteaga. The Arteagas took Alex in and lent him a sense of belonging.

Then, during Alex and J.D.'s sophomore year in high school, Juan Diego Arteaga suffered a heart attack and died during a football game in which the two boys were playing.

"First game of the season, second quarter," says Rich Hofman, the defensive coordinator. "He got up out of the stands, didn't feel good, and he just fell over. He never regained consciousness. It was such a sad thing."

Seemingly hardened by abandonment and loss—and left insecure by those same factors—Rodriguez by the end of high school was both more polished and more needy than Jeter.

"He was definitely not a jerk, but he was a bullshitter from the beginning," Caruso says of Rodriguez. "He was smooth. He was charming. But the thing about Alex was that he seemed to always need confirmation of his abilities. 'How did I do?' 'Do you think I was okay to do that in that game?' Derek never seemed to need that affirmation. Alex always did."

If A-Rod was a lot, even from the beginning, Jeter was as inscrutable then as he would always be.

"I remember going back to his house after a doubleheader," Caruso says. "[Derek's father] Charles invited me back to the house to have pizza. Derek could barely say three words. He was very shy. And very quiet on the field, too. Alex was not. Alex was not loud, but he was vocal. He was more animated in what he did. I don't know about similarities, other than their abilities. They were such different people."

As Jeter and Rodriguez's professional careers began, adversity further highlighted the differences in their personalities, and the differences in the support structures available to them.

When Jeter struggled in his first year as a minor leaguer, he confided his insecurities to his parents and kept his head down at work; Rodriguez, while close with his mother, had to make his own way in the world at a younger age.

After the 1994 season, A-Rod played winter ball in the Dominican Republic, living in the same building as his teammate, Montreal Expos outfield prospect Cliff Floyd. When overwhelmed by challenges, he turned to Floyd.

"He was struggling because [MLB veteran] José Vizcaíno was playing short," Floyd recalls. "He had never been in a place where he hadn't played before. We hung out every day. 'I know I'm playing today,' he would say. 'I have to be playing today.' 'Well, you ain't playing today. Swallow your pride.' That just never registered."

During long talks that lasted into the night, Rodriguez would cry.

"It was intense," Floyd says. "He had tears in his eyes in a couple of conversations we had. The frustration of not being out there absolutely destroyed him. It had to be entitlement—like, 'How could you bring me over here and not play me? You must not know who I am. I need to play. I'm about to be a star.'"

It was a heavy time for Rodriguez. That December his father, Victor Rodriguez, bought a ticket to a game and approached Alex during batting practice. Shocked, Alex agreed to have lunch with Victor the following day. When the appointed time arrived, he could not bring himself to show up.

Jeter never had an experience like that, but by the mid-1990s the two did share a connection that few others could claim: both were highly scrutinized young shortstops learning how to handle the onrush of stardom.

Because of that, they launched their big-league careers as long-distance friends. When A-Rod was in New York, he would sleep over at Jeter's apartment, and vice versa. When the Yankees and Seattle Mariners brawled on the field in 1999, Jeter and A-Rod chatted amiably to the side of the fight, earning public criticism from Yankees' outfielder Chad Curtis.

By the early 2000s, when the friendship had cooled significantly, Jeter had cemented his legend as Yankee champion. A-Rod was marooned in Texas, trying to prove himself as a leader worthy of the historic contract.

It was not going well. As the Yankees kept winning American League East titles, the Rangers posted losing records in each of Rodriguez's three seasons there. A-Rod was a perennial All-Star, led the majors in home runs, and in 2003 won the American League MVP award. And yet those who knew him then say he couldn't shake the perception that in some intangible but crucial way, the public viewed him as inferior to Jeter.

"He was in a tough situation in Texas," says Buck Showalter, the Rangers' manager in 2003. "I thought he was the best player in the sport, but he was expected to do everything on a team that was flawed from a pitching standpoint. It was quite a noose. He was expected to be anything and everything."

That pressure provoked attempts to lead that struck teammates and opponents alike as ham-fisted.

"Guys around the league used to call him 'the human hand job' when he was with Texas," says one opponent from that era. "He would try to be a leader, but it just came off as so phony, like he was stroking people off and didn't really mean any of it. 'Oh, your swing is so great,' when it obviously wasn't. That sort of thing."

Once in the early 2000s, a friend told A-Rod that longtime Baltimore Orioles' shortstop/third baseman Cal Ripken Jr. would sometimes usurp the catcher's authority and call pitches from the infield. "That is so cool," A-Rod said.

He then tried to do the same with the Rangers, but ended up infuriating pitching coach Orel Hershiser and catcher Einar Díaz. "I was like, I am the catcher," Díaz says. "Fuck that. He wanted to call every pitch. I was like, 'No.'"

"Our pitching was so bad, his heart was in the right place," Showalter says. "He was trying to help, but the route he was taking rubbed some people the wrong way. He was trying to be everything with his contract: 'Okay, I gotta help the pitcher. I gotta help the outfielders.' He wanted to bring everything that a guy making his kind of money could."

By the end of the 2003 season, it was clear to both Rodriguez and the Rangers that the marriage was not working. Texas and the Boston Red Sox agreed to a trade that would send A-Rod to Boston and slugger Manny Ramirez to the Rangers, but the deal was contingent on Rodriguez's reducing the value of his contract by roughly $30 million.

A-Rod was willing to do it, but the Major League Baseball Players Association would not allow the precedent. The deal fell apart.

On January 25, 2004, Rodriguez was in New York City to accept his MVP award at the annual Baseball Writers' Association of America dinner. Beforehand, he met for five hours with the Rangers' owner, Tom Hicks, general manager, John Hart, and Showalter. The sides pledged allegiance to each other, and the Rangers said that they planned to name A-Rod captain.

No one believed it, least of all Brian Cashman, who was scheduled to sit next to Rodriguez on the dais that night and who suddenly needed another infielder.

Nine days before the writers' dinner, Yankees third baseman Aaron Boone tore a knee ligament playing basketball. Boone's contract contained language that prohibited basketball. He admitted to Cashman what he had done, and the Yankees ultimately decided to release him.

The day of the dinner, Cashman says, "I was preparing for that conversation at the dais. We talked about how the Boston deal fell apart and what the union wouldn't allow them to do. Almost immediately after, I engaged the Texas Rangers."

Rodriguez recalled additional details of the conversation in *The Captain,* the 2022 documentary about Jeter.

"I ordered a cocktail," A-Rod said. "I'm not a big drinker, so you get me one, I'm already a little light-headed. He [Cashman] was having, I think, some scotch or something. And I think just in passing, totally playing around, he says, 'Too bad you're not willing to play third base, because you could be wearing pinstripes.' And I was one drink in, and I was like, 'Ha-ha, that's funny.' And it was about forty-five minutes later, and I said, 'Hey, were you serious about playing third base?'"

Cashman had planted a seed with subtlety straight out of Gene Michael's wily playbook. Within the month, A-Rod would be a Yankee, and Jeter would have his Ruth and Reggie, a tabloid frenemy for the new millennium.

21

The Long Parade

THE YANKEES' TRADE FOR Alex Rodriguez was the most dramatic move away from the cohesion of the late-1990s dynasty, but it was far from the first.

Beginning in earnest after the 2001 season, Brian Cashman was forced to remake the roster for a new age. The passing of time ensured that this could no longer be quite the team that Gene Michael, Bill Livesey, Brian Sabean, and the old gang had assembled with Cashman's help in the late 1980s and early 1990s.

The groundwork laid during George Steinbrenner's suspension a decade earlier and subsequent return included the acquisitions of Paul O'Neill, Tino Martinez, Scott Brosius, and Chuck Knoblauch, key to the championship years. All of those players participated in the 2001 World Series, and all were gone immediately after.

That series, a loss in seven games to the Arizona Diamondbacks, proved a dramatic coda to the era. As the city mourned the September 11, 2001, terrorist attacks on the World Trade Center, the Yanks captivated fans with walk-off victories in the Bronx in Games 4 and 5.

The first of those wins came on a Derek Jeter homer in the tenth and earned him a new nickname: Mr. November, because the blast came just after midnight on the first day of a new month for baseball (the attacks had paused the season and pushed back its conclusion).

The following night, Brosius homered with two outs in the ninth, tying a game that the Yankees went on to win in extras. The Diamondbacks recovered by mauling Andy Pettitte in Game 6 and stealing Game 7 on a broken-bat flare off Mariano Rivera.

The Yankees, who had won three consecutive championships and four in five years, would wait another eight seasons for their next one. In the wake of that defeat, Steinbrenner stormed through the Yankees' clubhouse, shouting that changes were coming.

Cashman could see two factors converging at once: an uptick in the Boss's involvement, which years of winning had kept somewhat at bay, and the natural turnover of an aging roster from the Michael-Livesey era.

The upshot would be a rapidly changing team around the remaining core of Jeter, Rivera, Jorge Posada, and Bernie Williams (in another year, Pettitte would leave for Houston, albeit temporarily).

O'Neill and Brosius retired. Martinez signed as a free agent with St. Louis. Knoblauch made a one-year stop in Kansas City before leaving the game. Cashman traded David Justice to the Mets for Brosius's replacement at third base, Robin Ventura.

From the outside, it seemed a loaded moment for the still-young Yankee GM—his first chance to put his full stamp on the roster and sink or swim on the choices.

True to his nature—this is a man who thinks not in narrative arcs but about the task at hand in any given moment—Cashman wholly rejects that premise. As he tells it, the fall and winter of 2001–2 was just another offseason on the job.

"No, I wouldn't say I was looking forward to putting a different marker on it," Cashman says. "It was more, how can we adjust and do what we need to do? How can we continue to maintain excellence? Is it something from the system, or is it coming from outside? It's like, what opportunities are available via trade? What's your financial flexibility?"

With several contracts coming off the books, Cashman did have the ability that winter to replace Martinez with Oakland Athletics star Jason Giambi. Giambi's weak defense did not fit Livesey's player profile for first base, which called for an average glove at minimum. But to Cashman, Giambi's power and ability to get on base outweighed this deficiency.

The seven-year, $120 million contract lavished on Giambi fulfilled the Steinbrennerian impulse for big splashes in the aftermath of a World Series loss. That impulse was often at odds with sound process, but in this case the organization was unified in its pursuit of Giambi.

"I supported the Jason Giambi signing," Cashman says. "The whole baseball group was on board."

That was not the case with every transaction that year, or in the three seasons that followed. Often Steinbrenner's involvement— and the advice he received from an ever-shifting cabinet based in his home city of Tampa—could disrupt the roster.

Assistant general manager Jean Afterman, who arrived in late 2001, was startled by the burgeoning problem.

"George had a shadow front office in Tampa made up mostly of non-Yankee employees," she says. "It was hangers-on from outside the organization and ambitious people from the organization. This shadow front office was constantly in his ear."

Afterman quickly became one of the most important advisers Cashman would ever have. Now that his first wave of mentors was fired, retired, or stuck in reduced roles, Cashman found in Afterman a partner he could trust in navigating the increasingly toxic work environment.

Her background was unique for baseball: a Bay Area native, Afterman held a degree in art history with a focus on ancient Greek gods and had spent time cataloging ancient artifacts for the University of California, Berkeley's Museum of Anthropology.

Afterman's first love, though, was the stage. In the 1980s, she became a well-regarded actor in the San Francisco theater scene before changing careers and heading to law school.

A lifelong baseball fan, Afterman found herself involved with the game soon after launching her legal career. In the early 1990s, she teamed with baseball agent Don Nomura on a rights issue involving baseball cards; as part of that work, she traveled to Japan and wondered aloud why the country wasn't sending its talented players to MLB.

Nomura explained that there was an agreement in place that prohibited Japanese players from signing with U.S. teams. That struck Afterman as unfair, if not unconstitutional, and she set about looking for loopholes. She found one in a "voluntary retirement clause" that allowed players who retired in Japan to play overseas.

In 1995, Nomura and Afterman used that clause to help Japanese pitcher Hideo Nomo "retire" and sign with the Los Angeles Dodgers. Nomo proved an instant All-Star and celebrity, blazing a path for Japanese stars to move more freely to MLB in the coming years.

Afterman impressed the Yankees when dealing with another of her Japanese clients, pitcher Hideki Irabu. Billed as the "Nolan Ryan of Japan," Irabu became a Yankee in 1997 and never fit in, especially after George Steinbrenner exclaimed to the press that Irabu was a "fat puss-y toad."

Once during Irabu's first year with the Yanks, Steinbrenner called Afterman, cursing and vowing to put her client on the next plane back to her. Afterman was not cowed.

"I'm going to be at the fucking airport," she shouted back. "You send him back with his fucking signing bonus check and we'll go right back to the bank and we'll cash it. Make sure he has that fucking check and I will welcome him with open arms and we'll sign him with another team tomorrow."

In the tradition of Michael and Cashman, Afterman—"a pit bull," as more than one colleague describes her—knew how to give it back to the Boss. After assistant GM Kim Ng departed for a job with the Dodgers, Cashman persuaded Afterman to replace her.

Afterman appreciated the Yankees' willingness to hire first Ng and then her in an era when virtually no women worked in baseball operations.

"George liked to say, 'I am a male chauvinist pig,' but the proof of the pudding is in the taste," Afterman says. "When I came to the Yankees, there were more women in senior positions in the organization than I've ever seen in any other organization. At that time, if Brian wanted to hire an assistant general manager, George had to approve everything. I don't think Brian and George get enough credit for this.

"When I came in as an assistant GM, then for like fifteen years after, there were no other women in the room for these GM meetings. At that time the GMs would [introduce their assistant GMs] by saying, 'This is my assistant.'

"When a man says 'This is my assistant' about a woman to another man, people just assume you're his secretary. I actually trained Brian [in this way]. We developed this whole patois. I said, 'I need you to say, "This is Jean Afterman, she is my assistant GM, she's a lawyer, we took her from the dark side, she stood up for the players . . ."' He

would basically give my whole résumé. That would give me validation. In the early days, that was necessary."

Cashman and Afterman became close friends, appreciative of the
other's toughness and bonded by their shared experience with the
ever-increasing meddling from Steinbrenner's shadow front office in
Tampa.

With roster suggestions coming in from Florida on a constant
basis—many of which the GM disagreed with but had to execute
anyway—Cashman and Afterman together developed a dark sense of
humor to cope with the situation.

"Brian and I once looked at each other and said, 'You know what?
A trained monkey could do what we do,'" Afterman says of her early
years with the team.

Cashman had always enjoyed playing practical jokes around the
office, which underlings said helped lighten a relentlessly tense work-
place. He had once called Gene Michael from a blocked number
claiming to be a reporter inquiring about his interest in managing
the Florida Marlins. Michael said that—off the record, of course, he
could not comment—he was interested. Cashman laughed so hard
that he cried.

On another occasion, Cashman teased the vice president of
domestic amateur scouting, Damon Oppenheimer, before the draft
by deploying a fart machine while Oppenheimer placed his order in
a Tampa restaurant.

Afterman, feeling that Cashman needed an upgrade, purchased for
him a higher-end model that he called the Fartmaster 400.

The group needed these moments of levity during a time of dysfunction, when multiple, disconnected factions assembled the major-
league roster. An example of this burgeoning problem came two
months into the 2002 season.

Paul O'Neill's primary replacements in right field, John Vander
Wal and Shane Spencer, were not producing, and neither was the
new left fielder, Rondell White. Steinbrenner—understandably, in
this case—wanted an upgrade in right, and Joe Torre was in his ear
about acquiring Raúl Mondesi from the Toronto Blue Jays.

Mondesi had decent power but a reputation as a player who was
difficult to manage. Even as the Yankees considered trading for him,

he was suspended by Toronto for arriving ten minutes late to a team meeting.

Cashman did not want him, but at the time Cashman was not in charge the way a GM typically is. In an act of protest, he recused himself from the trade talks.

"Mondesi wasn't me," he says. "That was Joe Torre. Torre was like, 'Oh, he'll play great for me.' I was against the Mondesi deal and fought hard against it. The Boss did that deal, and actually [team president] Randy Levine did the deal. I wouldn't do the deal, so I think Randy Levine finished it off.

"Mondesi's makeup was clearly an issue. Not a guy you would want here. The last I heard, he's in jail in the Dominican."

That is true: in 2017, Mondesi was sentenced to eight years in prison on corruption charges related to his term as mayor of his hometown, San Cristóbal.

But in late June 2002, Torre was lobbying for Mondesi. On June 29, he posted a provocative lineup for a Subway Series game.

"He played [infielder] Enrique Wilson in right field at Yankee Stadium against the Mets," Cashman says. "The Boss went ballistic. That's probably exactly what Joe wanted him to do."

Two days later, the Yankees finalized the trade without the involvement of their general manager. This was an ominous development for what the team's decision-making process, or lack thereof, was becoming.

Mondesi behaved just as Cashman feared he would. His exit from the Yankees came the following July, after he abandoned the team.

"In Boston in an extra-inning game on a Sunday night we pinch-hit for him," Cashman says. "We were on our way to Anaheim on an off day the next day. I guess he had showered up and left the clubhouse. I had him traded by Tuesday to Arizona. That's how I got Karim García."

García, an outfielder, was a productive part of a Yankee team that won the 2003 American League pennant. While Cashman was able to salvage that particular mess, the Boss continued to assert his power, next undermining a deal that would have been far more significant than the Mondesi trade.

After the 2003 season, Cashman pursued—and actually landed— free agent superstar outfielder Vladimir Guerrero.

"He had Vlad Guerrero signed, and the Boss said, 'No, no, no, we're going to do Sheff,'" says a Yankee official from that time.

Sheff was Gary Sheffield, a star in his own right but six years older than Guerrero. He was a Tampa native, which endeared him to Steinbrenner, and had met personally with the owner while Cashman was busy reeling in Guerrero.

Sheffield became a solid Yankee, especially in his first season, when he contributed thirty-six home runs and a hard-edged style of play that the Yankees had come to lack. In three seasons with the team, he batted .291 with seventy-six home runs and an .897 OPS (on-base percentage plus slugging percentage).

The problem? Guerrero signed with the Anaheim Angels, won the 2004 American League MVP award, and stayed in Anaheim for six of his prime years. He posted a .927 OPS as an Angel and later entered the Baseball Hall of Fame wearing that team's cap on his plaque. It could have been the Yankees who benefited from that historic production.

Still, as spring training opened in 2004, Sheffield was a welcome, professional presence in the Yankee clubhouse, strolling in with the kind of self-assured charm that folks expected from a player of his stature.

It was a very different scene across the clubhouse. Alex Rodriguez had just arrived in town to begin his tenure with the Yankees at the same time as Sheffield. But A-Rod proved to be an awkward fit from the start.

"Sheff walked in like, 'Hey, what's up, dawg? I'm doing my thing. If you need me, I'll be over here,'" says one teammate. "With Alex, it was, 'Hey, guys, I'm trying to be friends with everyone.' We were like, 'You're Alex Rodriguez, you don't need to do this.'"

From the first moment of that star-crossed season, Jeter did little to help his erstwhile friend settle in. While downplaying their feud and blaming the press for exaggerating it, the two rarely acknowledged each other in the clubhouse.

"Derek had his guys—Posada, Bernie [Williams]," the teammate says. "Alex was *never* going to be one of Derek's guys. It was tense."

It wasn't only Jeter who disapproved of Rodriguez's behavior. On February 29, just a few weeks into camp, a longtime member of Alex's Miami entourage, Eddy Rodriguez (no relation), wandered into several off-limits areas of the complex, including a spot behind the netting near the batting cage from which most club officials were barred. Eddy Rodriguez also walked through a tunnel clearly labeled "Authorized Personnel Only."

"A lot of us were looking at Alex like, 'This just isn't how we do it here,'" says the teammate.

Meanwhile, by the end of spring training, many players were fatigued by the icy vibes between A-Rod and Jeter.

Says a longtime friend of A-Rod's, "I don't think Derek wanted to be friends with Alex, and I don't think Alex wanted to be friends with Derek. I think Alex wanted to prove he was a better player than Derek, and that's a big part of why he wanted to come to New York."

Yankee officials who later had to manage the two egos saw a relatively simple reason for the continued disconnect: Rodriguez was a better baseball player than Jeter by any metric but championships, but was not as widely praised or adored.

A-Rod was insecure, which various amateur psychologists in baseball attributed to growing up without a father at home, a lack of a college education that led to stymied intellectual ambitions, secret shame over steroid use, the pressure of his historic contract, and general social awkwardness.

"Alex was very conscious of being accepted, being liked," says a Yankee official. "He did make an effort, and it was never malicious when he didn't do things well. He wasn't great with kids. If there was a Make-A-Wish kid in the dugout, Jeter would always engage with him. Alex wouldn't notice. But then, when we would give him feedback about that, he would try to do better."

As for Jeter, teammates saw a stark duality: He could be excessively kind to certain people, like when he befriended a young girl who wrote to him after her father died in the terrorist attacks on 9/11, kept in touch with her for years, and helped her through a cancer battle in adulthood. But around baseball folks, he wasn't always as warm. A longtime Yankee staffer compared Jeter's personality to a Yankee icon from a different era.

"He was like [Joe] DiMaggio," the staffer said, not meaning it as a compliment. "DiMaggio had a wall around him. And Joe could be a prick. He once refused to sign a baseball for Don Zimmer, for God's sake. Finally, DiMaggio is sitting in Torre's office and he says, 'I'll sign

Zim's ball now.' Zim tells him to go fuck himself. DiMaggio was cold and Derek was cold."

Jeter addressed this side of his personality in his 2022 documentary, *The Captain,* and offered a compelling reason for it.

"I have trust problems," he said. "I have trust issues. I have issues trusting people from the get-go.

"Even growing up, I remember I had a good friend of mine that was in high school. And after I graduated from high school, I found out that he had mentioned that he doesn't like to see interracial marriages [Jeter's mother is white and his father Black]. And I'm like, this is somebody I liked to hang out with. I trusted this person. So that's just an example of, it has been there for a while, but I think it has been magnified a bit as my career developed over time."

With insights like that many years away, the 2004 Yankees began on an awkward foundation. To make the challenge even more formidable, the division rival Boston Red Sox entered the 2004 season as a team on the rise.

The Red Sox had been under new ownership since early 2002 and after that season appointed Theo Epstein as general manager. Epstein was a twenty-eight-year-old wunderkind plugged into the new wave of data proliferating through the game. Boston also hired Bill James, the father of analytics in baseball, as a senior adviser.

By 2003, the Yankees–Red Sox rivalry had reached a new peak of intensity. In the ballparks, an air of menace reigned; for fans, donning the opposing team's hat or T-shirt at a road game was an invitation to real violence.

This antipathy extended to the organizations themselves. The new Red Sox president, Larry Lucchino, called the Yankees "the evil empire," a comment that left Steinbrenner apoplectic.

"The front offices didn't like each other," Afterman says. "Now we have relationships in other front offices, including Boston. It was different then. The players hated each other, too."

In 2003, with a lineup anchored by slugger Manny Ramirez and emerging star David Ortiz, the Red Sox led the major leagues in runs, total bases, OPS, and many other offensive categories.

In October, they nearly surpassed the Yankees to reach the World Series; only a home run by third baseman Aaron Boone in the eleventh inning of ALCS Game 7 briefly saved New York's season. The

Yankees then showed up flat to the World Series and lost in six games to the Florida Marlins.

The offseason brought a culture shock to both clubhouses. Two and a half months before the Yankees acquired A-Rod, with all his talent and baggage, the Red Sox traded for Curt Schilling, the star pitcher from the Arizona Diamondbacks. Like A-Rod, Schilling was the potential final piece of a championship-caliber roster. And like A-Rod, his big personality proved an awkward fit with new teammates.

During an early visit to Fenway Park in the 2004 season, the Yankees saw that they were not the only team trying to cope with new-found dysfunction.

"I vividly remember walking out to the bullpen at Fenway, and a couple guys on the team made a comment about Schilling: 'Fuck him,'" says a Yankee player. "It was bad. And they weren't playing well."

At that point, the Red Sox seemed too messy to be a serious threat. But the Yankees had their own issues, not least among them a shocking April slump from Jeter.

One of the most consistent players of his era, Jeter slipped into an 0-for-32 hole, the worst hitless streak for a Yankee since Jimmy Wynn in 1977. By the end of it, home fans were booing him, especially during a late April sweep in New York at the hands of the Red Sox.

Forty-three games into the season, Jeter was batting .189. Nearly twenty years later, in his documentary, he finally conceded that the pressure of A-Rod's arrival—or more specifically, the scrutiny on their personal dynamic—had affected his play.

"It's easy to say . . . it could have played a part, because there is so much attention now on individuals instead of the team and winning," Jeter said. "Fair to say it played a part."

Jeter was not the only struggling star. At one point in April, Rodriguez carried an 0-for-16 streak and heard the first of many boos from Yankee fans—the beginning of an issue that would later contribute to the fracture in Cashman and Jeter's relationship.

Despite this adjustment period, the Yankees outplayed Boston throughout the first half of the season.

On the afternoon of Saturday, July 24, they sat comfortably in first place in the AL East—nine and a half games ahead of Boston on the season, and up 3–0 in the third inning of a game at Fenway.

With two outs in that frame, Red Sox pitcher Bronson Arroyo plunked Rodriguez on the elbow with a 1-1 pitch. While taking his initial steps toward first base, A-Rod barked at Arroyo.

"Throw that shit over the fucking plate," he said, before shifting his gaze from Arroyo to catcher Jason Varitek, who was stepping in front of him.

"We don't hit .250 hitters," Varitek said, and while A-Rod was in fact batting .278 at that moment, the point that he was under-performing as a Yankee was accurate enough to sting.

"Fuck you," Rodriguez said to Varitek. "Fuck you, fuck you, motherfucker."

He then added "Come on! Bring it!" while beckoning the catcher with his hands.

Without removing his mask, Varitek pushed A-Rod's face. Players poured from the dugouts and bullpens, ready to fight. This was no baseball shoving match, but an actual brawl.

Yankees' pitcher Tanyon Sturtze pulled Boston's Gabe Kapler from the pile, provoking Kapler and a group of teammates to surround Sturtze in foul territory and beat him until blood oozed from his head.

In moments like these, a general manager can only watch, anxious, and hope that none of his key players is ejected or injured. From the stands, Cashman glowered at the field.

Theo Epstein was also in the seats, but he had a different reaction. The young Sox GM smiled and chuckled as his players mixed it up.

The actual fight was a draw—neither Varitek nor Rodriguez was able to take the other down—but it assumed an outsized symbolism for the teams and their fan bases.

Since the Red Sox sold Babe Ruth to the Yankees in 1919, they had won zero championships to New York's twenty-six. The "rivalry," as it was, was more akin to the rivalry between a nail and a hammer. And now, suddenly, the Sox were hitting back. A still photograph of Vari-tek's fist bearing into Rodriguez's cheek would live forever on book covers and desktop computers all over New England.

"I think the whole A-Rod/Varitek thing changed the season," a member of the 2004 Yankees recalls. "It's crazy how one incident could turn everything around, but it really did."

The Yankees hung on to win the division by three games. Rodriguez batted .286 with thirty-six home runs—excellent numbers, but below the .298 and forty-seven home runs he had posted the year before in Texas. And for much of the season, he had struggled in so-called clutch situations (for example, he hit .206 that year when batting with two outs and runners in scoring position).

One August evening in Toronto, Rodriguez was standing around the batting cage before the game, bemoaning the fact that he was not coming through in the clutch. Gary Sheffield was in the same hitting group and after a while had heard enough.

"Dude," Sheffield said, according to a person who was present for the exchange. "You're fucking A-Rod. Swing the bat and swing it like a man."

Rodriguez homered in that game and appeared to regain some of his pre-Yankee swagger after that.

The Yanks dispensed with the Minnesota Twins in the first round of the postseason, which set up a rematch of the previous year's New York–Boston ALCS.

That series opened in New York, and the Yankees began it in dynamic fashion, scoring twice against Schilling in the first inning, then four times in the third and twice in the sixth.

Sheffield, the Yankees' alpha that season, scored the fifth run, sliding into home to complete a bases-clearing double by Hideki Matsui. When he popped back up, Sheffield pumped his arm in the air, emitted a guttural scream, and chest bumped Rodriguez.

However much Varitek's July punch reset the dynamic between the clubs, October now seemed to bring a return to the natural order. The series had hardly begun, and Boston was at risk of total demoralization.

But the seventh inning, which opened with the Yankees leading 8–0, brought what proved an ominous development. The Red Sox—perhaps not so easy to demoralize, after all—scored five runs, startling the Yankees out of their romp.

New York hung on to win, 10–7, but not without needing their closer, Mariano Rivera, to complete a game that had once been a blowout. A weird vibe had already been allowed to creep in.

For the next two games, that vibe went away. The Yankees took Game 2 by a score of 3–1, then pounded the Red Sox, 19–8, in Game 3 at Fenway Park. Following that rout, they led three games to none, a margin that no team in baseball history had ever blown. The series seemed over.

The next four games would live on as the subject of documentaries, books, and endless postmortems among both fan bases. They would permanently change the psychology of Yankees–Red Sox and puncture the Yankees' sense of self in ways that proved irreparable.

In Game 4, the Yankees led 4–3 in the bottom of the ninth inning. Boston's first baseman Kevin Millar led off that frame with a calm at bat, watching a 3-1 pitch from Mariano Rivera sail high and inside for ball four.

The Sox manager, Terry Francona, inserted the speedy Dave Roberts as a pinch runner. There were no secrets to the strategy; Roberts was there to steal second.

After nearly allowing Rivera to pick him off on a throw over, Roberts dashed for second on the first pitch to Bill Mueller.

That pitch was high and outside to Mueller, a lefty hitter. Jorge Posada uncoiled from his crouch and fired to second, but his throw sailed a few feet to the right of the bag.

Jeter caught it and applied the tag, but it was too late; Roberts was safe.

Had the throw been on line, or a shade to Jeter's left, the trajectories of each franchise might have been different. As it happened, though, the Yankees sensed—intuitively then and now in clear-minded retrospect—that they had been forever altered by a single moment.

It took three more games to actually lose the series, but on some level they knew what would happen once Roberts slid in ahead of Jeter's tag.

"Pretty much when Dave Roberts stole second and then we lost that game, the tide was just turning," says Jean Afterman. "When you are an unstoppable force . . .

"Not to sound all Northern California, hippy-dippy, but that's where there used to be a magic around the Yankees–Red Sox rivalry. You could just sense the universe going one way or another. There were tidal changes going on. And that game showed that there was some magic happening on the other side."

Roberts scored the tying run on a Mueller single. David Ortiz homered in the twelfth to win it. The same burgeoning Boston icon won Game 5 with a run-scoring single in the fourteenth.

Back in New York, the Sox took Game 6 on a gem by Schilling, who was pitching through an ankle injury that seemed to bloody his sock (though to this day Yankees brass believes the bloodstain was fake).

The postseason is a time of powerlessness for any GM. He or she has already constructed the team, and now can only watch it perform. Cashman, Afterman, and the rest of the front office took in Game 7 from what passed as their suite at the old Yankee Stadium (it was really just three levels of desks, organized in rows like a small press box). They remained mostly quiet as the Red Sox finished up a blowout win that had come to seem almost inevitable.

The series ended on a Rubén Sierra groundout. Second baseman Pokey Reese fielded the ball, threw it to first baseman Doug Mientkiewicz, and the Red Sox poured from the dugout. Cashman and his staff remained in place, staring at the field.

"Most of us—Brian, myself—we stayed and watched the Red Sox celebrate on our field, because we wanted to remember that," Afterman says. "Then Brian went down to the clubhouse.

"It was incredibly devastating. It was also a gut punch to everybody's confidence. My sense is that it was a huge ego blow to a lot of those players, who had had nothing but success.

"And then I think there began to be an undercurrent in the clubhouse between the guys who had won a World Series and the guys who came in new and had never won a World Series. There was an artificial class system that began to develop after our success began to get sapped—after '04."

The Yankees had already fallen from their impossible perch of the late 1990s, and this loss seemed to underscore the reality that the decay had been gradual.

"In 2002, the Angels bounced us out in the first round," Afterman says. "In 2003 we went to the World Series, so we considered 2002 just a blip on the screen. But in 2003 it took Boonie's magic to get us to the World Series.

"Look, there is a great line from *A Streetcar Named Desire,* where [Blanche] tells Stella, 'You were never there—I was there, the long parade to the graveyard.' Stella left but Blanche was stuck with every relative, and one by one they died."

The full lines from Tennessee Williams, spoken by Blanche DuBois to her sister, Stella, go like this:

> I took the blows in my face and my body! All of those deaths! The long parade to the graveyard! Father, mother! Margaret . . . You just came home in time for the funerals, Stella. And funerals are pretty compared to deaths. Funerals are quiet, but deaths— not always. Sometimes their breathing is hoarse, and sometimes it rattles, and sometimes they even cry out to you, "Don't let me go!"

Concludes Afterman, "So in some ways for us it was like the long parade to the graveyard. It seemed that way for our fans, it seemed that way to the media, it even seemed that way to our front office.

"But in actual fact, unlike in the play, a new team rises. Baseball is not like real life. You get a do-over every year. Everyone did feel like one by one these players are retiring, but a new team does rise. And to me, that is one of Brian's unmatched great strengths as a general manager—he puts together a team that rises from the graveyard."

22

"It Was Literally Killing Him"

B RIAN CASHMAN, USUALLY SO dry and difficult to read, had to turn away from the reporters who asked about his future.

It was another funereal clubhouse at the end of a season, this one in Anaheim, California, on October 10, 2005. The Yankees had lost the division series to the Angels, and Cashman's contract was expiring at the end of the month.

He knew he was leaving, but couldn't untangle the contradictory threads of relief and devastation well enough to compose himself while talking to the press. Instead, he choked up and ended the interview.

Two Yankee officials, president Randy Levine and general partner Steve Swindal, George Steinbrenner's son-in-law, sensed the coming front-office shake-up and reached out to Cashman.

"Randy Levine tried to convince me to stay, and I said no," Cashman says. "Steve Swindal tried to convince me to stay, and I said no. Then they both went to George and said, 'He's out.'"

It had been a long time coming. Ever since the Yankees lost the 2001 World Series to Arizona, Steinbrenner's meddling had increased in frequency and decreased in rationality. Cashman would choose players like Vladimir Guerrero, and Steinbrenner would force on him Gary Sheffield or Raúl Mondesi or Kenny Lofton instead, then scream at Cashman if the moves didn't work.

It had happened again in late 2004, when Cashman was working to bring back the solid second baseman Miguel Cairo and the Tampa front office homed in on a player he did not want, Tony Womack.

"The different factions, Tampa versus New York, it just became [a situation where] there were a lot of different rosters put together by a lot of different people," Cashman says. "Tony Womack was an example of that. I was trying to re-sign Miguel Cairo, and Tony Womack was signed from down there. And he was a disaster."

"It became intolerable," says Jean Afterman, Cashman's trusted assistant GM. "Brian had to manage the owner. He had to manage the manager. He had to manage the press. He had to manage the front office. He had to spend an enormous amount of energy fending off stupid, bogus suggestions. And they were coming fast and furiously. It got to be almost manic how bad it was leading up to 2005."

In the aftermath of the playoff loss that year, a new opportunity arose: the Los Angeles Dodgers were offering twice as much money.

"He was down the tracks," Afterman says. "It was agonizing for him, but he was down the tracks. He is a lifelong Yankee. It would have ripped his heart out. But he also would not have survived under that situation. It was killing him. It was literally killing him."

That is an extreme comment, but Afterman stands by it. She recalls seeing Cashman physically shrinking under the strain.

"Brian, lucky man, when he was under stress, he would get thinner and thinner and thinner," Afterman says. "I used to say to him, 'Brian, if you stuck your tongue out and stood sideways, you would look like a zipper.' But he was really stressed out. And also working even more then—he was working thirty-six hours a day. The volleys coming out of Tampa, the cannon fire coming out of Tampa was getting—there were a lot of shots being fired from Tampa. At some point, he probably just thought, life is too short."

Levine and Swindal advised Steinbrenner that he needed to initiate a conversation with Cashman.

"He could charm a snake," Cashman says. "He called me and said, 'I've been told that you're leaving. Why are you leaving me?' I went through a litany of reasons."

"I want what's best for you," Cashman told Steinbrenner. "You've got to find someone you can trust. You do all these things that are against my wishes and then blame me when we're sucking, even though I didn't do these things. It's in our best interest if I leave."

Steinbrenner asked Cashman what he needed in order to stay

with the Yankees. What he needed, Cashman said, was the ability to centralize all baseball operations so that they reported to the general manager—as was the case in nearly every healthy organization. He needed Steinbrenner to shut down his shadow front office of Tampa cronies and make clear to everyone that Cashman was in charge.

He also felt a need to bring the Yankees into the modern age. The pro scouting department, responsible for evaluating trades and transactions involving major- and minor-league players, should move from Tampa to New York, where Cashman could remake it. The Yankees should jump on a nascent trend and hire a mental skills coach to help players cope with the emotional component of the game.

Finally, the team needed the budget and support to keep up with front offices like the Oakland Athletics and the Boston Red Sox, who were pushing forward in the area of analytics.

It was a lot to ask of a micromanaging owner steeped in Yankee traditions and hard-nosed football clichés. But Steinbrenner did not hesitate in his response.

"I want you to stay and do what you need to do," the Boss told Cashman.

Here again we arrive at a moment in the story that reveals the profound complexity of George Steinbrenner and his relationships.

Decades earlier, when the Boss was busy hiring, firing, and reassigning Gene Michael and Billy Martin, both were somehow compelled to remain in his orbit. It seemed impossible that they would want to work for a man who behaved as Steinbrenner did, but they kept coming back.

With Cashman, that history repeated, but with an added element: the ties between the Steinbrenner family and his own, and the pride that John Cashman derived from his son's position running the New York Yankees, baseball's crown jewel. This was a man who spent most of his own career working at Castleton Farm, a New York Yankee–level horse-breeding operation.

"My dad was a huge Yankee fan," Cashman says. "My dad wanted me to stay. I told him how difficult it was working here. It was impossible, blah, blah, blah. But at the end of the day, when George said, 'Why are you leaving me?' It was almost like your second father telling you he was hurt.

"I had an offer from the Dodgers that paid me—I think I stayed with George for $2.5 [million] a year for three years. The Dodgers offered me five a year for five years. And I stayed because I had loyalty.

"[Philadelphia Phillies GM] Pat Gillick was talking to me several times. He was retiring [in 2008]. He was trying to convince me to go to Philly. But the real two were the Mariners and the Dodgers. When I said no, the Dodgers hired Ned Colletti instead. Every opportunity but one, it was significantly more money. The Dodger deal was significantly more money. Maybe New York was just a place I wanted to stay.

"In the end, I turned down the opportunity to make more money in multiple markets because of my loyalty to one man. I was a nobody without him, if he hadn't handpicked me. I couldn't sleep at night moving forward with the rest of my life knowing that this man wanted me to stay. And if his family wanted me to be a part of them, I wasn't leaving."

As with Gene Michael, the stories detailing Cashman's interactions with Steinbrenner can leave an image of two men who hated each other. But the feeling was closer to love, even if that love bled into toxicity.

"Brian and George had respect and admiration; they were definitely bound together, and like family they loved each other, they hated each other, but they were closer than close," says Afterman. "There is still a photo of George hanging in Brian's office. But it was terrible leading up to 2005."

After the new agreement, in which Steinbrenner granted Cashman's every wish for how to restructure the baseball wing of the organization, the dynamic in the front office did improve. The Yankees continued to win in the regular season and disappoint in the postseason, but Cashman could withstand the results with a clear conscience, knowing that he was responsible for the choices that led to victories and defeats.

There did, however, remain one wild-card element that an understanding between Cashman and George Steinbrenner could not cover: The Boss was now in his late seventies, with his health and cognition in the early stages of decline. In 2006, Steinbrenner suffered a fall that left his speech and gait more halting than ever. By 2007, he was unable to oversee the team's daily operations.

Several years earlier, Steinbrenner had put in place a succession plan involving Steve Swindal, who was married to his daughter Jennifer. But in February 2007, Swindal was arrested in Tampa on a DUI charge; shortly after, he and Jennifer announced plans to divorce. As a consequence, Swindal would no longer become managing general partner of the Yankees (Swindal would plead no contest to the DUI and receive probation).

Into that void stepped Hank Steinbrenner as the next complication to Cashman's autonomy. This was not a personal conflict—Cashman, like just about everyone else in the Yankee orbit, carried great affection for George's garrulous older son—but it did present practical headaches.

Unaccustomed to life as a public figure, Hank picked up the phone for reporters and detailed sensitive information about trades and free agent pursuits. Cashman preferred to operate in the shadows, releasing drips of information strategically, if at all. Careless public comments tended to disrupt talks with teams and agents.

Early in Hank's time as the voice of the Yankees, Cashman was negotiating with Jorge Posada's agent, Seth Levinson. Posada, a free agent at thirty-seven years old, was seeking a four-year contract, and Cashman would not do it.

Cashman had a strong relationship with Levinson, who believed that the refusal to go four years was sincere. The sides were closing in on a three-year deal in November 2007 when a text from Levinson woke Cashman in his hotel room at the GM meetings in Orlando.

"I guess we're not done negotiating," the text read.

Cashman did not know what that meant until he logged on to the internet to see that Hank had been quoted in the morning papers saying that the Yankees would indeed give Posada a fourth year. The final agreement was for four years, $52.4 million.

As the offseason progressed, Hank provided reporters with play-by-play of the team's trade discussions with the Minnesota Twins for ace pitcher Johan Santana. And ownership negotiated with Alex Rodriguez, who had exercised an opt-out clause in his contract.

Cashman did not recommend re-signing A-Rod. It was nothing against the player, whom he supported in the cold war with Jeter and who had just won the American League MVP award; it was just that nearly any GM would rather spread that money around on the roster.

In any case, the Steinbrenners and Levine finalized a new ten-year deal with Rodriguez.

The situation was not nearly as challenging as it had been before Cashman agreed to return in 2005. He was still overseeing all of the baseball departments and growing the team's analytics capabilities. He was allowed to keep his prized pitching prospects Phil Hughes, Joba Chamberlain, and Ian Kennedy. And Hank Steinbrenner (who died in 2020 at age sixty-three) was, as Cashman puts it years later, "a sweetheart."

Hank also knew baseball, having spent decades learning from the best. "My brother worked in New York when I was in high school," says Hal Steinbrenner. "He worked under Stick [Michael] and got to know him well."

But as Hank emerged as a public voice, team officials worried that he was too trusting of a tabloid media that, in the words of one team executive, "created a character of Hank Steinbrenner as the Boss redux, and then it was like a runaway train. That's when the family had to get involved and Hal stepped up."

The emergence of Hal Steinbrenner as managing general partner of the Yankees—which became official on November 20, 2008, when Hal was thirty-eight years old—represented a significant moment for the organization, a shift away from his father's mercurial reign and his older brother's well-intentioned but disorganized stay at the top.

Reserved to the point of shyness, George's younger son had been largely unknown to the public before 2008, but, as it turns out, he had been immersing himself in baseball for many years prior. While working in the family shipping and especially hotel businesses, he kept his office at Legends Field, the Yankees' spring training facility where his father was also based.

"My office was right next to George's," Hal says. "I did develop a great liking of the hotel business, and also the tugboats that we have in Tampa and the ships on the Great Lakes. I got kind of entrenched with everything, but I would always be getting pulled into Yankee meetings, happily so. You may not have seen my face, but the reality was, George put my office right next to his."

Hal's temperament was a better fit for Cashman's attempts to modernize the Yankees by installing rational, evidence-based processes.

He exercised patience, listened to most recommendations, and rarely raised his voice.

Hal's personality was such a contrast to his father's, in fact, that it begged the question of whether he was acting in intentional opposition to the man he refers to as George.

"I think I know what you're asking," Hal says when presented with this question. "No, there was no intent to be different from him, but the reality is we're very different people. I would like to think I am far less impulsive, more patient, more analytical in my decision-making process. I don't like to be in the spotlight. That's not my personality. But no, there was no me going in and saying, 'I've got to show everybody I'm my own guy.' It was blatantly obvious.

"I'm big on delegation of authority. I don't like to micromanage. It wasn't a game plan to do that, so to speak, but it's just who I am. But at the same time, I was not going to try to be someone I wasn't. I was going to be me, and do the best I could for the family."

Hal's sense of loyalty paralleled Cashman's. George Steinbrenner died in 2010 at the age of eighty; by then, Hal and Cashman had developed a strong, almost familial working relationship.

The two would move forward together through an era in baseball that bore little resemblance to the wild 1980s—but before they could do that, Cashman had to massage the long end of what remained of a now-creaky dynasty.

23

Talkin' Shit

I HEAR YOU TALK SHIT about me," Derek Jeter said.

This was 2006 or 2007 at the old Yankee Stadium, by which time the clubhouse was more fractured than ever.

"Well, D.J.," Brian Cashman answered. "If talking shit is defined as me saying that you're not treating A-Rod well, and your teammates have a problem with it, that they're uncomfortable with that—I already talked about that to your face.

"If it's about your defense and your lateral range, then I've already talked about that to your face. If it's about you being so private and not letting people in, I talked to you about that. If that's me talking shit about you, then I have already dealt with you to your face."

Not many people spoke to Jeter that way, but that was Cashman's style. He continued, "Where do you think this is coming from? The intel is coming back to me from our clubhouse. People you've won championships with are the ones telling me these things. People you respect."

"Well, who?" Jeter asked.

"I'm not saying who," Cashman responded. "But it's my job to confront it."

"Brian always says, 'I don't have a very good bedside manner,'" Jean Afterman says. "He's not warm and fuzzy. He will tell them directly. But players know he's not going to lie to them, and that's a really big deal."

"The easiest thing is just to be direct," Cashman says. "Be firm and be strong."

Of all the concerns that Cashman expressed in that exchange, his primary worry remained that Jeter wasn't supporting Alex Rodriguez.

In his third season with the Yankees, A-Rod was still struggling in the clutch and still hearing boos from home fans. In fact, those boos were getting louder, and Cashman wanted Jeter to ask fans to ease up.

The sharpest visual representation of Jeter and A-Rod's relationship came on August 17, 2006, when the two converged under a pop-up hit to the left side of the infield, failed to call for it, and watched as the ball landed on the infield dirt.

"Brian went to Jeter and said, 'You're captain of this team,'" says Afterman. "'You don't get to pick and choose who you're captain of. You're captain of everyone on this roster.' That should have been incredibly persuasive."

"I did confront him when Alex was getting booed," Cashman says. "If you turn the clock back a couple years earlier when Jason Giambi was getting booed, he said publicly that fans shouldn't boo Giambi. They should support our players. He liked Giambi, so he defended him publicly. So I said, 'How is it that you would do it for that one?' Because his public stance on A-Rod was different. It was, 'I can't tell our fans what to do.'"

Jeter addressed these charges, sort of, in his 2022 documentary series. "What the fuck do you want me to do, man?" he said. "Yeah, I get it, but I don't know what they wanted me to do, actually."

Says Afterman, "In Jeter's defense, I don't know what anybody *did* expect him to do. I always enjoyed Jeter. I think he has a great sense of humor. But he's not a warm and fuzzy guy for most of the world. That's just not his style. I guess what everybody wanted was for him to defend Alex publicly, and that was a bridge too far for him."

Rumors about the Jeter/A-Rod relationship were widespread in those years—no one was fooled into thinking they were best friends—but there were uglier moments internally than nearly anyone realized.

In May 2007, the *New York Post* plastered a photograph on its cover of Rodriguez in Toronto with an unidentified woman.

"STRAY-ROD," blared the headline. "Alex hits strip club with mystery blonde."

Rodriguez was married, but adultery is not an issue that would disrupt a baseball team. The problem in this case, according to a Yankee official, was that a team staffer who was friendly with A-Rod tried to convince him that it was Jeter's people who had tipped off the photographer.

This was mere gossip—there was absolutely no evidence that Jeter had anything to do with the photo. But the accusation itself was telling of the levels of paranoia and disconnect swirling around the team and its two celebrities. As Jeter and A-Rod stood next to each another nearly every night on the left side of the Yankee infield, fans had no idea the levels of drama simmering just under the surface.

As Cashman said when Jeter approached him, A-Rod was not his only concern. In fact, the GM had been growing increasingly irritated with an issue that his shortstop couldn't control: the longtime reluctance of the manager and coaches to confront Jeter.

Cashman does not want to relive those conversations, but according to a team official, third base coach Willie Randolph in the early 2000s brought to the front office a concern that Jeter was goofing around with infielder Luis Sojo during infield practice and not properly focused on pregame preparation—and that the inattention was carrying over into games.

The official asked Randolph to address the issue with Jeter. A few days later, Randolph said that he had done so.

When the official mentioned it to Jeter, the captain said, "Willie hasn't talked to me at all."

A few years later, the view that Jeter would eventually have to change positions became prevalent in the baseball operations department. With his range declining, Jeter was still excellent going back on pop-ups, leading the team to believe that he would benefit from a shift to center field, as Hall of Famer Robin Yount had done later in his career.

Joe Torre told the front office that Jeter refused to change positions, according to two of the people Torre told.

When confronted, Jeter again said, "He never talked to me about it."

By this time, the once-tight bond between Cashman and Torre was fraying, too. The disconnect on talking to Jeter about moving to the outfield didn't help, nor did Torre's Jeter-esque reluctance to fully embrace Alex Rodriguez.

As the 2000s progressed, team officials saw a hardening in the clubhouse class system: there were Yankees who had won with Torre, and those who hadn't. When outfielders Gary Sheffield and Kenny Lofton complained that Torre was speaking to them differently because they were Black, the front office heard them out but offered a different theory.

"Lofton and Sheffield thought that Torre's treatment was racist," says a Yankee official. "We had to try to convince them that he wasn't racist, but played favorites. If you had a ring, you were treated one way. If you didn't, you were treated another way."

Torre has strongly denied Sheffield and Lofton's claims about racial bias.

"Joe changed," the official continued. "It became difficult to get into his office after the game, because of celebrities or his Bigelow tea sponsors. If you just wanted to go in and say, 'Hey, Skip,' you were blocked by all these people. It was like [longtime Dodgers manager] Tommy Lasorda toward the end, where the manager becomes too much of a celebrity. Whereas if Andy Pettitte or Bernie or Jeter wanted to get in, it was, 'Hey, come on in.'"

As can be expected when two people grow apart, it was Torre who thought that Cashman was different, not the other way around. In the manager's view, Cashman was becoming too dependent on new front-office hires and their data-driven ideas. He was not as trusting of Torre as he should have been.

In his 2009 book, *The Yankee Years*, written in the third person with Tom Verducci, he went public with those feelings:

"Cash, you've changed," Torre said.
"I have not," Cashman said.

A few paragraphs later, Torre dropped an intriguing detail, but did not elaborate:

"We had a falling-out in spring training," Torre said. "Then I apologized a few days later, because I really like Cash. I asked other people, 'Is this just me or has he changed?' It was his watch and he wanted to do it his way. I understand that. I would have liked to have him trust me. I was always a very loyal subject to him."

All these years later, Cashman does not want to speak about that "falling-out." But according to Yankee sources, here is the event that Torre hints at in his book and that caused a fracture in the Torre-Cashman relationship.

In 2006, Steinbrenner and Torre wanted Yankees legend Ron Guidry as the pitching coach, replacing the retiring Mel Stottlemyre. The suggestion came at a bad time for Cashman, who was trying to modernize his operation.

The front office viewed Guidry as a nice man—"everybody loves him," one team official says—and a knowledgeable pitcher, but not up to date with technology.

"Cash didn't want any part of it because Guidry had no experience," Torre said in his book. "He likes people with experience. I understand that. I was sort of in a tough spot, because I know I had mentioned Guidry in passing when I had [a] meeting with George. I know Cash went to George about Guidry's inexperience, because I know Billy [Eppler] didn't like Guidry. George, I think, hired him because he remembered me saying it."

Eppler, then the director of the pro scouting department and an increasingly important Cashman advisor, didn't in fact dislike Guidry personally. But primary among the team's concerns was that once spring training began, Guidry was not monitoring pitch counts during bullpen sessions, an old-school approach that the front office felt could put the health of pitchers at risk.

"It was a bad setup," a team official says. "All of a sudden we were vulnerable to injury."

The context for these front-office anxieties was Torre's long-established overuse of relief pitchers. From Ramiro Mendoza to Scott Proctor to Tanyon Sturtze, the manager tended to ride trusted relievers until they were tired—or worse.

Over the years Cashman would try to address it, but got nowhere.

"This guy has pitched five straight games," he would tell Torre.

"He says he feels healthy," Torre would respond. "He says he feels great."

"But of course he's gonna say that," Cashman would say. "You're Joe Torre. What do you expect this kid who is not making any money to say?"

The situation worsened to the point where, when the Yankees

called up top pitching prospect Joba Chamberlain in 2007 and put him in the bullpen, the front office created strict guidelines regarding when and how Torre could use him. Publicly, the Yankees called these "the Joba Rules." In reality, a team official says, "they were the Joe Torre Rules."

It was therefore a delicate time to introduce a pitching coach with a more old-school view of spring training workloads.

In their initial spring meetings in 2006, team officials asked Guidry how many pitches and innings per start each member of the staff would throw while ramping up for the season. Guidry's response—"Whatever they want"—left them concerned.

Guidry was not being confrontational; he was merely operating in a way that he was accustomed to from his own career in the 1970s and 1980s. This was an instance where well-intentioned people found themselves caught between two ways of operating.

"The guys pitching in our era, we did what we thought was good for us," Guidry says. "When I threw a bullpen, I would throw thirty pitches—about fifteen fastballs and fifteen sliders, depending on how I felt that day. Sometimes I would throw ten fastballs and fifteen sliders. Or five fastballs and I'd had enough. It wasn't based on time and it wasn't on pitches. It was on whatever we felt that we needed to do. And there were some times where I didn't even throw on a throw day. I just said, 'I'm taking the day off instead.' It was actually left up to us as pitchers, what we wanted to do in the bullpen."

By 2006, the game had evolved to a place where front offices wanted more information about throwing programs. Would starters throw a bullpen session every Monday, Wednesday, and Friday? What about relievers? At what rate would they build up their pitch counts?

Guidry said that he did not want to use pitch counts; he wanted to measure the bullpen sessions by time spent throwing—for example, ten minutes on Mondays, twelve minutes on Wednesdays, and fifteen minutes on Fridays. That left the front office to wonder if pitchers who worked quickly would throw an inordinate amount and pitchers who worked slowly would not throw enough.

Tension and mistrust boiled over after a bullpen session by Colter Bean, a reliever who was rehabbing from a knee surgery.

Each day early in camp, the pitching sheet submitted to the front office stated that each guy was throwing thirty pitches. The front office found that suspicious, considering that Guidry had said he was going by time, not pitch count. If that was true, how could everyone be throwing the same amount?

That spring, Cashman had ordered cameras installed throughout the complex so the team could quantify how many drills each player was doing, determine what worked and what didn't, and make changes for future years.

Wondering about the pitch counts, someone suggested looking at video of the bullpen sessions and counting the pitches.

The front office was stunned at what it discovered on the tapes. According to one source, Bean, an injured pitcher on a rehab program, threw approximately eighty pitches, exponentially more than he should have. By contrast, Mike Mussina, a healthy starter, threw about thirty.

Eighty pitches sounds nearly impossible for a 15-minute bullpen session; that's a pitch every 11.25 seconds. The tapes are long gone, making it impossible to resolve the exact count. But whatever the length of the session, and however many pitches Bean actually threw, the takeaway was that his workload was too heavy.

"I can't honestly say I even remember this issue," Guidry says. "I'm not saying it didn't happen. I'm not saying I wasn't there. I cannot remember. But if I was there, I probably was not privy to what went on after the session. If they had [an argument], it probably occurred later on. I don't recall anything about that going on in my presence. I like both of them. I loved working for Joe. He's a great friend. Cashman has always been great to me. He invites me to come to spring training every year."

"Maybe I did throw eighty pitches," Bean, reached by telephone in 2023 in the office of his Vestavia, Alabama, commercial insurance firm, recalled. "I didn't have a count. No one told me, we're going twenty-five or thirty today or whatever. As a guy who was trying to make it, your adrenaline is a little higher, so you would probably throw pitches quicker than a Mike Mussina, who was out there just trying to get through the day or get back and play golf."

It wasn't just Bean. Overall, starters were training like relievers, relievers were training like starters, rehab players were throwing way too much, and no one seemed to be counting. To make it worse, the paperwork claiming thirty pitches for everyone reeked of dishonesty.

"Half our payroll was tied up in pitching, and we didn't really have a pitching program," a team official says.

Cashman confronted Torre, and the two had a major blowout. The highly decorated manager felt that his boss was spying on him, and the GM questioned whether he could trust what Torre told him anymore.

In that way, the once-close partnership that included four World Series championships fractured over Colter Bean, an injured prospect whose major-league career would ultimately last six games.

But it wasn't really about Bean, and it wasn't about Guidry, a beloved Yankee whom Cashman likes and who has continued as a valued spring training guest instructor into the 2020s. This was merely the final crack in a long deteriorating and once-fruitful marriage between Cashman and Torre.

One can understand why new cameras and rules would offend Torre, and one can understand why a sheet that inaccurately claimed thirty pitches for everyone would anger Cashman. The upshot was that they were essentially done with each other.

"I do know that Cash and Joe, they weren't fond of each other, and I think I might have been a prime example of why," Bean says. "Cashman called me before '07 and told me that he had shared a bunch of numbers with [Torre and Guidry], and the way I took it, he was kind of fighting for me. I said, 'You're the GM; don't you make the decisions?' And he said, 'It's not that easy.'

"At that point I could tell there was more to it than meets the eye. I could tell there was strife going on. Obviously Brian had one way that he wanted to do the club, and Joe had another. I think Brian's way proved to work after Joe left. One thing I noticed, just the chemistry in the clubhouse when I was there versus when they won the World Series [in 2009] when they had [Nick] Swisher and all those guys, it was night and day."

Bean visited the clubhouse once in 2009, the second year of Joe Girardi's managerial tenure, and noticed that much of the tension he'd witnessed in 2006 and 2007 had dissipated. The 2009 team seemed to be having fun—a contrast to the few years prior.

"When I was up there, everyone scattered as soon as the media left," Bean says. "Everyone was gone. We had so many superstars it was like living in Hollywood or something. Jeter kept to himself a lot. He was always really good to me in the limited interaction I had with him. That guy was the superstar of all superstars, but he was always cool with me. But it was a weird dynamic with him and A-Rod, Giambi. It was a bad dynamic, in my opinion. From a team standpoint, if you spend that much time with each other, you gotta have some chemistry there. And they did not have any. And honestly that's one of the only reasons why they didn't win."

When Torre's contract expired after the 2007 season, the Yankees offered him a new, performance-based deal that Torre considered insulting—he didn't think he needed pay incentives to motivate him to succeed in October. He turned it down, and the partnership was over. As with any divorce, the final break came after years of drifting and resentment.

Following the blowup over Bean, another moment of significant disagreement between Cashman and Torre came at the end of the 2006 playoffs. Once again, the Yankees won the American League East that year. They routed the Detroit Tigers in Game 1 of the best-of-five division series, then fell into a slump and lost the next two.

Alex Rodriguez was one of the primary reasons that the offense went quiet. It had been another productive but emotionally challenging season for him as he struggled in big situations, heard vicious boos at home, and watched Cashman try without success to persuade Jeter to defend him.

Now A-Rod was 1-for-11 in the postseason, and the Yankees were facing elimination. When Torre and his coaches—an old-school group of ex-players that included Lee Mazzilli, Larry Bowa, and Don Mattingly, along with special adviser Reggie Jackson—reported to work on the morning of Game 4, they kicked around a radical idea.

"That day when we got to the yard, Joe was chatting with his coaches," Mazzilli says. "He says, 'I'm thinking about making a change, what do you think?' "

The change in question was to drop A-Rod down to eighth in the batting order, a spot usually reserved for one of a team's worst hitters. Mazzilli, Bowa, Mattingly, and Jackson talked it over.

"Joe thought hard about it, then posted the lineup," Mazzilli says.

"The decision to drop Alex down was agonizing. Joe was coming from a good place. It wasn't in any way a punishment. It was about putting a guy in position to succeed. We thought, take a little pressure off, maybe hit a three-run bomb from the eight hole and lengthen the lineup."

That process underscores just how much baseball changed between 2006 and the 2020s. In the contemporary game, front offices—including Cashman's—have strong input on lineups, especially during the playoffs.

Game planning is collaborative and based on data as minute as to how a particular hitter's swing path corresponds to the shape of the opposing pitcher's slider. A manager's gut instinct is but one ingredient. And no skipper would dare to implement a major change involving a star without informing the front office.

But that's exactly what happened here. No one even told Cashman about the lineup until it was too late.

He strongly disagreed with the decision, as did A-Rod, who told Bowa, the coach with whom he was closest, that it hurt him.

"But he never said a word to anyone else," Bowa says. "It probably burned him up inside, but he was professional."

Rodriguez went 0-for-3 in a Yankee loss that day. It was the final game of yet another largely successful but unfulfilling season.

A member of the front office recalls asking Torre if he was worried about embarrassing Rodriguez by dropping him that far down in the order.

"Fuck him," the team official remembers Torre saying (Torre firmly denies it). "Eighth is double cleanup."

24

Healing, Winning, Fighting

B Y THE END OF the 2008 season, when the Yankees missed the playoffs under their first-year manager, Joe Girardi, Brian Cashman had come to believe that his clubhouse was "broken," as he put it, and that Derek Jeter was part of the problem.

"We had a very stale clubhouse, where you basically weren't allowed to have fun, and the Yankee Way—this is how we do things," agrees one Yankee from that time. "I think Derek wanted to—there's only a certain way to win. You walk a straight line, and there's a certain respectful way to win, and you go about your business. But things had changed. And you are allowed to have fun and fist-bump and dance on someone's grave when you win."

Some team employees had taken to calling Jeter and his close friend Jorge Posada the "Grumpy Old Men," or comparing them to Statler and Waldorf, the cranks up in the balcony during *The Muppet Show.*

Their all-business approach, which worked so well in the 1990s, was starting to feel too severe for a younger generation of players like Joba Chamberlain, Phil Hughes, Robinson Canó, and Melky Cabrera.

Clubhouse dynamics are never simple, and opinions never unanimous. Through the middle and late years of Jeter's career, there were teammates who considered him, in the words of one, "the greatest leader I ever played with," a captain who knew how to command respect in a meeting with a perfectly chosen comment.

But many of the new kids connected more easily with A-Rod. Jeter confined most of his interactions to a small circle of trusted friends and family, which left an opening for Rodriguez to become more central to the Yankees' clubhouse culture.

"He bought me my first suit," says Chamberlain, who debuted in 2007. "I had never owned a suit. And there were times during games when I would look at Alex and he would call the game with me on certain pitches. He would give me a sign and I would think, 'Okay.'"

"Alex found his identity there when those younger players arrived," says Larry Bowa, the Yankees' third base coach in 2006 and 2007.

"I would see if they were in the same restaurant, he would pick up the check. He would pick up the check for Robbie and Melky. When you're a young player and someone is picking up a check and bringing in suits from a men's clothing store, that means something."

Rodriguez, for all his money and success, would also show up with Bowa on spring training back fields at 8:30 a.m., day after day, to help Canó take ground balls and improve both his work ethic and his fundamentals at second base.

The old guard seemed to stand on the other side of a fence from the newer arrivals, from A-Rod to Canó, Chamberlain, and Cabrera—anyone, really, who had not been a part of the dynasty. After the 2008 season, Cashman saw a need to heal this divide.

To address that need, he signed free agent ace CC Sabathia, a top pitcher known for his ability to get along with nearly everyone. He supplemented Sabathia in the rotation with A. J. Burnett, a talented and mercurial starter.

He landed Mark Teixeira on a massive free agent contract, not because Teixeira was a culture changer like Sabathia, but because he was the Platonic ideal of the Bill Livesey first baseman profile, an elite fielder who could hit for contact and power.

Cashman also traded for Nick Swisher, a high-energy goofball who grated on Posada but helped lighten the overall mood. And he already had Johnny Damon—amiable since his arrival in 2006 but muted by the Jeterian culture—as a natural to mix with the more garrulous new arrivals.

Suddenly the Yankees in 2009 were playing music in the clubhouse and smashing pies in one another's faces after walk-off victories. If this wasn't Jeter's style, he did silently acquiesce once the team started winning.

Even when A-Rod's long history of performance-enhancing drug use caught up with him for the first time, the group was strong enough to move past the distraction. In February, a *Sports Illustrated* report revealed that Rodriguez had failed an anonymous drug test in 2003. This shattered the image of A-Rod as a clean player and led to a New York tabloid firestorm.

A-Rod held a news conference at the Yankees' spring training complex and admitted to injecting performance-enhancing drugs during his time playing for the Texas Rangers.

"I'm here to say that I'm sorry," he said. "I'm here to say that in some ways I wish I went to college and got an opportunity to grow up at my own pace. You know, I guess when you're young and stupid, you're young and stupid and I'm very guilty for both of those."

Teammates were encouraged to attend, and most stood, grim-faced, wondering what in the hell they were doing there.

In previous years, an episode of Alex drama this severe might have sunk the group into a collective malaise. So many recent seasons had been slogs with high winning percentages as the team felt weighted down by the stares and sighs that marked the space between Jeter and A-Rod.

These Yankees had a lighter feel. They shook off the steroid news and moved on, though the team's early months together were not always smooth as the old guard and the new wave learned to mix.

On April 13, the Yankees lost to the Tampa Bay Rays, 15–5. Joe Girardi called on Swisher to pitch the eighth inning in order to save his bullpen. During a scoreless appearance, Swisher struck out Gabe Kapler.

Afterward, in an otherwise quiet visitors' clubhouse at Tropicana Field, Swisher was happy to discuss his unexpected mound debut.

"I had fun with it," he told the reporters gathered around him. "When am I ever going to get the chance to do that again? Probably never. . . . We know we didn't play very well, got to find something to laugh about in that moment."

Standing in front of his own locker, Posada glared at Swisher, scowling. A full ten years later, in an interview with authors Mark Feinsand and Bryan Hoch for their book, *Mission 27,* Posada stood by his disapproval of Swisher's post-blowout happiness.

"You just can't be laughing when you're getting your ass kicked," he said. "I know he took it as a fun time being on the mound, but I felt like even after that, he was doing interviews and he was laughing and stuff like that. It just doesn't sit well when you're losing and people are laughing. That's not our nature."

Well, it wasn't *his* nature. Or Jeter's. Or George Steinbrenner's or Bill Livesey's or Buck Showalter's or even Brian Cashman's. But the Yankees were changing, even if gradually. Some of the growing pains lasted until early summer.

On June 23, the Yankees lost in Atlanta, 4–0, their ninth defeat in thirteen games. The remade, expensive roster was just 38–32 on the season.

Watching the loss from home, Cashman decided that he needed to take the rare step of addressing the club, particularly the under-performing offense. He canceled plans to drive to Moosic, Pennsylvania, the next day to see the Yankees' Triple-A team and booked a flight to Atlanta.

The next afternoon he walked into the clubhouse and spoke to the hitters in an even but firm monotone. His message was that the Yankees had temporarily forgotten how good they were, how frightened opposing pitchers were of them, and how they should just relax and be themselves.

From there the Yankees took off, winning 65 games and losing just 27 the rest of the way. They finished with 103 victories and marched into the postseason more complete than they had been in years.

A matchup with the Minnesota Twins awaited in the first round. The Yankees typically dominated Minnesota, but were entering this postseason with significant pressure. Cashman's offseason spending spree and clubhouse overhaul, followed by the successful regular season, laid expectations on the Yankees to win the title that had eluded them since the Subway Series in 2000.

Sabathia started Game 1 and fell behind early. The game was tied 2–2 in the bottom of the fourth when Swisher batted with two outs and Robinson Canó standing on first.

Here, an insight that came directly from the Gene Michael scouting tree was key in helping the Yankees wrestle control of the series.

Ron Brand—Michael's friend from the Pirates' minor-league system in the late 1950s and the man who saw potential in Scott Brosius in 1997—had been scouting the Twins prior to this series, when he noticed a subtle tendency that became significant after Nick Swisher hit a 2-2 pitch down the left-field line.

The ball skipped into foul territory, then caromed off the wall and toward left fielder Delmon Young.

"Delmon Young always threw his relay throw at the feet of the relay guy," Brand says. "Never hit him in the chest. That made it difficult for the relay guy to scoop the ball and turn to make the throw. So we told [third base coach] Robbie Thomson, 'Hey, send a guy on a ball to left. Make him throw him out at home.'

"And in the first game, Nick Swisher hit the ball down in the corner and Canó scored. Canó wasn't a speedster, and it should have been a lot closer play than it was. But the throw was at his feet of the relay guy, and he was safe. So we won that game."

Indeed, Young fielded the ball, then bounced the relay throw to the cutoff man, shortstop Orlando Cabrera. Thomson sent Canó, and Cabrera's throw was offline. The Yankees now led, and they would not relinquish control of the series.

On the telecast, analyst Ron Darling complimented Thomson for his aggressive coaching, which came from heeding the scouting report.

"Delmon Young does a nice job of cutting this ball off," Darling said. "The problem is, when he gets it he one-bounces it to Orlando Cabrera, takes some of the steam off that throw. . . . I like that thought by Rob Thomson, the third base coach: push the envelope with two outs."

It was a moment of gratification for the scouts who did so much of the work that underlay surface success. And the fact that it was Thomson who executed the scouting report was another callback to Yankee tradition: nearly twenty years earlier, Thomson had been part of the group that first implemented the principles of the Yankee Way manual in the Yankees' minor-league system.

The Yankees ended up sweeping the Twins, then facing the Los Angeles Angels in the American League Championship. Sabathia came up big, winning Games 1 and 4 with dominant outings. Alex Rodriguez at last found his footing as a clutch superstar, batting .429 with three home runs in the series. The Angels had ended two Yankees seasons that decade with playoff wins over New York, but it wouldn't happen this time; the Yanks took the series in six games, with Sabathia earning MVP honors. A World Series matchup with the defending champion, the Philadelphia Phillies, awaited.

The AL and NL champs split the first two games at Yankee Stadium, then the series moved south on I-95 to a city eternally hostile to New York and its teams.

The Yankee front office did not have a suite at the Phillies' Citizens Bank Park, which was not atypical in the postseason, and had to watch from the stands. Phillies officials warned them not to wear any Yankees gear, lest they provoke drunken hostility from the home fans. As Cashman, Jean Afterman, and a few others settled in, all heeded that advice—until Gene Michael arrived.

Now in his seventies, Michael was about to watch his final Yankee championship. He shuffled through the aisle to his seat wearing a Yankee hat with white hair flying from it in all directions; a leather jacket with a huge Yankee logo on the back; Yankee rings on his fingers; and Yankee patches stitched into his clothing.

As Michael sat, a Phillies fan behind him began the predictable taunting and cursing.

Michael turned around, boomed, "You have a bad mouth!" and continued to watch the game. The fan stopped.

The Yankees won that night, and the night after that. They were simply the better team. After losing Game 5 in Philadelphia, they returned home to break in a new stadium with their first championship since 2000.

With Mariano Rivera on the mound in the ninth inning of Game 6, the Phillies' Shane Victorino hit a ground ball to Canó at second base, who threw it to Teixeira. The first baseman caught the ball, raised a fist, and ran to the dog pile that was fast developing on the grass.

On the left side of the infield, Jeter and A-Rod rejoiced, having finally collaborated on the title they were supposed to have captured upon A-Rod's arrival five years earlier.

The long parade to the graveyard was over. The Yankees had won again.

At thirty-five, Jeter had enjoyed an excellent year and was a key part of the title run. He batted .334 in 2009, with a .406 on-base percentage, eighteen home runs, and an .871 OPS—all upper-echelon numbers for a shortstop at any age.

The 2010 season, during which Jeter turned thirty-six, brought an abrupt decline. In the final year of his contract, Jeter's average fell 64 points, to .270, his power faded, and scouts inside and outside the Yankees organization continued to see slippage in his defense.

It was hardly the best platform year for free agency, but Jeter and his agent, Casey Close, did not think that should be the only factor. They felt that his iconic stature, and his remarkable body of work should elevate his value.

In early talks, Cashman believed that a three-year, $45 million offer did just that, exceeding what he would pay any other shortstop of Jeter's age and production. The Yankees, according to a team official, were also fielding unusual requests from Jeter's camp for an ownership stake in the team and/or its cable channel, the YES Network.

Despite these differences, Cashman assumed that the negotiation would wrap up with relative ease—until, that is, he read quotes from Jeter's agent that would reverberate for years to come.

It was a Sunday morning—November 21, 2010, to be exact—when Cashman woke up to learn he was in a public war with his captain.

That day, the *Daily News* columnist Mike Lupica published a rare interview with the publicity-averse Close.

"There's a reason the Yankees themselves have stated Derek Jeter is their modern-day Babe Ruth," Close said. "Derek's significance to the team is much more than just stats. And yet, the Yankees' negotiating strategy remains baffling. They continue to argue their points in the press and refuse to acknowledge Derek's total contribution to their franchise."

Reading that, Cashman says, "we were all caught off guard and pissed off."

In a meeting at the beginning of that offseason with Jeter, Close, Hal Steinbrenner, and team president Randy Levine, Cashman agreed with everyone else to keep discussions out of the press, per Jeter's wishes.

Cashman insists that he respected those wishes. While he says he can't be sure that no one in the organization leaked, he cannot figure out which article set Close and Jeter off.

In fact, while preparing to sit for his interview for *The Captain,* the

2022 documentary on which Close was a producer, Cashman asked the Yankees' vice president of communications and media relations, Jason Zillo, to go back through clips from that time to make sure he wasn't forgetting a provocative story in which he was quoted. Maybe it was his fault, and he just forgot? But Zillo found nothing to indicate Cashman had provoked Jeter.

"I don't know what it was," Cashman says. "I still have no idea."

In fact, sources say, it was not a single story that rankled Jeter and Close. Several articles reported from the GM meetings in Orlando, Florida, the week before Lupica's column contributed to a growing sense of irritation among Jeter's team.

On November 17, the *New York Post* published a column by Joel Sherman headlined "Yankees Prepared to Brush Jeter Back."

"GM Brian Cashman would not discuss the particulars of [their] meeting, saying, 'In fairness to the process, I am not talking about [the negotiations] in any way,'" Sherman wrote. "But confidants of Cashman said the GM is determined not to have the team get so lost in the past that it destroys the future by giving Jeter a contract that either lasts way beyond his effectiveness and/or overpays him to such a degree that it hurts financial flexibility elsewhere."

Another story emerged that day, this one by Wallace Matthews on ESPNNewYork.com and headlined "Rough Seas Ahead for Captain, Yanks?"

"If the New York Yankees could get Derek Jeter to agree to a three-year contract for $21 million per year, they would sign off on it today," the story began. "But they can't get him to agree to that, which is why we are a week away from Thanksgiving Day and a deal that was supposed to be a slam dunk is still on the shot clock.

"That is the word from a source with inside knowledge of the negotiations between the Yankees and Jeter. The source says the Yankees are willing to give Jeter more money than his play currently warrants, but fewer years than Jeter currently wants.

"Jeter, the source said, wants more. Four years, minimum, and preferably five or even six. Right now, it is a standoff, a dirty dance, a game of chicken in which one side or the other must eventually blink.

"And according to the source, who has ties to both the team and the player, there is at least one voice inside the Yankees hierarchy urging the front office to play its game as hard as Jeter plays his on the field.

" 'Tell him the deal is three years at $15 million a year, take it or leave it,' goes the hard-line approach. 'Wait him out and he'll wind up taking it. Where's he gonna go, Cincinnati?' "

In the November 18 edition of the New York *Daily News,* writer Anthony McCarron quoted Levine saying, "We think [Jeter is] a great Yankee, we think he's been a great Yankee and we've been great for him and this is the best place for him. But he's a free agent and he's allowed to test the market and do whatever he wants."

Cashman remains adamant that he had nothing to do with these or any other stories about Jeter's free agency prior to Close's comments in the Lupica column. Years later he can see how the "Where's he gonna go, Cincinnati?" comment in particular seemed inflammatory, but he strongly insists that it was not he who said it and that he does not know who did.

After Lupica published Close's comments, reporters reached out to Cashman.

"We responded," Cashman recalls. "If shot at, we'll fire back twice as hard. But we honored their 'Hey, let's keep it quiet.' And one day we wake up and there's Close going public. I didn't go public in response until every writer came to me in response to Casey Close's article with Lupica."

On November 23, Cashman told Matthews at ESPNNewYork .com, "We understand his contributions to the franchise and our offer [at that point, for three years and $45 million] has taken them into account. We've encouraged him to test the market and see if there is something he would prefer other than this. If he can, fine. That's the way it works."

In regard to Close's comment about the Yankees' "baffling" strategy, Cashman told Matthews that he was "certainly surprised. We have actually gone directly face-to-face with Casey and Derek and been very honest and direct. They know exactly where we sit."

No one in baseball had entertained the notion that Jeter, at thirty-six years old, would leave the Yankees. It was simply unfathomable. And now the GM was daring him to do just that.

"My fire off of 'shop it if you don't like it' was a response to Casey Close and Jeter's camp going public," Cashman recalls.

From that tense point, talks failed to progress. On November 29, Matthews quoted a source saying that Jeter and Close should "drink the reality potion."

With both sides now upset, they convened in Tampa for another face-to-face meeting. Cashman, playing hardball by this point, enumerated the reasons why he felt Jeter did not deserve more money than the Yankees were offering.

Jeter shot back by asking Cashman whom he would rather have playing shortstop. Cashman, put on the spot, named two younger stars, Florida's Hanley Ramírez and Colorado's Troy Tulowitzki. He hadn't intended to go there, but Jeter had brought it up.

"I'm not going to sit here and listen to this shit," Jeter said, according to his documentary.

That was the low point. Fearing that the deal could actually fall apart and Jeter would end up in another uniform before anyone knew what happened, both sides took a pause.

In early December they agreed to a three-year, $51 million contract and held a downbeat news conference at Yankee Stadium.

"I would be lying to you if I said I wasn't angry about how some of this went," Jeter said, standing at the lectern and frowning.

In his documentary series, he elaborated.

"It changed my feelings about the front office," he said. "I know now you were able to just throw me out. You were able to not treat me with the type of respect that I've shown you throughout my entire career. It's not a two-way street. It was a reminder that it was a business."

Jeter then changed his target from the front office to Brian Cashman himself, who in the 2020s is still wondering why he was the problem, when Close had been quoted first.

"Now I didn't want to have too many conversations with Cash," Jeter said. "I didn't. Didn't really want to speak to him, because I had lost that trust. Never say anything bad about him, but I didn't want to see him."

PART FIVE

INTO A NEW AGE

25

The Next Frontier

I N THE SPRING OF 1998, Yale University held its annual housing lottery for the next academic year. There was a freshman from Fairfield, Connecticut, who knew exactly which suite he wanted, but the randomness of the process left him unsure if he would get it.

The freshman set to studying the rules of the lottery to figure out if there was a way he could minimize that randomness and gain a measure of control over the outcome. He discovered that the selection order was weighted by seniority and room type.

Armed with that information, he canvassed the people who picked ahead of him. After persuading an upperclassman to change his selection—which he only knew was necessary because he had learned the specifics of the equation—the freshman ended up with the exact suite and suitemates for which he had hoped.

Six years later, that same freshman, now armed with a degree in mathematics, a job as an actuary at an insurance company, and a reputation as one of the top fantasy baseball players in the country, brought résumés and sample projects to the Winter Meetings in Anaheim, California.

A lifelong Mets fan, he had always dreamed of working in the sport. But there had never been a clear path into the industry for a shy math major who hadn't played the game at anything approaching a high level. Even Brian Cashman had been a college singles hitter.

With the publication of Michael Lewis's bestselling book *Moneyball* in 2003, that changed. The book detailed Oakland Athletics general manager Billy Beane's use of analytics to propel his low-budget team into the playoffs. It suddenly became trendy to look for brains, even at the expense of baseball experience.

The Yale graduate with a math degree and an actuary job, whose name was Michael Fishman, managed to score an interview with Beane himself. He presented Beane with his sample projects, one on how in-game moves affected win probability and one on how to value relief pitchers.

Beane was impressed. He had the budget for one hire, and nearly went with Fishman. But late in the process Beane met an engaging young man with a degree in mathematics from MIT and a doctorate in economics from the University of California, Berkeley.

That candidate, Farhan Zaidi, got the job. He would go on to become general manager of the Los Angeles Dodgers and president of baseball operations for the San Francisco Giants, widely regarded as one of the brightest executives in the sport. Fishman left the meetings with his dream still unfulfilled.

The following year, 2005, is when Cashman threatened to leave his job as general manager of the Yankees and George Steinbrenner persuaded him to stay—by finally giving him full control over baseball operations and permission to modernize the Yankees by investing in analytics.

"If you're going to be about history and tradition, you have to be about the future," says Jean Afterman. "Because history and tradition move on and on, and you have to move with that river. You can't just be encased in amber and wait for some David Attenborough to come in and create Jurassic Park. You have to be able to move with the times. And Brian reads everything."

At the time, many of Beane's competitors were hostile to his *Moneyball* fame. For everyone who loved the book, there seemed to be as many baseball lifers who derided Beane as an unaccomplished attention seeker. Not Cashman.

"Brian, to his credit, there was a humility and a curiosity there," Beane recalls. "At the time it was easy to kind of pile on with the book. And Brian, because he was Brian, was more curious.

"He said, 'I'm kind of interested in some of this stuff, you got any recommendations on where I can start?'"

As Cashman and Fishman remember it, Cashman first took note of Fishman because the latter listed Beane as a reference on the application he sent to the Yankees. The way Beane tells it, he suggested Fishman to his friend in response to Cashman's question about where to start.

Fishman's work samples impressed Cashman. As he considered making Fishman his first analytics hire, he consulted with Afterman.

"Brian gave me his résumé to look at, and he had listed Billy Beane as a reference," Afterman says. "I said, 'If he's so fucking good, how come Billy Beane didn't hire him?' Brian said, 'You know, I'll ask him.'"

Cashman called Beane.

"This guy is amazing," Beane said. "I would have hired him if I had the budget to hire both."

That was good enough for Cashman and Afterman, though one other consideration remained: Fishman had also been honest with Cashman during the interview process that he had grown up rooting for the Mets.

A decade later, when front offices prided themselves on cold rationality, this would have been a meaningless detail.

"But at that time, shit like that might have actually counted for something," Afterman says. "Teams and front offices, there was no collegiality. At the time a Mets fan working for the Yankees would have been like a Red Sox fan working for the Yankees."

While Cashman was still deliberating, Afterman went to midtown Manhattan for a doctor's appointment. There she spotted Fishman walking around in a tattered, clearly beloved Mets T-shirt that looked as if it had been through hundreds of spin cycles in the washing machine.

She returned to the office and told Cashman, "I saw Michael Fishman! In a Mets T-shirt! In midtown!"

This certainly wasn't a detail to share with George Steinbrenner, but Cashman knew that the game was changing. He hired the Mets fan, who instantly became a former Mets fan.

In the coming years, Fishman would help to steer the Yankees through a time of breathless change in the industry. Soon even *Moneyball* ideas would seem outdated as teams experimented with precise data on pitches and batted balls, outfielder sprint speed and first-step quickness, and so much more.

Terms like "exit velocity" and "spin rate," not even invented at the turn of the millennium, would become fully integrated into basic locker-room chatter.

When Cashman was a Yankee intern in the late 1980s, he spent his mornings transcribing answering machine messages from each minor-league manager detailing the results of the previous night's game. By the 2010s there would be high-tech cameras in the ballpark of every affiliate, measuring biomechanical data and other advanced information collected from the field. Nearly every movement in every game could be captured and evaluated.

In fact, this contemporary version of baseball presents a problem that is the opposite of that which Fishman and Cashman confronted when they first began working together in 2005. Back then, there was not enough data available; now there is an information overflow. The question has become how to best communicate all of it to the human beings who play the game.

Beane's mentor in Oakland was Sandy Alderson, the general manager who preceded him. Though Alderson is a minor character in *Moneyball*, it was he, not Beane, who first brought what was then called sabermetrics into an MLB front office.

In the early 1980s, when Alderson became GM of the A's, he was an attorney and former U.S. marine with no experience in baseball operations. He dealt with that deficiency by relying on the work of the pioneering baseball analyst Bill James.

When Alderson walked into the ballpark with mimeographed copies of James's self-published *Baseball Abstract*, he was unwittingly firing the first shot of what would become a revolution.

In the early 2020s, Alderson was in his seventies and wrapping up his long career in the game with a stint as president of the Mets. I asked him, as the father of analytics in baseball organizations and a pioneer (in parallel to Gene Michael) of on-base percentage as a transformational metric, what the next frontier of the movement would be. What was the next big stat or metric?

"The next frontier isn't a stat," Alderson said. "It's empathy and implementation."

In other words, information is abundant in the contemporary game. The project for analytically inclined teams—a group of which the Yankees stand at the forefront, having by the 2020s built out three separate data-driven departments and embedded analysts in every other wing of baseball operations—is to communicate this information in ways that players and coaches can appreciate and understand.

In 2005, Fishman and the Yankees began a two-decade project that consisted of attempts to not only innovate but break down the silos, insecurities, and power struggles that change can create. It was not always smooth or easy. Into the 2010s and 2020s, Yankee players sometimes felt grateful for all the new information, and sometimes they pushed against or resented it.

But if George Steinbrenner's toxic work culture was the front office's primary challenge in the late twentieth century, massaging the influx of data has been the main project of the twenty-first.

In fact, it has been the central theme of the game itself this century. There is a tidal wave of new information that didn't exist before. Much of it can be helpful, but it can also be difficult to communicate and understand. The key to both remains a human touch.

26

Inventing a Stat

A. J. Burnett was pitching. Jorge Posada was flinching. The umpire was, too. And strikes were becoming balls.

This was early in the 2009 season, and Michael Fishman and Billy Eppler were watching a game from Brian Cashman's Yankee Stadium suite. Both were executives on the rise in the Yankees organization, and they were about to invent a metric.

Fishman had earned extra credibility with Cashman the previous offseason when recommending a trade for the Chicago White Sox first baseman and outfielder Nick Swisher. Swisher had a down season in Chicago in 2008, but Fishman noticed that his underlying numbers, like how hard he was hitting the ball, were strong.

Cashman was surprised by the advice but followed it. Now Swisher was on his way to a productive tenure with the Yankees.

Eppler was just as important to Cashman's vision of the twenty-first-century Yankees. In contrast to Fishman, who flashed his quiet wit to only those he knew well, Eppler was a sociable former college pitcher with a degree in finance. The two shared an office wall at Yankee Stadium and, despite their superficially divergent personalities, became fast friends over a shared interest in innovation.

Eppler's entry into professional baseball came through a random connection with Damon Oppenheimer, the Yankees' director of amateur scouting: both Eppler and Oppenheimer had fathers who owned Chevron stations in San Diego.

In 2000, Oppenheimer connected Eppler to the Colorado Rockies, who hired him as a scout. Eppler's boss in Colorado was Bill

Schmidt, who had scouted for the Yankees when Bill Livesey was still a towering figure in the organization. As Eppler worked to learn the craft, Schmidt put him in touch with Livesey as a mentor figure.

"The first time Billy [Eppler] got into the player profile was in Colorado because of Bill Schmidt and Bill Geivett, who were both disciples of ours," Livesey says. "They told Billy to come down to the stands and sit with me at a game. That's how far I go back with Billy [Eppler]."

In 2004, the Yankees hired Eppler for a dual role in scouting and player development under Oppenheimer and Mark Newman. He worked out of the minor-league complex on North Himes Avenue in Tampa, which is around the corner from the major-league field and office.

"When Billy would come over for something, you could tell he was capable of doing more for us," Afterman says.

Having caught Cashman's attention, Eppler became a centerpiece of the GM's Yankee reorg after the 2005 season, when George Steinbrenner gave him more autonomy. Prior to that, the Yankees had a pro scouting department, but it lacked an overarching vision and was based in Tampa.

Cashman took charge of the department, moved it to the New York offices, and named the thirty-year-old Eppler as its director. In that role, Eppler tried to sharpen his evaluative skills by shadowing Gene Michael and tried to improve an area further from his comfort zone by working with Fishman on the data side of the game.

"I gravitate toward analytics because I understand blind spots," Eppler says. "Fish gravitates toward qualitative assessments, in addition to quantitative, because he understands blind spots. When you have that vulnerability with another person who has an extreme strength in a particular area, you're going to accomplish great things, because you put the egos down and make yourself vulnerable to the other person."

In 2007, Eppler and his pro scouting group made updates to the long-vaunted Yankees secret sauce, Livesey's player profile. They added more specific skill elements like plate discipline, arm accuracy (rather than just arm strength), and baserunning skill (rather than raw speed).

This was not a departure from the Yankee Way but an attempt to augment and modernize it. Eppler showed his loyalty to Livesey and his philosophies by bringing a sixty-eight-year-old Livesey himself back to the organization as a pro scout for a few years beginning in 2008.

On the day in 2009 when they watched Burnett throwing to Posada, Eppler and Fishman noticed a troubling pattern: Burnett was throwing fastballs for strikes that the umpire was calling balls. But a closer look revealed that it might not have been entirely the umpire's fault.

Burnett's mix of pitches included an elite "12-6" curveball, so named because its downward break mirrors the drop from 12 to 6 on a clock. He also threw a high-velocity fastball that he was not always able to control. Sometimes, he airmailed it all the way back to the screen.

This is where Eppler's time watching Stick Michael observe the game in extreme detail came in handy. He noticed that, on certain fastballs, Posada's head would rise a bit, as if flinching in anticipation of wildness. It was just a reflex. But because the umpire's head was right behind Posada's, he would flinch, too. And when an umpire flinches, he tends to call the pitch a ball. It's human nature.

"Fuck!" Eppler yelled at one of those missed calls. "That's a fucking strike! The fucking umpire missed it!"

He turned to Fishman.

"Fish, I bet there are six or seven pitches a game when that fucking happens to him," he said. "And when A. J. walks hitters, it starts to snowball. You can see his shoulders start sinking. You can see him shake his head a little bit."

Then he asked the key question: "Is there any way we can look at this with the new systems that have been put into the ballpark?"

"Yeah," Fishman said. "Actually, I think we can."

Those new systems to which Eppler was referring were technologies that had, three years prior, quietly begun to change the way certain teams evaluated their players.

Back in 2006, a Mountain View, California–based company called Sportvision, best known for creating the yellow first-down line for television viewers of football games, first sold to Major League Baseball its PITCHf/x cameras, which tracked the velocity, break, and location of every pitch. Fans could see the results on MLB's Gameday app, and teams could mine the underlying data.

The first MLB game to use PITCHf/x cameras was an American League Division Series matchup between the Oakland A's and the Minnesota Twins at the Metrodome in Minneapolis on October 4, 2006. It's hard to overstate the significance of that day in the history of the sport.

The *Moneyball* era was all about identifying surface statistics, like on-base percentage, that other teams undervalued. PITCHf/x data represented a completely new frontier from that which the Oakland Athletics pioneered: collecting brand-new stats that revealed an underlying game which never before had been visible.

"It started with ball tracking," Eppler says. "Pitchers started first, like being able to capture accurate velocities. It was velocity and location based. Then came the batted-ball data, and it was like, how hard are they hitting the ball? At what angles are they hitting the ball? And then you can start to do hit probabilities and home run probabilities."

To put this in lay terms, it went from "he hit the shit out of that ball" to "he hit that ball 107.7 miles per hour at a launch angle of 12.4 degrees and a sweet spot percentage of 31.6." That level of specificity could help front offices determine which players, like Nick Swisher on the White Sox in 2008, were maintaining their underlying skills while enduring a season of bad luck.

In 2007, PITCHf/x was in some major-league parks; by the following year it was in nearly every one. The Yankees were among the clubs to aggressively seek advantages in this new trove of information.

"We jumped into the research of that data right away," Fishman says. "Baseball statistics—the surface stats—can be misleading at times. The sample size in baseball is not big enough to really know the true talent levels, so this technology really provided some underlying data happening with the actual ball. We started trying to evaluate players based on the pitch rather than the result.

"It was a massive, massive shift. This new data was game changing."

Within a decade, ball-tracking data would be widely available to every team, and to the general public via the MLB-run website baseballsavant.com. Anyone could look under the hood and beyond the surface stats of any player. But in those early years, much of the data remained in the shadows but available for a curious mind like Fishman's to explore.

After Eppler asked Fishman if he could use the PITCHf/x cameras to determine if Burnett was indeed being robbed of strikes, Fishman left Cashman's suite for the area in the Yankee offices where his quantitative analysis department worked (by then, Cashman had fought for and won the budget to increase the head count under Fishman).

He huddled with Alex Rubin, an analyst with the Yankees at the time. The two talked about the concept of receiving the baseball and if that affected ball and strike calls. Did some catchers get more balls called strikes than others, and vice versa?

The next day, Fishman circled back to Eppler.

"We looked at it," he said. "And it's not to the level that you think, but yeah—we're costing A. J. a couple of strikes per game. Now we understand the value of a strike."

As they tried to figure out what their discovery meant, Eppler and Fishman wondered how much of a variable the individual umpire represented. Eppler called Josh Paul, one of his pro scouts and a former major-league catcher.

"Josh, when you caught in the big leagues, how many times in a season was the same umpire behind you?" Eppler asked.

"Well, I didn't catch every day," said Paul, a career backup. "But if you caught every day, I would say a maximum of four."

That told Eppler that the issue was not umpire dependent, because the umpires rotated too much. It must have to do with the pitcher-catcher pairing.

Catchers, it turned out, could present—or frame—pitches to the umpire in ways that made those pitches more or less likely to be called strikes.

"Well," Fishman said, after digging deeper into these numbers. "I've got some good news."

"What's that?" Eppler asked.

"The best one at this in baseball is on our roster, too," Fishman said. "It's José Molina."

Molina, a thirty-four-year-old veteran catcher, was Posada's backup on the 2009 Yankees.

"Get the fuck out of here," Eppler said.

Fishman assured him that what he was saying was true.

"Well, shit," Eppler said. "Let's go talk to Cash."

The two marched into Cashman's office to detail their discovery. They showed him the evidence and asked permission to go downstairs to the clubhouse and ask the manager, Joe Girardi, if he would consider pairing Molina with Burnett.

Girardi, a former Yankees catcher hired to replace Joe Torre in part because of his openness to data-driven ideas, looked down at the numbers, then up at Eppler and Fishman.

"This makes sense," he said.

The Burnett-Molina pairing continued into the postseason, which was relatively rare; typically, a team's primary catcher remains in the lineup for every game in October, no matter what worked during the regular season. Posada handled it with professionalism in public, though friends said that it wounded him.

With the Yankees down 1–0 in the World Series, Burnett threw seven strong innings to Molina in a crucial Game 2. Had the Yankees lost that night, they would have traveled to Philadelphia in a 2–0 hole, their chances of winning a championship suddenly minuscule. But they won and took control of the series soon after.

The issue with Posada and Burnett was generally overstated by the public as a problem of personal chemistry. But that wasn't the entire story: the pairing was almost entirely based on the newfound concept of catcher framing.

Over the next decade, this would become a widespread metric by which teams evaluated catchers. Eppler and Fishman can't be sure that they were the only ones who discovered it—by then, several clubs had analysts digging through PITCHf/x data—but at minimum they had invented the stat in an unwitting parallel to their rivals.

"You never know what other teams are doing individually," Fishman says. "There could have been other teams that were doing this then. But years before it became a public stat, we were doing it on our own. That doesn't mean there weren't other teams doing it. Baseball people, scouting people, always knew that there was some element to it that some catchers get more strikes than others. Obviously, pitchers knew that as well. Pitchers would request certain catchers.

"But what nobody really knew was the extent of it—the extent of the value that was there. With the actual data we were able to quantify exactly how much value a catcher was giving you from ball/strike calls."

With every recommendation like this that yielded results, Cashman came to trust his data people more and more.

27

A Loose End from the Old Days

Shut the Fuck Up

ALEX RODRIGUEZ WAS IN trouble again. In fact, trouble doesn't even begin to cover it this time.

It wasn't so much the performance-enhancing drugs; those had been prevalent in the sport for years, and everyone knew that A-Rod had indulged before. It was the drama, which once again engulfed the Yankees.

Not long after his first drug scandal in 2009, Rodriguez had begun working with Tony Bosch, a Coral Gables, Florida–based entrepreneur who provided pills, gummies, and other methods to deliver substances banned by Major League Baseball like testosterone and human growth hormone.

Although baseball's so-called steroid era had occurred in the late 1990s and early 2000s—when sluggers like Barry Bonds and Mark McGwire destroyed home run records and even middle infielders sprouted Popeye forearms (Bonds consistently denied steroid use despite ample reporting that suggested otherwise, while McGwire later admitted to it)—demand for an edge had continued unabated.

There was simply too much financial incentive to cheat. Teenagers saw the chance to lift themselves out of poverty, minor leaguers saw the chance to become big leaguers, big leaguers saw the chance to be well-paid stars, and well-paid stars saw the chance to maintain that level of excellence and stay healthy during the grind of a season and career.

As longtime MLB manager Buck Showalter puts it, "I've been to the Dominican Republic. Okay, I could cut sugarcane for a quarter an hour, or I can roll the dice here and see if I can go to the States and do this. What would you do? I'd go, 'Where's the fucking syringe?' It's not black and white."

Providers like Bosch recognized this and were ready to capitalize. When Bosch appeared on *60 Minutes* in 2014, reporter Scott Pelley glared at him and asked, in a deeply serious baritone, "Did you ever think about the *integrity of the game*?"

Bosch struggled not to laugh at the question. "I love the game of baseball," he told Pelley, who appeared stunned by the comment.

"How can you love the game of baseball and do this to it?" Pelley asked.

"Because, unfortunately, this is part of baseball," Bosch replied. "When you ask these guys to play a hundred-plus games, back-to-back, jump on a plane, get off the plane, all these road trips, their bodies break down."

"At the end of the day," Bosch added years later to me. "I wasn't black; I wasn't white. I was in a gray area."

Bosch was also savvy enough to position himself on the cutting edge of PED trends.

In the 1990s and early 2000s, players injected classic, heavy-duty steroids like Winstrol. Beginning in 2004, MLB introduced random testing. Soon after, under pressure from Congress, it increased penalties and hired former U.S. senator George Mitchell to assemble a report on the drug issue in the game. Over the ensuing years, Commissioner Bud Selig became more aggressive in trying to catch and punish users.

The testing program created a boom in business for a new wave of providers. Bosch explains the progression: "There is a right way and a wrong way to do [PEDs]. Before, it was a free-for-all, [José] Canseco–style. Then all of a sudden it's banned in 2004. Oh my God! Now we gotta do it differently. When you want to get Winstrol, you can go to any gym. You can pick whatever car you want to meet [a dealer] in, and it's in the car. I was saying no to that. Don't do that; that's for idiots. That's for amateurs. And they keep on getting popped. When Manny [Ramirez] got popped again and again, that wasn't me."

Bosch made use of old standbys like testosterone and HGH, but he also worked with amino acids called peptides that more easily eluded MLB's drug-testing program.

"Peptides are a bunch of amino acids put together in a certain sequence in a very short chain in order to create signals for the body to do something," Bosch explains. "You have your own natural peptide production, or synthesis, in your body. So the idea is to manipulate your body; basically, to hack your body. I was known as the biohacker.

"You want to jump higher? I've got a peptide for you. You want to fuck more? I've got a peptide for that one. You want to focus more at work? I got a peptide for that one that will trigger the neurotransmitters so you can up the serotonin, the dopamine, so you can—bam, focus. You want to lower anxiety, reduce diabetes? I've got peptides for that. For physical performance—I want to run faster, have better bat speed, quick hips, I want to turn around faster—I have a peptide for that."

Players like Ramirez and Robinson Canó—and surely many others—stayed on the heavy stuff. But the alternatives that Bosch provided, like testosterone gummies and peptides, were tougher to detect. In fact, his ballplayers were caught not by failing a drug test but when a disgruntled former client stole records from the Biogenesis office and shared them with journalists.

In early 2013, the newspaper the *Miami New Times* broke the story of Biogenesis, to which A-Rod and thirteen other ballplayers were linked. Those thirteen accepted suspensions from MLB, but Rodriguez took a different strategy: he fought back in an increasingly public and dramatic fashion.

By this time, tension between Jeter and A-Rod was mostly behind Cashman as a management challenge. The two had won a championship together and, pushing deep into their thirties, were no longer premium players in the sport. The world had moved on to other interests and obsessions.

Cashman, along with his twenty-first-century cabinet—Jean Afterman, Billy Eppler, Michael Fishman, and Tim Naehring, a former Red Sox infielder whose sharp evaluations marked him as a rising star in scouting—was mostly focused on the continued project of modernizing the Yankees. Gene Michael was still hanging in as an adviser, taking an interest in the PITCHf/x data and noticing how it validated many of his long-held observations and instincts.

The Yankees were thinking about the future. Then the Biogenesis story broke, and dysfunction returned.

The winter of 2013 brought two separate but parallel events: MLB was investigating A-Rod and Biogenesis, and A-Rod was rehabbing from offseason hip surgery that would keep him out for much of the year. As the season began, it was unclear what would happen first, Rodriguez's return to the field or his drug suspension.

Jeter had fractured his left ankle in the 2012 postseason, then experienced a setback early in 2013. The Yankees, fueled by far less star power than usual, teetered all summer on the edge of playoff contention.

They were a boring, mediocre team and could not compete for intrigue with the off-field story line of A-Rod and his potential return. Would the Yankees welcome him back once his rehab was over? Would MLB try to ban him for life?

On June 25, Rodriguez escalated the drama with a tweet that he did not clear with the Yankees' medical staff or front office.

"Visit from Dr. [Bryan] Kelly over the weekend, who gave me the best news—the green light to play games again!" he tweeted.

This carried several problems. One, teams like to announce injury updates themselves. Two, Kelly was not the Yankees' team physician. Three, the Yankees' own medical staff had not yet deemed A-Rod ready for game action.

As the unsanctioned update circulated, Cashman sat at his desk in his Yankee Stadium office, looking at the flat-screen television mounted on his wall and settling in to watch a game that promised an interesting pitching matchup. He was not yet aware of the tweet.

Then his phone buzzed with a call from Andrew Marchand, a reporter who covered the team for ESPNNewYork.com.

"I remember we were playing the Texas Rangers and it was [Yu] Darvish versus [Hiroki] Kuroda, two Japanese pitchers," Cashman says. "Andrew Marchand calls me and says, 'Alex said he was cleared.' Which was not true, and it wasn't even our doctor.

"There was something about the way the question was asked, and what it was about, and me just not wanting to deal with Marchand, and I was trying to watch the game and this was distracting me from it. I just said, 'Alex needs to shut the fuck up,' and I slammed down the phone."

The exact quote, relayed soon after by Marchand in a tweet that would reverberate around the sports world, was "You know what, when the Yankees want to announce something, [we will]. Alex should just shut the fuck up. That's it. I'm going to call Alex now."

Yankee fans old enough to remember George Steinbrenner's most combative period, when he took on Dave Winfield and even the beloved captain Don Mattingly in the press, might have recognized the moment as part of a long tradition. But quotes like these simply did not happen in professional sports anymore—and actually a GM directing an on-record f-bomb at his star player would have been noteworthy in any era.

Cashman's "shut the fuck up" hit in the social media age, and it blazed like a digital wildfire through the pregame evening.

Rivals had wished many times to say the same about their players. "Other people around the game called me and were like, 'Way to go,'" Cashman said.

A friend in the game sent Cashman a charcoal-colored figurine of a round bomb, emblazoned with the letter *F.* Cashman displayed it at the front of his desk at Yankee Stadium for years, before moving it to his home office, where it still occupies a prominent spot on the desk there.

While he didn't exactly apologize to Rodriguez—whom, after all, he had supported for years in the cold war with Jeter—he did take the time to explain why he was upset. And he chastised himself for the public loss of control.

"Normally I'm pretty good with the media," Cashman says. "But that was just a glimpse of the raw me. I felt like I was dealing with the circus over here, and then my team over there, and then the circus and my team."

As the summer of 2013 progressed, the atmosphere around the Yankees became more circus-like, to use Cashman's analogy, than it had been at least since the days of Steinbrenner versus Winfield.

With MLB aggressively investigating A-Rod and its suspension drawing closer, Rodriguez and his legal team mounted a pugnacious PR campaign.

On August 2, A-Rod played a rehab game for the Yankees' Double-A affiliate in Trenton, New Jersey. Afterward he shared with reporters the theory—or at least the strong implication—that MLB and the Yankees were conspiring to end his career.

"I will say this: There is more than one party that benefits from me not ever stepping back on the field," A-Rod said that day. "And that's not my teammates and it's not the Yankee fans. I think it is pretty self-explanatory. I think that is the pink elephant in the room. I think we all agree that we want to get rid of PEDs. That's a must. I think all the players, we feel that way. But when all this stuff is going on in the background and people are finding creative ways to cancel your contract and stuff like that, I think that's concerning for me, it's concerning for present—and I think it should be concerning for future players, as well."

Meanwhile, the situation was about to boil over in other ways. Rob Manfred, then baseball's chief operating officer, went on *60 Minutes* and accused one or more of A-Rod's people of being involved in a death threat delivered to Tony Bosch, who was now a paid witness for MLB.

"Are you saying that Alex Rodriguez or his associates were involved in threatening to kill Tony Bosch?" Pelley asked Manfred.

"I don't know what Mr. Rodriguez knew," Manfred said, without offering further details. "I know that the individual [of greatest concern to Bosch] has been an associate of Mr. Rodriguez for some time."

An atmosphere of paranoia defined the period, and folks were left to wonder if seemingly random events were connected. One day in the summer of 2013, Cashman returned home to Connecticut earlier in the afternoon than usual to find a suspicious scene.

"Something happened, but there's no proof of where it came from," Cashman says. "I wound up home one day—if you had my normal routine down, I was back home one day when I wasn't supposed to be, in the afternoon. I left work early or whatever. And when I came home in the early afternoon, my door was open. And I was like, I never leave my door open, ever. It was unlocked and wide open. And then all of a sudden when I was in my bedroom, I heard a *beep beep*.

"I had an alarm, and a door was open. And I thought, 'Holy crap, somebody was in my house.' When I got home, somebody was in my house. Because I had shut the door and went upstairs, and then heard the alarm *beep beep*. And then I ran downstairs.

"All of a sudden, antennas were up. [Other] people were experiencing odd behavior. It was all around the same time, so I was led to believe that this was not a coincidence."

Cashman did not call the police, so there is no report of the break-in. Neither A-Rod nor any of his "associates," to use Manfred's term, were ever linked to the incident—it was just office speculation, and probably nothing.

But the gossip itself was a telling indicator of the mood and tone of that time. It was not normal for a future commissioner to accuse a star player of involvement in a murder threat. This naturally led to widespread nervousness and suspicion.

It was into this increasingly toxic and paranoid environment that Rodriguez returned to the team on August 5 for a road game against the Chicago White Sox. On that very same day, MLB handed down a record suspension that would keep him off the field through the 2014 season, though A-Rod could play while awaiting his appeal.

Jeter was on the disabled list and absent, but A-Rod's arrival caused division in the clubhouse nonetheless. In a locker room overflowing with not just baseball reporters but representatives of national news networks and celebrity gossip websites, CC Sabathia strongly defended Rodriguez, saying he was glad to welcome a player so accomplished back to the team.

On the other side of the room, just a few lockers down from A-Rod's, the first baseman Lyle Overbay stood talking to two reporters and shaking his head.

"Why did he feel he needed to do that?" Overbay asked. "I don't think I could have lived with myself if I had taken stuff."

Rodriguez told reporters that he apologized to his teammates for causing the distraction. Teammates pushed back.

"He might have talked one-on-one with a few guys, but it wasn't like he addressed the group or anything," Overbay recalls. "There wasn't some big apology."

A-Rod played out the string while awaiting appeal. The hearing took place at MLB's Park Avenue headquarters that winter and was yet another circus, a war between Rodriguez and a commissioner in Selig, who wanted to appear tough on steroids before retiring and hoping for a spot in the Baseball Hall of Fame.

On the streets below the MLB offices, an impromptu group of pro-Rodriguez protesters held signs, including one that referred to the Yankees president, Randy Levine, as "the devil."

Cashman had long since stopped talking to Rodriguez, not so

much out of anger as because the environment had become so liti-gious; eventually, A-Rod was suing the Yankees' team physician, MLB, and even his own union.

The arbitrator ended up reducing the suspension but still banished Rodriguez for the 2014 season.

Fast-forward one year: Preparing to make his return in 2015, Rodriguez sought out Cashman to make amends about the gener-ally chaotic atmosphere of 2013 and early 2014—just as he had with Manfred, now the commissioner, and several others. The contrition allowed him to once again play for and ultimately retire as a Yankee, then begin a career as a broadcaster for the Fox network and ESPN. He briefly served as a special adviser to Hal Steinbrenner.

"The way he has acted since, I would say his apology was sincere," Cashman says. "I appreciated him saying [he was sorry], and I had a decision to make about whether I was going to accept it. I was going to be working with him moving forward, so do you, like, hold a grudge? I knew I wasn't doing anything wrong, so I could live with myself on that.

"He's walking the path, and part of that path was apology. So did I want to try to allow him to move forward, at least in my small world? I was not going to waste any energy or time on negativity toward him for that. I would rather just leave the past in the past and look for-ward to a better day. So did I appreciate that he took the time to say he was sorry? I appreciated it. It made things easier to move forward."

The two would be doing so without Jeter, who retired after the 2014 season. Because of his ankle injury in 2012–2013 and A-Rod's suspension the following year, the Yankees' most famous frenemies since Ruth and Gehrig had already played their final game together.

For Cashman—and surely for the Hall of Fame–caliber players themselves—it was the end of an exhausting era.

28

Replacing an Icon

I N THE HOURS BEFORE a Single-A game in Lynchburg, Virginia, in July 1989, a twenty-two-year-old infield prospect in the Boston Red Sox system named Tim Naehring was taking infield practice when a batted ball struck him on the cheek.

Still in uniform, Naehring hurried to the hospital, underwent X-rays, and returned to the ballpark to pinch-hit. Three days later the team traveled to Frederick, Maryland, where he had oral surgery. He emerged from the procedure with his front teeth pushed back, his gums black and blue, and a set of braces holding the top half of his mouth together.

That afternoon, the Red Sox promoted Naehring all the way up to Triple-A and told him he was needed immediately for a doubleheader against the Yankees' affiliate. Naehring flew back to Lynchburg to retrieve his car and then drove more than six hundred miles to Pawtucket, Rhode Island, arriving in the middle of game one.

"What happened to your face?" was the first thing the manager, Ed Nottle, said to him.

Nottle told Naehring he would be the designated hitter in the second game, which was delayed by rain. While Naehring sat at his new locker, looking around a room in which he barely knew anyone, a veteran named Rick Lancellotti approached and looked him over, bruised mouth and all.

"Stay hot," Lancellotti said. "You're facing Ron Guidry in game two."

Gulp. Guidry was one of the great left-handed pitchers of his time.

Now thirty-eight years old and in the minors on a rehab assignment, he was near the end of his career but still a presence.

The first time that Naehring stepped in against the Louisiana Lightning, he struck out. His next at bat was a battle. With a misty rain filling the air between them, Naehring fought off one Guidry slider after another—that once-great pitch that now only occasionally had its old bite—before driving one down the left-field line for a double.

When Naehring trotted into second base, Guidry turned around and gave a small nod, as if to say, "Not bad, kid. You got me."

Flash forward twenty years. Guidry and Goose Gossage are eating in the staff cafeteria at the Yankees' spring training complex, along with Naehring, now a top scout for the Yankees.

"Gator, my first Triple-A at bat was against you," Naehring says.

"Yeah, I remember that night," Guidry says in his pacifying Cajun drawl. "Pawtucket, Rhode Island. Rain delay."

"How in the world can you remember that particular game?" Naehring asks.

Answers Guidry, "That was the last game I ever pitched."

For Naehring, this is a neat coincidence, a harbinger of his future connection to an organization for which he never played but which he later helped shape.

In the years after Gene Michael's prime, Brian Sabean's departure, and Bill Livesey's ouster, no person with a traditional field or scouting background was more important to the Yankees than Naehring, and at no time would he be more urgently needed than when the team had to seek a replacement for the retiring captain, Derek Jeter.

Brian Cashman would come to regard Naehring as the Platonic ideal of a contemporary baseball thinker, able to speak languages new and old and empathize with all viewpoints. "He's my Gene Michael," Cashman would often say—meaning that just as Michael was George Steinbrenner's most trusted evaluator, Naehring was Cashman's.

Prior to joining the Yankees' front office, Naehring spent most of the 1990s as a popular player for the Red Sox. An Ohio native, he had the down-to-earth charm that, as he aged and grayed, recalled Jake Taylor, the sage if hard-living Cleveland Indians catcher played by Tom Berenger in the film *Major League*.

A shoulder injury brought Naehring's playing career to a premature end in 1997, when he was just thirty years old. He took a job in player development for his hometown Cincinnati Reds and, through the 2000s, built a reputation around the game for his eye for talent and affable demeanor.

Back in New York, Yankees' pro scouting director Billy Eppler, empowered by Cashman to rethink what the department should look like, had his own eye on Naehring. They would see each other at industry events and end up talking shop over long group dinners or bottles of wine that kept coming into the wee hours.

Because of baseball's strict rules about tampering with competitors' employees, Eppler had to be careful how he expressed his growing interest in Naehring. But the purposeful way in which he made sure to ask how things were going in Cincinnati telegraphed his true feelings.

In 2007, a shake-up in the Reds' front office left Naehring unemployed. He considered leaving the game altogether for a business opportunity in Cincinnati but decided that he would listen if the Yankees called. He liked Eppler and was intrigued by what was happening in that organization.

Eppler reached out almost immediately. "I saw there were some changes in Cincinnati," he said. "Would you be interested in coming to the New York Yankees in a pro scouting gig?"

So much for the business opportunity in Cincy. For Naehring, the pull of the game was too strong.

He was a perfect fit for Eppler and Cashman, who were seeking to fill job openings with former players who had not only a scout's eye but a mind open to data. In the years after *Moneyball*, oversimplified jock/nerd silos persisted in the game; the Yankees wanted to break them down by seeking complex, versatile people who carried both personas within themselves.

"We had a foundation of people who had scouted for a long period of time," Eppler says. "Some for decades in the amateur world. We had people who had decades or more of pro scouting experience, and we just wanted to diversify the group. So we brought in [former catcher] Josh Paul, [longtime coach and manager] Pete Mackanin, and [former outfielder] Kevin Reese, among others."

The Yankee hierarchy came to see in Naehring a unique ability to scout a player, summarize how analysts might diverge from his evaluation, and offer a fair-minded combination of the perspectives. They quickly began using him to scout their own system in order to get a holistic view of Yankee prospects.

"[Cashman] can call me any time and I can give him a pretty good understanding of where we're at in terms of our organization," Naehring says. "I give it to him through my lens, but blend some of the analytical stuff with that, so I can speak to him in regard to, say, 'Listen, here's going to be the challenge. Here is what the analysts are going to say about this guy, rather than the scout lens.' So I can help define exactly what that looks like for when he's trying to make his decision. Just describe the landscape as thoroughly as possible as he makes his decision on a player."

Says Eppler, "He had his playing experience and a general thoughtfulness. He doesn't run with the first idea or the first thought or the first evaluation. He thinks his positions through. He asks critical questions of himself before presenting an opinion or an evaluation. That mindfulness really sticks out. You stack that on top of a playing career, and he's just really somebody who checks a lot of boxes. He brought a diversity of thought and a really well-rounded approach to his role."

From the beginning of his Yankees career, Naehring found himself interacting frequently with Cashman. In his early years he was assigned to scout the entire National League plus the Yankees' own organization.

When it came time to discuss potential trades, Naehring was often at the front of a meeting room in Tampa or at Yankee Stadium, presenting to Cashman, Eppler, and Fishman and taking questions on players the team was considering trading or acquiring.

"They get a sense pretty quickly of what you're made of, in terms of your evaluation skills, your presenting skills, and your report-writing skills," Naehring says. "They have a pretty good understanding early on of what you're bringing to the table."

Although he had been with the Yankees since late 2007, Naehring's most significant task came in 2014. That February, Jeter announced that he would retire after the season.

The Yankees had less than one calendar year to replace a legend. This required that they find not only a productive shortstop but a person who could handle the unique pressure of following one of the most beloved players in franchise history.

The entire scouting department dove into the project. In a nice bit of symmetry, both Michael and his spiritual successor, Naehring, were significant figures in the process.

"I relied a lot on Tim," says Eppler, who by then was an assistant general manager. "Tim had a lot of information and very thoughtful and technical evaluations."

Michael, at seventy-six years old, was not traveling as much as he once did, but while in New York he looked at videos of candidates. Just as important, he trained his off-ball eye on potential Jeter replacements in stealth pregame scouting sessions.

"I would get Stick down to the field early at Yankee Stadium, during batting practice," Eppler says. "We would watch the guys take ground balls and watch them play a little bit, and I would piece Stick's evaluation together from what he was seeing."

In the initial meetings about replacing Jeter, the Yankees' brain trust considered punting for a year or two by plugging the position with a stopgap veteran.

"We sat back and said, 'If somebody said, "How are we going to replace Jeter?"' Well, you're probably not going to replace Jeter," Naehring says. "We completely understood how difficult it would be to replace Jeter.

"I remember watching the Big Red Machine as a kid in Cincinnati, thinking about how many of those guys were Hall of Fame–type players. I remember people having conversations like, 'How are you going to replace Pete Rose or Johnny Bench?' You're probably not going to replace those guys. The next person in line has big shoes to fill.

"And I remember talking with Stick casually in the war room about, 'Is the best game plan going out there and finding a stopgap-type guy? Finding a veteran who can handle the pressure? Do you get a guy for a year or two who can step in and bridge the gap to a younger, higher-ceiling, more talented guy, and take the pressure away from that person by having someone be there in between Jeter and him?' There were all sorts of concepts going around about how we were going to go about it."

As the 2014 season began, the Yankees started to narrow their attention to a group of shortstops that included both veterans and youngsters: Elvis Andrus of the Texas Rangers, Jed Lowrie of the Oakland Athletics, J. J. Hardy of the Baltimore Orioles, Andrelton Simmons of the Atlanta Braves, and Didi Gregorius of the Arizona Diamondbacks.

Kevin Reese, the former outfielder, was now pro scouting director. He, too, fit the profile that both Cashman and Eppler wanted: field experience plus data curiosity (the next two men who would serve in the job, former MLB pitchers Dan Giese and Matt Daley, were of the same mold, and Reese's name began to circulate in internal speculation as Cashman's ultimate successor).

Reese deployed many of his scouts to look at these shortstops. Naehring's sharp, Stick-like eye for off-ball behavior stood out when he recommended against one candidate because of his subtle behavior between pitches.

Typically, when a runner is on first base, one of the middle infielders gives a sign for who will cover second. Often this sign is an open or closed mouth. Naehring sought a shortstop who, like Jeter, would take charge and give that sign.

"I happen to think that if you're the shortstop, you should have leadership qualities—be a guy who takes control," Naehring says. "That helps everybody around them. They help move guys. They want to make sure they're helping everyone get positioned correctly. You want a leader, right? And how do you figure out if someone is a leader if you're not in the dugout with them? How do you figure it out when you're sitting in the stands?

"Like a center fielder. When you watch [2023 Yankee center fielders] Harrison Bader or Aaron Judge, you watch them moving other players. 'Hey, I'm moving five steps to my left, and I want the backside guy to know where I'm moving.' Constant communication. When I'm watching a shortstop, I want to see communication with the other infielders. I want to make sure they know in a shift situation who is or is not going to be on second base. Who's communicating with the pitcher and making sure that gets done.

"And most notably to me, when you get a guy on first base, there are signals typically given on who is taking second base on a steal and who is not. Open/closed mouth. On one particular day I saw a veteran-type shortstop who was not giving those signs, and the rookie second baseman was. It could have been that the veteran was trying to teach the rookie how to do it. I didn't know for sure. But I saw that was happening, and I made a note of it."

As the first half of the 2014 season progressed, Naehring began a close and lengthy observation of Gregorius, a twenty-four-year-old infielder born in the Netherlands and raised in Curaçao.

This was in part a happy coincidence because of another Yankee target who played for the Diamondbacks, pitcher Brandon McCarthy. McCarthy was underachieving for Arizona, having posted a 4.53 ERA in 2013 and a 5.01 ERA for that team in the early months of the 2014 season.

"I happened to see Arizona a lot, because I was on Brandon McCarthy for what felt like forever," Naehring recalls. "With my scouting eyes, I was like, 'Why is this guy not producing better numbers?' I think that was one of the first times where the scouting lens blended with David Grabiner [the Yankees' director of qualitative analysis after Fishman's promotion] in his department.

"They recognized numbers on pitch quality, pitch movement, pitch usage, and saw some low-hanging fruit that we could put into play right away. The scouts saw McCarthy and were like, 'Wow, this stuff should play. He should produce better than what he's doing.' It was one of the first moves where both departments really liked it."

In McCarthy, Yankees scouts saw good stuff and a chance for better results, and the team's data folks identified how that could happen: by having McCarthy throw his cutter more. That pitch had strong underlying qualities, but the Diamondbacks had told him to minimize it.

The Yankees' acquisition of McCarthy on July 6, 2014, was therefore a significant moment for the organization in how it combined the insights of scouts and analysts. After arriving in New York and emphasizing the cutter, McCarthy posted a 2.89 ERA for the Yankees.

While scouting McCarthy, Naehring got a long look at Gregorius. The shortstop had signed with the Reds as a teenager, then was traded to Arizona in 2012. Though evaluators around the league saw potential in Gregorius's athleticism and left-handed swing, the Diamondbacks had a glut of middle infielders who blocked his ability to receive daily playing time.

"During that process of sitting on McCarthy and seeing the Diamondbacks over time, seeing Didi play short, Didi play second, I really liked the upside with the bat," Naehring says. "I thought there was pull-side power. I thought the swing would play in Yankee Stadium. I liked some of the things he was doing with his swings, and I thought there was upside versus right-handed pitching."

Good scouts are also reporters, working their contacts around the league to learn what the games do not tell them. In this case, Naehring's old colleagues with the Reds had intel on Gregorius as a human being.

"Friends of mine who I knew going back to the Reds organization, where Didi was signed, liked the makeup, the person, the baseball intellect," Naehring says.

Naehring brought his observations to Eppler, who was able to cross-check them with an inside view from his latest ex-player/scout/analyst hybrid, Eric Chávez. A seventeen-year MLB veteran, Chávez had played for the Yankees in 2011 and 2012 before signing with Arizona in 2013.

"When I played for the Yankees, Billy said, 'Once you're done playing, I'm going to give you a call and you're going to come work for us,'" Chávez says.

Chávez retired midway through the 2014 season and months later was in the Yankees' front office—just in time to contribute to the project of finding Jeter's replacement.

"He played with Didi in Arizona," Eppler says. "Tim had a lot of information on him, and Chavy could speak from a teammate's perspective."

Says Chávez, "I was like, 'Hey, man, Didi is one of the best defensive shortstops that I have seen.' And I said, 'Arizona is overvaluing some of these other infielders, and Didi is unbelievable. You can't replace Derek as the player, as the icon. But you can replace some of the intangibles. Didi brings reliable defense and that left-handed bat at Yankee Stadium.' I felt that he was the perfect fit."

On September 25, 2014, with scouts still gathering opinions and the future of the shortstop position still unresolved, Jeter's Yankee career ended with the type of drama he seemed uniquely capable of producing.

In the ninth inning of their final home game of the season, the

Yanks led Baltimore 5–2. Jeter stood at shortstop, soaking in the chants of his name, drawing deep breaths, and blinking through tears, a rare display of public emotion.

He was moments away from his final bow when closer David Robertson, 39-for-44 in save chances that season, allowed a two-run home run to Adam Jones. That made it a 5–4 game, but Robertson still had the lead.

With two outs and Jeter still fighting tears, Baltimore's Steve Pearce sent a fly ball deep to left field.

Nearly everyone in the ballpark watched the flight of the baseball, as their eyes were trained to do. Back at shortstop, an off-ball moment that the world had never seen occurred: Jeter put his hands on his knees, lowered his head, and cursed the turn of events. A master of stoicism seemed nearly overwhelmed.

In the visitors' dugout, the Baltimore manager suspected that Jeter would be just fine. That manager happened to be Buck Showalter, who had been the Yankees' field general when Jeter debuted in 1995.

Showalter had helped codify the Yankee Way that Jeter rode to glory. He had managed A-Rod in Texas and had been a Yankee in exile for nearly two decades. Later, with Billy Eppler, he would bring Gene Michael and Bill Livesey's ideas to the New York Mets. Baseball is almost too symmetrical sometimes.

On this night, Showalter saw that Jeter was due up third in the bottom of the ninth. He knew enough to sense the potential for magic.

José Pirela led off with a single, and manager Joe Girardi replaced him with pinch runner Antoan Richardson. Brett Gardner sacrificed Richardson to second, bringing up Jeter with one out and the potential winning run in scoring position.

Showalter could have called for an intentional walk to set up a double play. As Jeter walked from the on-deck circle, he looked into the Orioles' dugout, and the two made fleeting eye contact. Showalter decided to pitch to him.

It did not take long for the magic to arrive. Jeter drove the first pitch from Baltimore's closer Evan Meek to right field, Richardson dashed home to score the winning run, and the retiring captain leaped in the air, arms outstretched, as teammates raced from the dugout to greet him in the dirt behind first base.

Up in the press box, where reporters never allow ourselves to appear in awe of what transpires on the field, a brief silence fell, followed by a smattering of *can-you-believe-it* noises. We should have been typing furiously to update our deadline stories with this development, but for a moment we just stared at the field. A few of us laughed. Goddamn. That really just happened.

Yankee officials were immediately curious about Showalter's strategy, wondering why the Orioles infielders seemed shifted to the left side for Jeter, when Jeter was known to hit the ball the other way, to right field.

"It's almost like Showalter purposefully gave him the hit," says one Yankee executive, noting that the Orioles had already qualified for the playoffs at that point and the Yankees had already been eliminated. "You don't play Jeter that way. He's a guy that goes the other way. It was like an homage to Jeter. The way he defended him, it was just very odd. And he could have walked him in that situation." Showalter, of course, wholly rejects this premise.

Jeter's career was over, save for a weekend series in Boston to close the season in which his participation was minimal. Now the front office had to turn fully toward the impossible task of replacing him.

Cashman concluded that he would not be able to get J. J. Hardy, who ended up quickly re-signing with Baltimore. Eppler ran point on trade talks with Texas for Andrus because his counterpart there, assistant general manager Thad Levine, had been in Eppler's wedding party. But Andrus, who had once seemed like a burgeoning star, was showing signs of decline, and he held a player option on his contract that could trigger an extra three years and $43 million starting in 2019.

The Rangers wanted catching prospect Gary Sánchez. The Yankees wanted Texas to pay a share of Andrus's contract option. It was too complex, and the Yankees moved on.

While Cashman and his brain trust liked Gregorius, they were also drawn to the defensive wizardry of Simmons in Atlanta. Trade talks with the Braves commenced.

In exchange for Simmons and outfielder Jason Heyward, Atlanta wanted a package that included prospects Aaron Judge, Luis Severino, and Sánchez (imagine Judge as a lifelong Brave). They also wanted the Yankees to take on the burdensome contracts of veterans B. J. Upton and Chris Johnson and expressed interest in prospects

Ian Clarkin and Manny Bañuelos. It was too much to ask, and talks did not progress.

Cashman's attention then turned fully to Gregorius, with Naehring's endorsement at the top of both his and Eppler's minds.

"Tim talked a lot about Didi and thought he was a guy who could play everyday shortstop for us," Eppler says. "Bringing it in front of Cash and saying, 'This is a guy we should really zero in on.'"

"I had already thought that Naehring was a young Gene Michael," Cashman says. "This was an actual baseball person. So we started talks with the Diamondbacks, but essentially we didn't have anything we were comfortable with. I tried to get Didi from Arizona ten different ways. Every time I tried, I could not lock up directly with the Diamondbacks. I was surprised. I was like, 'God, these are good players we're offering.'"

Unable to match up directly with Arizona's chief baseball officer, Tony La Russa, and general manager, Dave Stewart, Cashman had to think creatively. He knew that the Detroit Tigers GM, Dave Dombrowski, and manager, Jim Leyland, liked young right-handed pitcher Shane Greene, who had performed well as a rookie for the Yankees in 2014.

"At the time I was talking to Dave Dombrowski in Detroit, and they coveted Shane Greene," Cashman says. "I didn't want to move Greene, but I desperately needed a top shortstop. Or any shortstop. At the time I couldn't yet tell you if Didi was legit, but they had a shortstop factory going on in Arizona of young guys.

"Dombrowski and Leyland loved Greene. Dombrowski said, 'What are you guys looking for?' I said, 'Listen, I'll tell you straight up. If you can get Didi Gregorius from Arizona, I'll give you Shane Greene.' I didn't want to do that, but it was a validation of Tim Naehring's belief in what Didi could be. Dave said, 'Okay.' And within forty-eight hours Dave was like, 'I got him.' I was like, 'What the fuck? I've been trying to get this fucker forever and you make one, two calls.' But yeah, it was a three-way deal."

Before agreeing to the trade, Cashman called Naehring at home in Cincinnati.

"You really like this guy?" he asked.

"Yeah, I do," Naehring said.

"I think we might be able to work something out here," Cashman said. "I'll call you back. We might have a three-team trade in the works."

Naehring walked upstairs and found his wife, Kris.

"Hey," he said, "this is going to be pivotal for our time as Yankee employees. If this goes well, our time with the Yankees could go well. If this doesn't go well . . ."

In the very early going, it did not go well at all. Gregorius batted .206 in March and April 2015 and .232 in May. The fans at Yankee Stadium were starting to boo, and the pressure of replacing Jeter seemed to weigh on Gregorius.

If this was an uneasy time for the player, it was for the man who recommended him, too.

"The offensive struggles, yes, it was obviously stressful," Naehring says. "Scouts always make comments like, 'Once you bring them in, it's on to the next person.' Well, that's true, but I will tell you that you become a pretty big fan of the people you have your name on. You're watching every night. You want that person to come in and be an asset that helps put a ring on everybody's finger. Yeah, those first months were tough."

Naehring drew reassurance from his knowledge that the Yankees' hitting coach, Jeff Pentland, was working with Gregorius on adjustments to his swing that had yet to click. Sure enough, he finished that first season in pinstripes with a respectable .265 average, defensive play far superior to Jeter's, and an overall winning style of play and attention to detail.

From there, he took off. In five years with the team, Gregorius was not only productive but popular with fans and teammates. He just seemed like a Yankee.

"He was everything and then some," Cashman says. "He was fantastic. He was as good as they came, and he was a good person. The fans loved him. He performed. He was great."

Gregorius would also contribute big hits in the postseason. Before leaving in free agency after the 2019 season, he did nearly everything required to become a vaunted Yankee, save for one accomplishment that he alone could not control: he never played in a World Series.

For all the continued Yankee excellence, even dominance, that ultimate success eluded them after 2009. By the mid-2010s, with

Jeter, A-Rod, and the previous generation gone or leaving, Cashman and his front office were at work trying to build yet another core.

The process served as another reminder, as if they needed one, of how rare and special the 1990s group had been, but it did deliver the franchise's next generational superstar—an heir to Jeter, but without the clubhouse baggage.

In fact, by the time Jeter knocked that last single past a mysteriously shifted Baltimore infield, Aaron Judge was already crushing homers in the low minors.

But before he arrived in the big city, there would be more Yankee drama—and more Yankee change.

29

New Core, New Culture, and Very New Challenges

Midway through the 2016 season, it was obvious to Brian Cashman that his team was not good enough to win a World Series and that the best move was to trade veterans for prospects.

Retooling, let alone the dreaded concept of rebuilding, simply did not happen in Yankeeland, at least not anymore. Not since 1989, when the Yankees traded Rickey Henderson to Oakland in the middle of a losing season, had the team acted as "sellers" at the midsummer trade deadline.

But every farm system can use a reset, especially one still depleted by years of chasing a dynasty and acquiring expensive stars. Cashman made his case to Hal Steinbrenner.

On the other side of the debate were voices from the business side of the organization who felt that conceding a season would be too much of a departure from the Yankees' brand, which sells winning.

Steinbrenner weighed both arguments. "There were certainly people in the organization who felt that it completely blew our chances to win that year, and that included even people in my own family," he recalls.

Cashman was able to convince Steinbrenner that his path gave the Yankees a better chance for sustained success in the future. And he tried to appease the business folks by trading for veteran reliever Tyler Clippard and promoting some of the prospects about whom the fans were excited. Cashman was able to present this as something less than a white flag.

For weeks, Tim Naehring—now a Yankees vice president and

Cashman's top baseball man after Billy Eppler left to become GM of the Los Angeles Angels—and the Yankees scouts fanned out across the country, evaluating potential trade targets. In what would be his penultimate trade deadline, Gene Michael watched video of the prospects.

Then, on July 25, the sell-off began. Cashman traded closer Aroldis Chapman and three other players to the Chicago Cubs for infield prospect Gleyber Torres.

Six days later, he moved ace reliever Andrew Miller to Cleveland for outfield prospect Clint Frazier, pitching prospect Justus Sheffield, and two others. On August 1, the day of the deadline, he sent veteran hitter Carlos Beltrán to Texas for pitching prospects Dillon Tate, Erik Swanson, and Nick Green.

"As far as trading Beltrán, I remember that our offense was just not performing," Steinbrenner says. "And I didn't think that they were going to start performing magically. As far as trading Chapman and Andrew Miller, I wanted to get the young guys in. [Gary] Sánchez, Judge, [first baseman] Tyler Austin, were part of that. Guys who every other team had been asking about for three, four years previously. Every trade deadline, every offseason. And I refused to trade them.

"Yeah, there was disagreement [about whether to sell], but I just felt we weren't good enough to win, period. And let's get the young guys up, let's get the fans excited about it, and let's see if they can perform here. Every other team thinks they can, because that's why they wanted them in every trade that was discussed. The results, as we sit here now [in 2023] are the results. Obviously with Judge, they were good results."

Though not all of these moves proved successful, the Cubs trade was a triumph. Not only did Torres become an All-Star in New York, but after the 2016 season Cashman re-signed Chapman as a free agent.

Frazier, on the other hand, never blossomed, and Cashman hung on too long to extract trade value from him. The Yankees ultimately cut Frazier after the 2021 season; on that one, their scouting and projection had missed.

Some of the other acquired players proved valuable in more subtle ways. Cashman traded Sheffield and Swanson to Seattle for two years of starting pitcher James Paxton. Paxton was often injured, but effective in key spots for the Yankees, including the 2019 postseason. In 2018, Cashman used Tate to acquire reliever Zack Britton from Baltimore. Britton spent several years as an effective setup man and important clubhouse leader.

On August 13, twelve days after the Beltrán trade, Judge made his major-league debut, setting up a historic season in 2017.

But for all the hope and renewal that came with trading veterans, taking a breath, and introducing younger stars, the next season—2017—ended up, on several levels, as a crushing one. On September 7 came news of Michael's sudden passing from a heart attack. The loss hit friends hard. From the moment he arrived in New York in 1968 and routed Mickey Mantle in late-night card games, Michael had touched nearly everything significant that happened with the franchise. He was a Yankee before and after George Steinbrenner and had loomed large in the design and retention of their final dynasty while mentoring Cashman.

Few were closer to Michael than Buck Showalter, whose Orioles—of course—happened to be playing the Yankees on the night of Michael's death. When he learned the news, Showalter flashed back to a scene in his kitchen a quarter century earlier.

"He would drive from New Jersey to spring training in Florida, and he would stop at my house at like seven o'clock in the morning," Showalter says. "Come in and have breakfast. Have some coffee, get back in the car, and continue to drive. He was a crazy driver, too. But I can remember his voice like yesterday."

Dishes clanking in the sink. Coffee brewing. Stick Michael, his unmodulated baritone in its prime, talking baseball in the kitchen.

"God, I miss him," Showalter says.

The Yankees' brass had to shake off the loss and prepare for a postseason run that came a year or two earlier than expected. When Cashman executed the sell-off in 2016 and made room for the kids, he figured it would take time before the Yankees developed into serious contenders again.

But several of those youngsters bloomed quickly, including pitcher Luis Severino and especially Judge, who set a new rookie record by hitting fifty-two home runs and finished second in AL Most Valuable Player voting to Houston's second baseman, Jose Altuve.

The Yanks won ninety-one games, then defeated Minnesota in the Wild Card game and Cleveland in a five-game division series. They found themselves in an American League Championship Series against the ascendant Houston Astros.

Over the past few seasons, Houston's general manager, Jeff Luhnow, had rebuilt that organization with a focus on data and efficiency. A former consultant for the morally ambiguous McKinsey & Company, Luhnow made effective use of technology, fired experienced scouts, and created a work culture in which underlings felt relentless pressure to innovate.

That environment gave rise to one of the most significant cheating scandals in the history of the game.

Over the next three years, the Astros' front-office officials, coaches, and players would collaborate and utilize technology like cameras and algorithms to steal the signs of opposing catchers.

In a larger sense, across the sport, the era of electronic sign stealing began in 2014, when MLB expanded instant replay and introduced the replay room near the dugout. In that room a team employee watched games from multiple camera angles and advised the manager on whether he should challenge an umpire's call on a particular play.

With so many close-ups available, players began to drift into the replay room and peek at the catcher's hand to see what pitch was coming next. The Yankees participated in this trend, as did the Boston Red Sox, Los Angeles Dodgers, Milwaukee Brewers, and other clubs.

Those clubs relayed the signs from the dugout to base runners, who then used a complex set of signals—touching the brim of their helmet, running a hand across the letters on their jersey—to convey the sign to the batter.

This was an ethical gray area, but in line with what teams had done for more than a century. It required some art and design, because of the signals required.

The Astros, however, took sign stealing a giant step further, making the crucial decision to do it with no one on base—in other words, alerting their batters regularly to oncoming pitches. Using audio cues like telephone rings and the banging of a bat on a garbage can, the Astros passed stolen signs directly to the hitter. This was far more egregious than what other clubs did: there was no art to the theft, no need for players on the field to develop signals or use their brains to figure out the signs. In the eyes of opponents, it was just bald, naked cheating. No other team was credibly accused of this. After the 2019 season, the Astros were caught, and the wave of electronic sign stealing crested.

In the 2017 postseason, the Yankees and other clubs were beginning to suspect the Astros but did not yet know the extent of the problem.

According to a member of the Astros who participated, the team's cheating in that ALCS (and in their subsequent World Series victory against the Dodgers) went like this: before home games at Minute Maid Park, club personnel mounted a television showing a live feed of the catcher's crouch on the wall behind their dugout. That TV had hung there consistently during the season, but during the playoffs league officials patrolled clubhouses before and after postseason games, so Houston had to step up the sneakiness. As soon as the final out of a game was recorded, the Astros removed the television from the wall in order to hide their actions.

The Astros beat the Yankees in seven games, and while they did not hit well at home during the series, it's impossible to know how their razor-thin margin of victory would have been altered by a series played on the level.

In some ways, the Yankees organization never got over the resentment.

"That was our year," one team executive says.

"You didn't earn it," Aaron Judge said in 2020 of the Astros' 2017 championship.

"The only thing that stopped us was something so illegal and horrific," Cashman told the online sports publication *The Athletic* in 2022.

The Astros' cheating continued in various forms through the 2019 postseason. In Game 6 of the ALCS that year, the Yankees noticed a pattern of flashing lights in the outfield. The lights were blinking on and off in a pattern that indicated whether a fastball or off-speed pitch was coming.

"Watching it, we knew every pitch that was coming—so they did, too," says a Yankee official.

"That's a crock of shit," one member of that Astros team tells me in response.

The Astros won that series on an Altuve home run in the ninth inning of Game 6. Rumors followed that Altuve was wearing a buzzer under his jersey that gave him the pitch. My own extensive reporting on this turned up no evidence to support the buzzer theory, but plenty of Yankees players and officials will go to their graves believing that the allegation against Altuve—which Altuve strongly denies— is true.

After that ALCS loss in 2017, Cashman and Steinbrenner made a significant change, deciding not to offer manager Joe Girardi another contract. While Cashman had decided to move on earlier that season, a World Series appearance might have complicated the plan; in a way, Houston's cheating had yet another major effect on the Yankees.

Back in 2007, when Cashman hired Girardi to replace Joe Torre, the GM saw him as a perfect partner in the new world of information and technology.

The two collaborated on a championship in 2009, then Girardi shepherded the team through the challenging period of conflict between the front office and a declining Derek Jeter and Alex Rodriguez.

By 2017, when a younger generation of Yankees was emerging, Cashman was hearing reports from the clubhouse that Girardi's all-business personality was not meshing with the kids. The public would come to assume that an inability to relate to younger players was Cashman's reason for moving on from Girardi. But actually, that wasn't it.

Cashman didn't need his manager to be best friends with every twentysomething who emerged from the minor leagues, but he did need to remain aligned with him philosophically and personally.

Beginning during the 2017 regular season, Girardi and Cashman were no longer that way, as Cashman now reveals.

"I was his biggest supporter, the reason he lasted so long, because I thought he checked a lot of boxes and did a lot of great things for us," Cashman says. "It's hard to separate when the players aren't on board: Is it because he's a tough taskmaster? Or are the players not on board because he couldn't connect? It's hard for me, in my chair, to separate that.

"As long as we're winning and he's doing the job and having success in it, it's not something you focus on. But obviously alignment is very key, and at one point we got off-line about something. It was repairable, but he chose not to try to repair it, so I moved on."

Cashman declines to offer further detail about this issue. Other sources say it was a conflict involving communication and honesty, though it was not a rift on the level of his break with Torre over Ron Guidry and injured reliever Colter Bean. The very next year, when managerial openings emerged for other teams, Cashman would work his contacts in front offices and the media to push Girardi's candidacy. He retained genuine affection for the man.

"I love Joe Girardi," Cashman says. "I think he was an impactful New York Yankee player, an impactful New York Yankee coach, and a world champion. We have a lot to be proud of. But like everyone else, family members have disagreements that can lead to separation, and that was ultimately what happened. I think the world of him."

As Cashman and his inner circle interviewed potential replacements, no one clicked. Cashman began to worry that he had made a mistake and would not be able to find a manager to equal the guy he had dismissed.

Then Aaron Boone walked in. Cashman knew Boone from only two deeds in the distant past: the eleventh-inning home run that propelled the Yankees to the World Series in 2003, and Boone's subsequent decision to tell the truth about an injury that cost him his Yankee playing career (when he tore his knee playing basketball—an activity that his contract prohibited). Cashman remembered Boone's ethical behavior. Rather than concoct a lie, which many players would have done, Boone and his agent told the Yankees the full story. The team did release him, but the parting was amicable.

In late 2017, after spending eight years as a prominent broadcaster for ESPN, Boone was looking to get back on the field. A third-generation big leaguer—Boone's grandfather Ray debuted in the big leagues in 1948, and his father, Bob, in 1972, and his brother Bret played contemporaneously with Aaron in the 1990s and early 2000s—Boone was known around the game as an intelligent and affable person, but he had never managed or coached on any level.

The Yankees granted him an interview. During a grueling, approximately nine-hour process, Boone was quick with his answers to game strategy questions, on point with the analytics people, and down-to-earth enough for the traditionalists. When he left, Cashman and a few others turned to one another and asked, "Is he for real?"

"He checked every single box that day," Cashman recalls. "It was an extensive interview involving a number of different departments."

Cashman's mind was made up: Boone—smart, tough, and caring—had a chance to become a special manager.

Boone got the job and quickly became the first skipper in baseball history to win a hundred games in each of his first two seasons. His feel for in-game strategy was a work in progress, improving vastly after his first year or two at the helm, but he brought two qualities that Cashman needed: an empathic demeanor with players of a generation that the front office considered more sensitive, even coddled, than their forebears, and a willingness to collaborate with the increasingly influential data people.

"He's an exceptional manager," Cashman says. "He was a risk worth taking, and I really hope our fans will eventually realize that. And I hope he gets a championship, because he deserves it."

"He cares about people," says Zack Britton, a veteran relief pitcher who became a clubhouse leader after Cashman acquired him from Baltimore in 2018. "He is very good at keeping things internal. When the team is struggling, he is so positive. I know our fan base is probably sometimes like, 'God, I wish he would just rip somebody!' But that's not who he is. Boonie is not going to sit there [in a press conference] and air you out.

"But the dude is super passionate. He'll have these team meetings and go off. You see it with his ejections. That's where you see the real fire in him. And he will do that behind closed doors. But he doesn't embarrass anyone in front of the group. If we have a group meeting, he'll be general, and then he might call guys into his office separately."

Indeed, Cashman and most players agreed that Boone was the right fit for the clubhouse. But that did not erase all tensions related to the most contentious area in the modern game: the implementation of analytics.

For a deeper understanding of that defining issue, I turned to Britton and another thoughtful pitcher, Yankees' ace Gerrit Cole.

30

Gerrit Cole and Zack Britton

Analyzing Yankee Analytics

I T IS A RAINY Sunday evening at Yankee Stadium in September 2022, too wet for the Yankees to take batting practice on the field. They have a night game scheduled on ESPN, and Aaron Judge is sitting on sixty home runs.

A few minutes after 5:00 p.m., Gerrit Cole is throwing a bullpen session, and Zack Britton is sitting with me in the dugout, looking out at the drizzle and reflecting on how analytics have changed the Yankees, not to mention the sport itself.

Cole is one of the best starting pitchers of his generation, and Britton one of the top relievers. They are also two of the most cerebral players on the Yankees' roster. Both were leaders in the Major League Baseball Players Association during tense negotiations with owners in the 2021–22 lockout, and both have long utilized data to improve their performances.

By now, the analytics movement within the Yankees has grown from Michael Fishman alone in 2005 to three entire departments: qualitative analysis, performance science, and baseball systems. The team also embeds analysts into every other wing of baseball operations, from scouting to player development to the major-league coaching staff.

If the final frontier of the data revolution in baseball is, as the analytics pioneer Sandy Alderson says, the human arts of empathy and implementation, Britton and Cole are well equipped to discuss how that is going.

Britton came into the league in 2011, Cole in 2013. They have played on both sides of the Statcast era, and Cole was a member of the Houston Astros in 2018 and 2019, the final years of that team's culture of extreme analytics.

The Yankees acquired Britton in a trade from Baltimore in July 2018. Britton underwent elbow surgery in 2021 and spent most of 2022 rehabbing at the Yankees' complex in Tampa. There, he had an up-close view of the profound changes in player development that had come to the industry since he was a prospect.

"I spent almost a whole year in Tampa, where the hub of this is," Britton says. "The biomechanics and the analytics and all that. In that environment, the young kids are getting almost immediate feedback [with data], an immediate understanding."

That, to Britton, is an improvement from the Yankee culture of four years prior, when the front office provided granular information about each of his pitches—how they break, how they spin, what results they produce—but without sufficient explanation or context.

"I came from a place that had none, in Baltimore, to here, where I had an iPad put in my locker with anything or everything I needed or wanted," Britton says.

"I would say the communication, at first, was confusing when I got traded over here. It was kind of an overload because I came from somewhere that had nothing, and I wasn't really sure how to interpret it and apply it. I would look at it one way, and think, 'Oh, wow, something that I thought I was good at, it's not really saying I'm good at.' But then [the analysts] would come down and say, 'No, you're good at it.' Interpreting the information was difficult."

As the Yankees' union representative, Britton interacted with the front office more than most players, especially during the 2020 season, when the team grappled with logistics during the height of the COVID-19 pandemic.

Brian Cashman and Jean Afterman came to appreciate Britton's maturity and collaborative nature and sought feedback on their implementation of analytics.

"I've had so many conversations with Cashman and Jean Afterman about communicating analytics," Britton says. "Every year that I have been here, at the end of the season I've sat down with either Jean or Cash, and they've been like, 'How are we communicating?' They take the initiative. My honest opinion has always been that sometimes for the young players it was information overload. Maybe they didn't know how to interpret it that well.

"But it has evolved over the years to where the team is very specific now about who communicates the information to the player. When I first got here, it was four or five people, whether it was somebody in the front office or the coaching staff, and the message would be different [depending on who delivered it]."

After the 2019 season, Cashman moved to streamline this process. He fired the experienced pitching coach Larry Rothschild and hired Matt Blake, a thirty-four-year-old pitching coordinator in the Cleveland organization. Blake was a relative unknown in the industry, but impressed Cashman during his interview with a profound knowledge of cutting-edge technology and ability to discuss it in lay terms.

The change came after Cashman watched other organizations, particularly the Astros and the Tampa Bay Rays, turn good pitchers into stars by using pitch data to identify strengths and weaknesses.

In 2017, the Astros traded for fading Detroit Tigers ace Justin Verlander, then utilized high-speed cameras and advanced metrics to revive his career. The following year, they acquired Cole from Pittsburgh and showed him data that persuaded him to ditch his sinker and throw more four-seam fastballs high in the strike zone. Cole quickly transformed from a very good pitcher to a great one.

The Yankees did not bid for Verlander but did talk to the Pirates about Cole. But the Yankee front office knew that had they acquired either pitcher, they would not have been able to provide the information that led to their success as Astros.

"To be objectively fair, Verlander goes from Detroit to Houston, instead of to the Yankees," says a Yankee official. "At that time, Houston is using NASA sticky stuff to increase spin rate. But they also had all the tech and the data and the alignment to get guys to significantly improve.

"The metamorphosis of Verlander and Cole that happened in Houston would not have happened with us. Not at that time. It would now, with Blake. Cole was a middle-of-the-rotation starter at best in Pittsburgh, and Verlander was looking like he was at the back of his career. They found a whole new gear when they went to Houston because of [pitching coach] Brent Strom and [GM] Jeff Luhnow knowing how to develop pitchers better than anyone in baseball."

That is a damning self-assessment, and that gap might have cost the Yankees a championship in 2017 and/or 2018. Another example came when the young power pitcher Nathan Eovaldi posted a 4.45 ERA for the Yankees in 2015 and 2016, then went on to improve in Tampa Bay and excel in Boston. Why, Yankees brass wondered, were they unable to unlock the best Eovaldi when other teams could?

In an attempt to fix this problem and achieve balance between old school and new, the Yankees in late 2019 hired Blake but retained longtime bullpen coach Mike Harkey, a former major-league pitcher.

"Now it is designated who gives you the information," Britton says. "You bring in Matt Blake, who can give you any and all information. Whatever you want, Matt can break it down. And Hark can be more of a guy who—you can say old-school mentality, but he understands analytics.

"So, if there is something I want to do that is more of a feel thing, I'm probably going to go to Hark. But Matt can walk me through the numbers. Let's take my slider. It has evolved to where it is a weapon, but I wouldn't understand that if I didn't have the analytics to show me. I would just be sinker, sinker, sinker.

"So the communication has improved. Can it always be better? I think so. We can simplify the message, especially with younger players. As veteran guys, we already know who we are as players, but the younger guys, the more precise you can be with the communication, the better. And I think Cashman understands that. And I think Hal Steinbrenner understands that. I have talked to Hal about it. And Jean. I think everyone is aware that the communication could improve."

Now Cole is finished with his bullpen session. He walks through the misty air, down the right-field line toward the dugout. As Britton speaks while sitting on the bench, Cole leans on the railing above, listening and nodding. Then he descends the steps and sits with us.

This tracks with Cole's hyperactive, hyper-curious, hyper-involved personality. Since his arrival in New York in 2020 after signing a nine-year, $324 million free agent contract, Cole has served not only as ace of the staff but as a self-appointed assistant pitching coach.

He talks strategy in the clubhouse. He watches his teammates' bullpen sessions, looking at the real-time analytics and providing feedback. When new Yankee pitcher Carlos Rodón threw off a mound for the first time in spring training of 2023, Cole was standing on the infield grass, arms folded, alongside Boone, Blake, and the analytics staffers. On days when he is not pitching, he sits at his locker and offers lengthy digressions on the art of pitching to interested reporters.

Now Cole is preparing to jump in as Britton discusses the pros and cons of using data to identify which pitches are most effective.

Britton became an All-Star in Baltimore by throwing one of the best sinkers in the game. When he arrived in New York, the Yankees' analytics folks told him that the data on his slider was better than he might have thought. They encouraged him to throw it more.

"I get here in '18," Britton says. "I've been an 80, 90 percent sinker guy and had a lot of success. I get here, and they're like, 'We want you to use your sinker 70 percent of the time. We want you to increase that slider percentage by 10, 20 percent because it is extremely effective.'"

Hearing that, Britton suspected that the numbers, while technically correct, were not capable of reflecting the context in which he had thrown the slider.

"My pushback was like, 'Well, it's effective because everyone is sitting on my sinker,'" he says. "Sometimes the analytics can't decipher that. They see this high swing-and-miss percentage on my breaking ball, but it's because of my sinker. One thing is attached to another. And analytics can't, like—"

Cole is ready to pipe up.

"Correct," he says. "Say there is expected OPS on a guy of .850 on a changeup, right? And so nobody throws it to him anymore. But out of the seven times he has seen it this year, he's swung and missed every time."

Britton nods and turns to me. "Does that make sense?" he asks.

Sort of. It's a lot of jargon, but I think I mostly get it: you can't always rely on the numbers. "This sounds to me," I say, "like the flaws of a non-pitcher or non-athlete giving the information, because—"

Britton jumps back in.

"Well, I wouldn't characterize them as that," he says, ever diplomatic. "It's more about being out on the field. The computer won't identify the fact that the reason my slider was really good was because [the opponent's] scouting report was 'sinker, sinker, sinker.' And then I throw a slider. It might surprise some guys, but if I throw my slider as often as my sinker, it's not as good of a pitch.

"But the computer cannot decipher that. It just sees the raw numbers and says, 'This pitch gets 50 percent swing and miss, so he should throw it more.' But the reality is, it's tied to something else.

"That is my point. We weren't digging as deep as that. We just kind of saw the number and were like, 'Well, just increase the usage of it and it should retain this 50 percent swing-and-miss rate.' Where I was sitting there going, 'If I'm throwing it more, it ain't getting that swing and miss 50 percent of the time.' Because it's my sinker that makes that pitch better than maybe what it is."

"That would seem like a good example of where you need people in the organization who have a feel," I say.

"Correct," Britton says. "But now I think we have evolved, because they have been around longer. I'm pretty sociable, and I'll go up to them and we'll have these conversations. I don't know if it affects how they go about it."

"I don't think it affects how they go about it," Cole says.

"You're more skeptical about how open-minded they are?" I ask.

"No, no," Cole says. "It's just—they're analysts. It's a lot of ones and zeros."

"It's a lot of raw data," Britton says. "I don't think it affects how they compute the data."

"Their job is to collect it, decipher it, filter it, find trends, present trends," Cole says. "Understanding how a player is going to apply that, and having more comprehension of a situation in general by talking to [Britton], that's not their job."

I mention that it is interesting talking to these two in particular because they came to the Yankees with very different analytics backgrounds. While Britton's Orioles did not even have an analytics department, Cole's Astros used data as much as any team.

The Orioles did have one data processor, however: Buck Showalter's brain. Showalter, the Zelig of this book, managed the Orioles from 2010 to 2018 and employed his own self-collected information to, among other things, shift and position his fielders.

"Showalter has this black book," Britton says. "He was always documenting strikes, walks, outs. Now let's say I'm pitching and giving up a lot of weak contact to third. All of a sudden he would start shifting the defense. Just by him watching the game and taking notes. He was doing his own version of analytics before it was a thing.

"He didn't really need the computer. He would just do his feel, and all of a sudden I would start to notice, 'Wow, [third baseman] Manny Machado is on the grass right now, and those weakly hit balls are now outs.'"

But unlike the Yankees of those years, Baltimore did not have designated numbers people. When Britton needed data, he had to ask his agent, Scott Boras, for it.

"Boras has somebody that's doing that," Britton says. "He would send over spray charts for me. So I came from basically nothing to all of this. And I do feel like I have communicated okay with [the Yankees]. Whether or not it has changed anything that they have done, I'm not sure—"

"I think it has changed," Cole says.

"I do feel like they have made a conscious effort to ask whether or not it is being communicated well and what they can change," Britton says.

"I think it's always an evolution," Cole says. "There is a balance between both ends of the spectrum, and the ideal amount of analytics can shift with the types of players you have, or the type of coaches you have. There is not one right way to do it. The best way to do it is probably to check in with the players every year and see if you can make any adjustments."

"How were the Astros with that?" I ask.

"They had a system that was so user-friendly," Cole says. "The most user-friendly thing I have ever seen. Then there was a culture where players were their own analysts to a certain extent. There is one huge computer room where coaches and players and everyone is mingling. There's like ten computers in there. There's a large room in spring training and a larger one in Houston.

"If you were to apply that to [the Yankees'] clubhouse and try to make parallels, when we're not in the clubhouse when the media is in there, we're either in the food room or the training room. And in Houston, when you're not in the clubhouse, you're either in the food room or the video area. It's a hangout."

"So the culture there was, it's more a part of your day to study that stuff?" I ask.

"One hundred percent," Cole says. He then goes on to name some of the players central to the Astros' run of success: first baseman

Yuli Gurriel, second baseman Jose Altuve, and third baseman Alex Bregman.

"Yuli watches what Yuli watches," Cole says. "Jose watches what Jose watches. Breggie watches what Breggie watches. And then at some point it all finds its way into a conversation, whether it's in the cage or in the computer room. It's very neat."

Britton returns the conversation to the Yankees.

"There is a desire on their part to know if they're doing a good job or not," he says. "In spring training we put on an event with all the front office, including the analysts, to get them out on the field. Because one thing I thought ever since getting here was that there was a disconnect between the players and the analysts in the front office.

"It was like everything was going on behind the shadows. The players would get the information and be like, 'Well, who is saying that? I don't know that person.' And so in spring this year I asked Boonie if we could do this, because I was just tired of hearing—and I think a lot of people were tired of hearing [information] and being like, 'Who's saying this?' And we had that, and I thought it was good."

"I thought it was good," Cole says.

"I thought it would help," Britton says. "And immediately, all the analysts—to their credit—were like, 'This is awesome.' Because they felt the same way. They felt like the players were looking at them like, 'I'm gonna mess you up if you come in the clubhouse,' when in reality that wasn't true. So it went for both sides."

"You're humanizing each other," I say.

"Now I can see them in the food room, and we can have a conversation," Britton says. "It's not like, 'Oh, this is the guy who told me that this pitch sucks.'"

Cole stands.

"I've gotta go lift," he says, walking away with an offer to further discuss the topic another time.

(I took him up on this, and an important addendum to Cole's comments on that September day came the following April, when he was 4–0 with an 0.95 ERA in a season that would end in him winning his first Cy Young Award. I circled back one afternoon at Yankee Stadium to ask him about the flow of information from the analyst Zac Fieroh, who works in the clubhouse, to Blake to Cole and his catcher, the elite defender Jose Trevino.

"The game plans have been very crisp this season," Cole said. "Since spring training we have been identifying what makes me good. And Blake just keeps getting better. A lot of the things he's learning are trends in game management. That one pitch or that one sequence—the types of things that, the more experience you have in those situations, the better gut feeling you develop, and the more command you have in those situations. Not that he is calling the pitches, but he can provide that continuity between Zac and us.")

With Cole gone, I mention to Britton that the Yankees' acquisition of Trevino suggested a move away from pure analytics, back toward old-school scouting and feel.

"That makes sense," he says. "I think it's evolving."

The Yankees have drawn public criticism for becoming too reliant on analytics. One would expect Cashman and Michael Fishman to push back on this, which they have. But it's important to note that Tim Naehring—a field guy whose voice would be minimized in an analytics-only front office—also objects, and emphatically.

"I absolutely disagree [that the Yankees are too reliant on analytics]," Naehring says in a separate interview. "I can understand if someone wants to just throw that blanket statement out there. It's easy to do in our industry right now. But I have lived this whole process. I want scouts to still be scouts, and I want them to tell me what they see from a scout lens. Then we're going to have an analyst say what they see. And then we're going to have the people in the office blend the two and we'll come up with the true value. Cash from the beginning—and Billy Eppler—thought it was important that we have continuing education.

"Our scouts understand all the numbers. We can sit in the stands and do what we normally do, and evaluate through the statistical numbers what our eyes are seeing on how the person does what they do. How do they produce, or how are they not producing? We can match up the how with the what.

"We still have one of the largest pro scouting departments period. There is a nice mix of ages and different types of backgrounds. The whole concept, from the beginning, has been to try to blend."

That attempt to blend is not always successful. Personalities and ideas can lead to conflict. Some analysts enter the clubhouse overly comfortable and confident in their views.

One moment of disharmony came during the 2019 season, when Yankee players developed a custom of turning to the dugout after a hit and wiggling four fingers at their teammates, who returned the gesture.

Few in the media or fan base knew what this meant. Well, here's what it was: a shot at a particular employee without a playing background who seemed too comfortable in the clubhouse. This employee would wave four fingers at the cook in the food room—in a rude and dismissive fashion, players felt—when he wanted four eggs.

Once, Cashman was watching a game with that employee and Carlos Beltrán, a former player who served as a Yankees special assistant in 2019. The players on the field did the four-finger gesture.

"They're talking about you!" Beltrán said, laughing.

A more consequential symbol of analytics-driven tension came during the 2020 postseason, when the Yankees faced the Tampa Bay Rays—widely regarded as the smartest, most cutting-edge organization in this area, without the ethical baggage of the Astros—in the division series.

With the Yankees leading 1–0 in the series, the team deployed a strategy that the Rays had pioneered a few years earlier: The opener.

An opener was a relief pitcher who started the game. He would be followed by a "bulk pitcher," typically a starter and typically with opposite handedness of the opener. This forced opponents into difficult lineup decisions, unfavorable platoon matchups, or early pinch-hit moves once the bulk pitcher took over.

It was a clever bit of strategy devised by a small-market team with a limited payroll. When the Yankees decided to try it, they underestimated the degree of clubhouse blowback that would follow.

For Game 2, Boone named the twenty-one-year-old right-hander Deivi García the opener and planned to use the thirty-seven-year-old lefty J. A. Happ as the bulk guy. Happ was upset by the disruption to a routine he had followed his entire life, and his teammates felt that the front office was trying to be unnecessarily cute. The idea was rooted in logic but implemented without obtaining buy-in from the player.

García allowed a home run in the first inning. Happ entered in the second and struggled. The Rays won the game, took control of the series, and soon ended the Yankees' season.

"That ruffled feathers," Britton says. "That's a good example. J. A. was a veteran, an older pitcher. We started Deivi. All the players were kind of scratching their heads, going, 'Hey, we had an advantage over the Rays; why are we thinking about tricking them?' And they didn't even take the bait, which was worse. It didn't even prevent them from putting any of their righties or lefties in there against us.

"We felt like J. A. had been steady for us. He's older. He's used to his routine. Let's just let him start and let Deivi come in after him. I think it upset him. You're very routine-oriented. And it obviously didn't work. It actually flipped the series.

"There was definitely frustration. I didn't say this, but I heard it a lot: Some guys were like, 'We're the fucking Yankees. We don't need to try to out-analytic the Rays. We have the best talent.'

"And that actually stuck with me, because in my head I was like, 'You're damn right. We're the New York Yankees. The Yankees go out and get the best players. And the analytics is a bonus. The reality is, we have the talent on the field to beat anybody. So let's let the talent play, and if the analytics can help us, that's what we want.'"

Britton takes a breath. He wants to be clear that he's not complaining, just providing the unvarnished clubhouse perspective for which I asked.

"Cash has been great," he says. "I have nothing bad to say about Cash and communication. He has communicated well with me since I've been here. There was just an awkward middle period [with analytics]. We travel with analysts. I consider those guys, like, in the fire with us every day. Those guys aren't getting the cheers out there like us, being rewarded by fans, but they are grinding with us."

Five days later, Britton left a game with arm fatigue, and his season was over. As it turned out, so was his distinguished career; though he would not officially retire until late 2023, Britton would never again pitch in the big leagues. His Yankee tenure lasted fewer than five years but came at a time of dizzying change in the way the team operated.

There were flaws and bumps during the transition, but as Britton left the dugout that afternoon when we talked, he turned around to make one final point.

"I don't know," he said, "if there is anywhere better to play than here."

31

A New Leader

O NE SPRING DAY IN 2013, the Yankees' vice president of amateur scouting, Damon Oppenheimer, called Chad Bohling with an urgent request.

"Hey, I've got a guy," Oppenheimer said. "I want you to go fly."

Bohling, who oversees the team's mental conditioning department, had received this call many times before. But never would Oppenheimer ask him to visit a player as important to the future of the team as this one.

Bohling boarded a plane in New York bound for Fresno, California. He landed, rented a car, and drove to a Marie Callender's restaurant, where he met with a junior at Fresno State named Aaron Judge. Then Bohling hopped on a plane back to New York.

It was all the time he needed to make a recommendation to Oppenheimer: This young man was mentally and emotionally prepared to join the Yankees organization. Judge's earnest personality was even more striking than his six-foot-seven frame, and his gap-toothed smile, especially when he tilted his head to the side, betrayed a hint of smart-aleck twinkle that saved him from blandness.

"He checked off all the boxes for me," Bohling, who operates in the background of the Yankees' world, says in a rare interview.

"From the on-field to off-field stuff to character to makeup as a baseball player and teammate, to the way he goes about approaching things to how coachable he is. I said, 'On and off the field, 100 percent I would sign off on this guy.' It was only a small piece of Damon's decision. He has all these other areas that he has to check, too. But he checked all the boxes for me."

Bohling's involvement in the predraft evaluation told much about the direction of the franchise and the lasting effects of Cashman's Yankee reorg way back in 2005. Bohling was the least known piece of what became the GM's vision for a twenty-first-century team.

Back in 2005, when Cashman extracted a pledge from George Steinbrenner to stop heeding random roster suggestions from the shadow front office in Tampa, he also obtained clearance to either expand or create three departments: pro scouting, analytics, and mental skills.

He promoted Billy Eppler to run pro scouting and hired Michael Fishman to jump-start analytics. The third department was the most mysterious, and remained so for two decades.

Bohling, whose official title is now senior director, organizational performance, describes mental skills as "making sure your mind is right and having the mind space needed to go in the right direction that day."

In practice, that involves individualized work with players and the entire team, all aimed at sending them out to the field in a positive frame of mind—everything from listening to talking, from showing video examples to creating situations that might arise in games.

In 2005, there were only four or five mental skills professionals working in baseball. But given the chance to design a modern version of the Yankees, Cashman saw value in helping players maximize their talent in this way.

This was a time when the simmering tensions between Derek Jeter and Alex Rodriguez were eroding the Yankees' clubhouse culture. For this and other reasons, Cashman was looking for creative ways to address the abstract but important issue of team chemistry.

His friend Mark Shapiro, the Cleveland Indians' general manager, was one of the only baseball executives at the time to utilize mental skills professionals. Shapiro worked with sports psychologist Dr. Charles Maher, who had heard of Bohling's work as the director of mental conditioning at IMG Academy, a multisport facility in Florida. Cashman asked Shapiro permission to speak to Maher.

Maher gave Cashman a list of candidates, including Bohling. Bohling had worked for legendary tennis coach Nick Bollettieri and with the Jacksonville Jaguars when Tom Coughlin was head coach. That proved a lucky connection, because Cashman had shared a New York apartment with Coughlin's son Timmy when both were in their twenties.

Bohling's first official day as a Yankees employee was April 1, 2005. News of his appointment as director of optimal performance was greeted with both mocking headlines—*New York Times:* "Steinbrenner Hires Motivational Coach (Don't Laugh)"—and derision from some players.

In that *Times* article, Gary Sheffield said, "I don't believe in it. I think it's for people who are weak-minded. I think there are people who need someone there for them. It's not for me."

As he began the job, Bohling faced multiple challenges. He was tasked with connecting with a team that not only included skeptics like Sheffield but also might as well have been the Beatles of baseball, a traveling rock show with stars like Jeter, A-Rod, Randy Johnson, Jason Giambi, and Hideki Matsui. And he had to convince the players that he was not a mere spy, planted in the clubhouse by the front office.

"In my interview with Cash, he and I discussed that," Bohling says. "[I said] if that's what you're looking for, don't hire me, because that's not me. And he was like, 'No, no, that's not what I want. I want you to gain the respect of these guys.'"

Starting out under manager Joe Torre and a veteran team, Bohling employed a gradual approach.

"It took time," he says. "It was more like, 'I'm not coming here to try to change some of these guys who are elite already. I'm just going to be a sounding board. If anyone needs me, I'm here to provide different perspectives.' We weren't going to push anything."

Bohling developed close relationships with Andy Pettitte, A-Rod, and Robinson Canó, among others. He even accompanied Pettitte to the World Baseball Classic in 2023, in which the former Yankee served as pitching coach for Team USA.

"Canó came in [nearly every day]," Bohling says. "Alex did it. A few pitchers, every day that they started, they would come in. Andy Pettitte would come in to just kind of get something off his chest where he felt better when he was out there and pitching."

In 2009, the same year that Cashman brought CC Sabathia in

to help heal the group, he asked Bohling to integrate fully into the major-league team in New York, rather than work out of Tampa. Bohling has been a constant presence since both at home and on the road, meeting with individual players like Judge, holding periodic team and staff meetings, and working with the front office and support staff on strategies to ensure the well-being of the entire group. He can often be found in the dugout.

Bohling's department has grown to employ six full-time professionals to work with people at all levels of the major and minor leagues while also helping with the draft, which Oppenheimer began to request around 2006.

"I credit Cash for seeing that this wasn't something that was just going to help individuals, but it could help departments," Bohling says. "It could help the organization. Damon's department is an example of that. He's utilized the heck out of this department over the years. We were one of the first teams to do this in the draft space."

The relationship that Bohling built with Judge began at that Marie Callender's in California in 2013. It continued through Judge's time as a minor leaguer in the Yankees' system, when he and Bohling kept in touch, and bore fruit during Judge's big-league career, including the historic 2022 season in which Judge hit sixty-two home runs to top Roger Maris's American League record from 1961.

Before each game, Judge visits Bohling's office, which is near the manager's office at Yankee Stadium. There, they watch video of Judge making great plays and hitting home runs, interspersed with clips of legendary athletes. This places Judge in the focused, confident mindset that he needs while competing.

Says Bohling, "It's not just working with players who are struggling, but it's working with a Judge who [in 2022] was one of the best, but he would come in every single day. He has been doing that ever since he was a rookie."

"It's a lot of positive reinforcement," says Judge. "This is not like the NFL, where you get ready on Sunday, once a week. It's not even basketball, where you've got a couple games to focus on, then a couple off days to relax and refocus. We're playing every single day. So to get locked in and get focused—you just traveled across the U.S. for a couple of games. You're getting beat up. Your body is not feeling great. And all of a sudden you've got a game in Oakland [where attendance and energy tend to be low], which is tough to get up for.

"Having someone like that to give you a positive message, show you some highlights—it just kind of puts everything in perspective and gets you locked back in after the game."

As Bohling noticed immediately, Judge had the potential to be a special person within a baseball team. And sure enough, he would later become the most effective and unifying clubhouse leader that Cashman's Yankees ever had.

After Judge's dynamic first season in 2017, in which he set a new rookie record for home runs with fifty-two, the Yankees had a chance to acquire Giancarlo Stanton, the reigning National League Most Valuable Player, from Miami.

In yet another baseball-is-a-small-world moment, the new CEO of the Marlins was . . . wait for it . . . Jeter. And when Jeter took over the club with venture capitalist Bruce Sherman, he planned to lower payroll and rebuild the team.

This meant trading Stanton and his thirteen-year, $325 million contract. After the 2017 season, Jeter and the Marlins' president of baseball operations, Michael Hill, met with Stanton and delivered a message in a way that the slugger did not appreciate: agree to a trade or be stuck here with a losing team.

"That was the team's play," Stanton recalls, still shaking his head six years after the encounter. The six-foot-six, 245-pound giant is subtle but clear in conversation, and has a way of adding an extra layer of meaning with a raised eyebrow.

"Those specific words were from another person in the meeting. But [Jeter] was the representative of that."

Miami attempted to deal Stanton to the St. Louis Cardinals or San Francisco Giants, but Stanton had no-trade protection in his contract and did not want those destinations.

The Yankees, meanwhile, were trying to sign Shohei Ohtani, a pitcher/DH hybrid from Japan. Not confident of Ohtani's willingness to play on the East Coast, they also considered engaging the Marlins on Stanton.

Stanton was in fact starving for playoff baseball and wanted to go to a contending team. But he was not going to allow Jeter to push him around. According to a Yankee official, when Jeter tried to force Stanton into a trade to the Cardinals or Giants—or remain in Miami, where the team would be gutted around him—Stanton said, "Fine, I choose to be here."

With Stanton and Jeter locked in a staring contest, Major League Baseball tried to help. According to a league source, Commissioner Rob Manfred's chief legal officer and soon-to-be deputy commissioner, Dan Halem, asked Jeter to call Cashman.

Jeter, according to that source, responded that he was at the ownership level, so it was more appropriate for Cashman to speak to Hill.

"At a certain point Dan Halem said, you [and Cashman] have got to get on the phone, but [Jeter] wouldn't call," the source said.

With Halem facilitating, the teams were able to work out a trade that Stanton accepted. Next came the same gesture that Cashman had made back in 2004: calling his current face of the franchise to feel him out about adding a star.

This conversation proceeded much differently than the talk with Jeter about A-Rod had (though in fairness to Jeter, Stanton had never criticized Judge in an *Esquire* magazine article). Judge had not won any championships or earned Jeter's status, but he had just been named American League Rookie of the Year and was at the center of the Yankees' clubhouse culture and marketing efforts.

Cashman reached Judge in Stockton, California, where Judge was at an event with the apparel and memorabilia company Fanatics.

"I was excited about it," Judge says. "I was at this Fanatics appearance, and I got this phone call from Cashman. 'Okay, this is either good or bad. I don't know what's about to happen.' But he called me to just give a heads-up. He's like, 'Hey, we're thinking about making a big trade for Stanton. What do you got on that?'

"He said, 'I know he's a right fielder and he just won MVP. What do you think?' I said, 'You're adding an MVP guy to a team that was just one win away from the World Series. I'm all for it. I'll do whatever I can. If it's me playing left field, center field—whatever I've gotta do, I'm here to bring that guy in.'"

Stanton and Judge had met the previous summer at the pre–All Star Game Home Run Derby in Miami. Stanton was the hometown star, and Judge the young upstart who ended up winning the Derby. Because both were tall, good-looking, marketable athletes of color, they often found themselves lumped together—or, as they saw it, pitted against each other.

Their initial bond came through a shared interest in de-escalation.

"The media was trying to make some tension between us with the Home Run Derby stuff," Judge says. "We talked before that. We just said, 'Let's go out there and have some fun. Screw what everybody keeps asking us about, like 'Is there a competition?' and this and that.' It was like, 'Let's just have fun.' So for us, it started there in Miami, getting to know each other.

"And once he came to spring training, it was like, 'Hey, let's go get dinner. Let's find a place to just hang out.'"

Adds Stanton, "I think we both opened it with, 'We want to make it clear that it's not a competition. You help the team tonight and I'll help the team tonight. That's most important.' And I think that was the best way for something like this to work."

There was Ruth versus Gehrig. There was Reggie versus Munson. And, boy, oh boy, was there Jeter versus A-Rod. There would be absolutely no Judge versus Stanton. In fact, they became friends, Yankee stars who actually liked each other, as Mickey Mantle and Roger Maris did before them.

"We have the personalities so it didn't become what it previously was with some of those other dynamics," Stanton says.

As the years progressed and Judge grew from young man to player in full, his inclusive style of leadership was also a relief to Cashman, who, after all, had heard privately from prominent Yankee veterans that Jeter was not an open enough captain, especially to those who arrived after the late-1990s dynasty.

In the Judge era, no one is asking, "Whose clubhouse is this?" It's clearly Judge's, but he does it in a way that does not provoke jealousy. This works because Judge does not protect the clubhouse as if it were his territory.

"We have been blessed with so many great stars that come in here and check their egos when they walk through that door," Judge says. "They understand that there is a bigger picture here. This game is grueling. This game is hard. If we're going to win a lot of ball games, we need every single person in here pulling on the same rope.

"When you're able to welcome in an MVP, and then welcome

another MVP [third baseman Josh Donaldson]. With certain guys here, it's like, 'How can we get you comfortable?' And if you're comfortable, you're going to play your best.

"That's one thing I want to do as a leader: It's like, your role adapts. Sometimes you have to be the guy who stands up in front of the room and talks. Other times, you have to be that guy that sits back and it's like, 'I've gotta let Stanton do his thing. I've gotta let him be the guy who leads us out there that time.' I've gotta let Cole be the guy where it's, 'Hey, you're on top of the world. Go lead us.' So it's just about understanding that and adapting to whatever the team needs."

The only other star player during the Cashman era whose leadership philosophy resembled Judge's was CC Sabathia, but he was a starting pitcher with an individual routine. Position players are more connected to the daily rhythms of an entire team.

It wasn't all stress-free between Cashman and Judge. As he did with Jeter, Cashman felt the need to raise difficult topics.

A few years into Judge's career, he objected when a camera for the YES Network, which was owned by the Yankees, shot the slumping catcher Gary Sánchez in the dugout. On other occasions he would block the camera operators from filming other teammates.

"He threw sunflower seeds at the camera and stared down the cameraman," a team official says. "Finally, there were complaints."

Cashman asked Judge to stop, and Judge agreed to do so. Before long, the behavior resumed.

"Dude, you have to stop," Cashman would say. "This is the Yankees-owned network. You can't do that."

"I'm just protecting my teammates," Judge responded.

The answer was clearly sincere; Judge wanted to help Sánchez avoid scrutiny. Cashman understood that the behavior was coming from an impulse to lead and support.

One late night after a game in 2023, Judge and I stood near his locker in Yankee Stadium. I asked if it was true that he had done that to the camera operator.

"Hell yeah," Judge said. "I really don't care about the media. I don't care about anybody who is not in this room. I can see when guys are going through it. I can see when guys have a weight on their shoulders and the last thing they need, in my opinion, is another million people staring at them when they just gave up a three-run homer or lost a game for us or struck out for the fourth time. That's the last thing we need.

"I'll be the guy who stands in front of it and kind of blocks him from that. They told me to stop it, and I said 'Tell me all you want, but it ain't gonna stop.' I can be the bad guy."

That, I told Judge, sounds an awful lot like a certain general manager we both knew. He smiled.

As Judge's free agent year of 2022 began, he kept the front office guessing about his intentions. In spring training, Cashman granted an interview to Andy McCullough of *The Athletic* in which he criticized the Houston Astros' illegal sign stealing from 2017 to 2019.

"I get offended when I start hearing we haven't been to the World Series since '09," Cashman told the publication. "Because I'm like, 'Well, I think we actually did it the right way.' Pulled it down, brought it back up. Drafted well, traded well, developed well, signed well. The only thing that derailed us was a cheating circumstance that threw us off."

Judge, approached by a few reporters on the field before a Sunday morning spring training game in Dunedin, Florida, seemed to push back on Cashman's comments.

"We just, we didn't win, you know," Judge said. "In my book, we didn't win so that doesn't count in my book. We didn't win so I can't take credit for it."

Front-office officials could have sworn they'd heard Judge making comments similar to Cashman's in private. They wondered if he was putting on one face for the clubhouse and front office and another for the media. Was his answer taken out of context? The Yankees didn't have a grasp on his true thoughts.

As that same spring training began, the Yankees and Judge set about negotiating a long-term contract extension that would prevent Judge from hitting the open market at the end of the year and make him a Yankee for life.

It was a tricky calculation for the team to determine what Judge was worth: On the one hand, he was a prodigious power hitter, elite defensive outfielder, and by far their most marketable star; on the other, injuries had prevented him from playing 150 games in a season all but once in his career. Historically, players as tall as the six-foot-seven Judge did not remain healthy deep into their thirties.

But he was Aaron Judge, budding Yankee icon. What was a team to do?

During those initial talks, Judge set a deadline of Opening Day to reach an agreement. If he and the Yankees failed to strike a deal by the first pitch of the season, Judge would cut off talks for the rest of the summer and become a free agent at season's end.

Like many of his impulses, that one appeared to come from a genuinely thoughtful place of not wanting his status to become a distraction for the team while they competed for a championship.

Five days before the opener, the sides realized the gap between their financial positions was too vast to be bridged. The Yankees were offering $213.5 million over seven years. Judge rejected the offer and did not counter.

At 11:30 a.m. on Opening Day, April 8, the team convened a news conference at Yankee Stadium. Cashman walked into the room, sat at the table in the front, and spoke in his usual public monotone.

"We were unsuccessful in concluding a multiyear pact," he said. "Obviously, our intent is to have Aaron Judge stay as a New York Yankee as we move forward, and I know that is his intent as well, which is a good thing. We're going to be entering those efforts in a new arena, which would be at the end of the season when free agency starts, and maybe that will determine what the real market value would be, because we certainly couldn't agree at this stage on a contract extension."

Then Cashman laid out the details of the Yankees' offer.

After that game, Judge sat in the same chair for his own news conference. Asked about Cashman, he shook his head.

"It's something I felt like was private between my team and the Yankees," he said.

According to two Yankee officials, in the final days of spring training Cashman informed Judge's agent, Page Odle, that he planned to share the Yankees' offer with the media, because he believed it would leak out anyway. He had arrived at this decision in consultation with Hal Steinbrenner; the team president, Randy Levine; the vice president of communications, Jason Zillo; and other high-ranking team officials.

The club's reasoning was that in a less-than-ideal situation announcing the offer was the most honest and straightforward strategy. Details like that tend to leak eventually, and the Yankees did not want a significant update about Judge to emerge at random and via anonymous sources. The team felt that it had nothing to hide; consistent with his annually high payrolls, Steinbrenner had made the face of the franchise a legitimate offer. Why not just share it on the record?

According to Yankee officials, no one from Judge's side asked Cashman to refrain from announcing the offer.

Judge's camp has a different recollection of the timeline. A source from that side says that Cashman informed them around 9:00 or 10:00 a.m. on Opening Day, April 8, that they were announcing the offer. According to that person, Judge's phone was off by then because he was preparing for the game, so he didn't speak to anyone involved in the negotiations until after the game. Yankees people remain adamant that their version is the correct one.

A little more than a year later, I asked Judge himself if he knew in advance that the announcement was coming.

"You know," he said, "it was kind of news to me. And then we kind of figured from my team that they were going to do it just to put pressure on me, pit the fans against me, and pit the media against me. I found out—I'm trying to think here—I know I talked to [Cashman] in spring training before it was over. We kind of just discussed what they offered, and my opinion and his opinion.

"We discussed through the whole process, 'Hey, we don't need to put this out in the media. So you really want to get this done? Then there is no need to put it out.' So, it was kind of a shock to me and, I think, a shock to everyone else when that happened.

"It was upsetting to us, and news to me when he came out and did it. We were discussing, 'If you guys want me here and want to get this done, let's just keep this between me and you. No need to get the media or anyone else involved.' What really ticked us off was the fact that he did it anyway. He can do what he wants, though."

By turning down the offer, Judge placed a significant bet on himself. But as the season unfolded, he outperformed his career norms—playing nearly every day and launching his pursuit of Maris's American League record sixty-one home runs. True to his word, neither he nor his agent negotiated with the Yankees during the season.

In July, the Washington Nationals made superstar right fielder Juan Soto available in a trade, and the Yankees inquired about him.

"It's a no-brainer that you would rather have Soto than Judge for the next ten years," a team official told me at the time, citing Soto's age (twenty-three) and Judge's (thirty) and the fact that both were generational superstars. Why not swap Judge out for a newer model, albeit one whose defense was significantly weaker (bear in mind, this was before Judge's historic home run chase and MVP award)?

But the San Diego Padres won the Soto sweepstakes, taking a potential replacement for Judge out of circulation for the time being (the Yankees would ultimately acquire Soto from San Diego in December 2023). Now the Yankees had no obvious alternative to Judge—and they still couldn't get a read on him.

In September, with Judge nudging closer to Maris's record, Tom Verducci of *Sports Illustrated* asked him what he considered the true single-season home run record—Maris's sixty-one or Barry Bonds's steroid-tainted seventy-three in 2001.

"Seventy-three is the record in my book," Judge said. "No matter what people want to say about that era of baseball, for me, they went out there and hit seventy-three homers and [Mark McGwire's seventy homers in 1998], and that to me is what the record is. The AL record is sixty-one, so that is one I can kind of try to go after."

Reading those comments, Yankee officials wondered if Judge was earnestly answering a question or catering to the people of San Francisco—his future fan base?

Judge had grown up in Linden, California, rooting for the Giants, a team that was widely expected to pursue him in free agency. If Judge wanted to be a Yankee, team brass wondered, why wouldn't he just say Maris? It might have been nothing. Or it might have been something. Who knew?

Judge passed Maris on October 4, the penultimate game of the season. He had turned down more than $200 million before Opening Day and gone on to enjoy one of the greatest seasons in the history of the sport. This staggering feat of self-confidence provoked awe in teammates, opponents, pundits, and fans.

Neither Cashman nor his front office had the luxury of pausing to feel awe. After the season Judge had, the Yankees simply had to find a way to retain him.

32

Aaron Judge's Very Weird, Very Stressful Free Agency (Which Only Determined the Course of the Next Yankee Decade)

L ESS THAN AN HOUR after the Yankees' 2022 season ended in a meek American League Championship Series sweep at the hands of the Astros, Aaron Judge stood surrounded in the middle of the clubhouse at the stadium: writers hoisted their iPhones in the air to record him, television reporters angled their microphones toward his mouth, camera operators stood on stepladders—all were pushing one another forward in an effort to hear what the free-agent-to-be had to say.

Were his days as a Yankee over?

"It was a special time," Judge said of his years in New York—and wait: *Was* a special time? Judge was speaking of his life with the Yankees in the past tense?

"I just kick myself for not bringing home that championship for them."

Them?

But then: "When we finally get there and secure this thing, it'll make it a lot sweeter, going through the tough times like this, that's for sure."

So . . .

Once the scrum dispersed, Judge spent another ten minutes or so chatting informally with many of the beat reporters who had covered him throughout his career. On his way out, his comments to several team staffers led them to assume he was leaving: "Thanks for everything"; "hope to see you sometime down the road"; and other ominous pleasantries.

It wasn't just reporters, clubhouse attendants, and fans at home who were confused by the apparent contradictions in Judge's behavior and phrasings. Brian Cashman, Hal Steinbrenner, and the Yankee hierarchy itself was grasping at clues about the inscrutable player's intentions.

As the offseason began, Cashman's gut told him that Judge wanted to leave, but he had no concrete information to back that. No one in the front office knew if Judge truly enjoyed playing in New York, and that was before the startling events of the 2022 postseason.

Appearing exhausted by his chase for history and the attention that came with it, Judge struggled in the first round of the playoffs, a division series matchup against Cleveland. In those five games, Judge had just four hits in twenty at bats, though two were home runs.

In Game 2 of that series, Judge went hitless in five at bats, striking out four times. As he walked away from the batter's box after the fourth strikeout, a sound that seemed unfathomable just days earlier followed him to the dugout: fans were booing Judge at Yankee Stadium.

Sure, they booed everyone around here at one point or another. Derek Jeter and Mariano Rivera even heard it, though that was early in a season, not in October. And booing Aaron Judge? In New York? In October 2022 after he had just completed one of the most remarkable seasons in baseball history?

"Given the context of when and to whom it was happening, that was a whole new level of negativity," says one Yankee executive.

Surprising as it was, team officials had already begun to notice in recent years, and especially in 2022, an increasingly adversarial dynamic between the ballclub and its customers.

Part of this came from self-inflicted expectations. George Steinbrenner had long since set the bar for success with the unrealistic view that any season not ending in a championship was a failure.

Yankee fans paid steep prices for tickets, cable packages, and merchandise, and were tired of investing financial and emotional capital in seasons that did not include a World Series appearance. They did not want to hear that it was impossible in the modern game to duplicate what the Yankees had done from 1996 to 2000. They wanted the visceral thrill back. This was understandable, but also unattainable.

The dilemma facing the Yankees and their fans in the 2020s

recalled a quote from Lee MacPhail, general manager of the Yankees during the pre-Steinbrenner years of CBS ownership.

Then the team found itself exhausted by constant comparisons to the halcyon days of the Ruth/Gehrig/DiMaggio/Mantle/Ford years.

"You know," MacPhail said in 1972, "the Yankees are in a strange spot. They are not competing against the Tigers, Orioles and the rest of the league. They are competing against ghosts, and that's a battle you can't win."

It seemed, at first, that the 2022 season might vanquish some of the ghosts of the 1990s that haunted the rest of the Cashman era. The Yankees began with forty-four wins in their first sixty games and looked like a contemporary version of the 1998 team in their grit, fight, and seeming refusal to lose.

Then came a long, anxious denouement that brought injuries, losing streaks, and a risk of blowing the whole thing. After a 22–6 June, the Yankees were 13–13 in July and 10–18 in August.

It got ugly at the stadium. Aaron Boone, a manager widely respected in the clubhouse and around the sport, heard the occasional singsongy chant of "Fire Boone" at Yankee Stadium during the season.

True to his subtly proud character, Boone would walk to the top step of the dugout and, as the jeers buffeted his back, straighten and square his shoulders.

The manager was hardly the only one to hear it that year. Fans booed Hal Steinbrenner during on-field ceremonies for Paul O'Neill and Jeter. Friends of Hal's within the organization noted that the jeering hurt him, and further alerted every Yankee to the growing problem of external toxicity around the franchise.

It wasn't just booing that bothered players. Boone and the front office also noticed that it was difficult to persuade contemporary athletes to stop looking at social media, even though the worst of the tweets directed toward or written about them were abusive and even occasionally threatening.

To download the Twitter or Instagram apps, as many players did, was to carry a particularly nasty and addictive jeering section in one's pocket. The front office began to suspect that it needed a plan to help players in dealing with this new form of taunting.

The ugliness might even have affected Yankee leadership in a significant way: One team official recalls an ominous sense around the organization in October that Steinbrenner would have responded to fan anger by firing Boone, a manager he respected, had the Yankees failed to make it out of the first round. If that was true, it never got to Cashman.

The Yankees did squeak by Cleveland, so Boone remained safe. But the sudden bad energy directed by fans toward Judge continued intermittently through the ALCS.

While the Astros completed their four-game mauling of the Yankees, Judge had just one hit in sixteen at bats, and the boos grew louder.

Teammates, opponents, and members of the front office expressed disbelief that the player who had just treated fans to a once-in-a-lifetime season could become the subject of scorn so quickly. As one Yankee official said during the ALCS, "Why would he want to play here after that?"

It was hardly the ideal context in which to resume the Yankees' most consequential negotiation since the heyday of Jeter and A-Rod.

Within days of his team's elimination, Cashman reached out to Odle in order to restart the talks that had stalled in April. Hal Steinbrenner contacted Judge to personally express his commitment to him, and he pledged to spend enough on payroll to build a winning team around Judge.

Soon Steinbrenner and Judge met face-to-face in Florida. The team upped its offer to eight years and $300 million; while no one thought that would be the final bid, the Yankees believed that the conversation between the two men had been positive.

Then came yet another twist. Unfortunately for me, I caused it.

On November 3, I published an article on the website for SNY, the regional sports network in New York for which I worked, reporting that the New York Mets would not be bidding for Judge.

Steinbrenner and Mets owner Steve Cohen, I wrote, "enjoy a mutually respectful relationship, and do not expect to upend that with a high-profile bidding war."

Within a few hours, I received a text from Bruce Meyer, the deputy executive director of the Major League Baseball Players Association, asking, "What's this based on?!"

To the union, my story reeked of collusion. Per the terms of the sport's collective bargaining agreement, teams are barred from discussing with the media the markets for players, let alone agreeing not to pursue them.

This is a particularly sensitive area in baseball, because owners were caught colluding against free agents in the 1980s and forced to pay $280 million in fines. Now I had accidentally stirred up old and deep grievances.

Upon receiving Meyer's text, I was obviously unwilling to indicate where or from whom I received information. But I did feel it was appropriate to say that I had no knowledge of a conversation between the clubs or their owners; if my story had implied otherwise, it was the result of sloppy phrasing. I stood by my reporting, but the words "mutually respectful relationship" were not intended to describe collusion.

The union, and presumably Judge's camp, remained unconvinced. Judge himself would later tell me that he was initially upset by the possibility that his free agency might not have been as unrestricted as it was supposed to be.

A few days later, both the Yankees and the Mets received a letter from Major League Baseball, at the behest of the MLBPA, instructing the teams to turn over all communications with me regarding Aaron Judge.

At the time, the public had no knowledge of this drama. The last thing I wanted was to be in the news. Then, just before 11:00 p.m. on November 16, I received a text from Ken Rosenthal, a prominent national baseball reporter for Fox Sports and *The Athletic,* asking if I could talk.

Rosenthal wanted to give me a courtesy heads-up that he was publishing a story in a few minutes about the collusion investigation sparked by my report.

Over the next twenty-four hours, the news blazed a scorching path across social media, sports talk radio, and print, ensuring once and for all that Judge's free agency would not be a smooth and controversy-free reunion.

On that very day, Commissioner Rob Manfred addressed reporters at the quarterly owners' meetings at MLB headquarters in New York. Asked about the investigation, he said, "I'm absolutely confident the clubs behaved in a way that was consistent with the [collective bargaining] agreement. This was based on a newspaper [*sic*] report. We will put ourselves in a position to demonstrate credibly to the MLBPA that this is not an issue. I'm sure that's going to be the outcome."

Hours later, on a conference call with reporters after winning the American League MVP award, Judge said that he had read a few articles about the collusion allegation and wanted to learn more.

On November 22, MLB concluded its investigation by finding the teams innocent. In reality, there were no communications between me and the Mets or me and the Yankees that proved collusion. My report about the Mets' deciding not to pursue Judge was accurate, but not because Cohen and Steinbrenner had conspired to make it that way.

Still, it left a sour taste for all involved—another piece of weirdness in a free agency that was about to get even more difficult to predict.

The day after MLB's collusion investigation concluded, a video surfaced on MLB Network's social media channels of Judge standing in what appeared to be a hotel lobby, wearing a beige hoodie and a black baseball cap.

"Aaron Judge in San Francisco!" a female voice said from behind a phone camera. "What are you doing in the city?"

Judge offered an awkward chuckle, then said, "Visiting some family and friends. That's about it. That's about it."

"Any fun plans?" the woman asked.

"We've got something," Judge said, now walking away as if trying to make a genial escape from paparazzi. "Have a good one."

Soon after the fourteen-second clip began to circulate, two MLB Network reporters tweeted that Judge was set to visit with the Giants. It looked as if he had been busted, TMZ-style.

Here's what actually happened. Planning to visit with the Giants, Judge and his wife, Samantha, flew into Oakland that afternoon.

Giants officials met them at the airport, then drove them around to look at potential homes. The group then crossed the Bay Bridge into San Francisco, where the Giants planned to showcase their beautiful stadium, introduce Judge to his favorite player from childhood, former Giants infielder Rich Aurilia, and entertain the couple in the city at night.

Before all that, Aaron and Samantha wanted to check into their hotel, the St. Regis on Third Street. All parties agreed to sneak in the back entrance in order to avoid publicity. At the last moment, the Judges, Odle, and the rest of their group said they wanted to exit the car at the front lobby.

The Giants agreed, but team officials felt troubled by the last-minute change; they had now joined the Yankees as teams who liked Judge but felt unable to read him.

As the woman took out her phone and shot the video, a member of Judge's group turned to a Giants official and admitted that the whole thing had been a setup (perhaps intended to put pressure on the Yankees), according to that official. Watching back east, the Yankees suspected this but did not know for sure.

As November drew to a close, Cashman and Odle continued to negotiate. The team expected a resolution during the Winter Meetings, the annual transaction extravaganza that began that year on Monday, December 5, at the Manchester Grand Hyatt in San Diego.

On that morning, when Cashman landed and checked into the hotel, he had no idea if Judge would choose the Yankees or the Giants. He was confident that the Yankees' final offer would be competitive, but neither he nor any other Yankee official had a window into Judge's mind and heart.

The afternoon brought the first of a few developments that left the team uneasy—a feeling that soon escalated into panic and even resignation.

Bryan Hoch, the Yankees reporter for MLB.com, tweeted that Judge was expected to arrive at the Winter Meetings the following day.

At first, this seemed to the industry like a strong sign that the Yanks and Judge were closing in on a deal. Could word of a news conference be next?

But Cashman dispelled this notion when speaking to reporters on Monday evening. The Yankees, he said, had no meetings scheduled with Judge or any knowledge of his travel itinerary.

This did not seem good. In fact, it felt as if the Yankees were losing the thread. They were now in the dark during a crucial point in negotiations, unaware even where Judge was or planned to be.

Sitting around a table in the San Diego Hyatt lobby bar that night, sipping red wine, Boone and several high-ranking Yankee officials debated whether Hoch's report was correct. Cashman remained up in his suite, working.

Judge had been spotted talking to Tampa Bay Buccaneers' quarterback Tom Brady at the Monday Night Football game in Tampa, one official noted.

"What's he gonna do, take a red-eye to San Diego after that?" the official asked.

"He's not coming," another official said, his voice lilting upward with hope, not certainty.

When someone suggested to Boone that he simply text Judge and ask him, the manager picked up his phone. He then realized it was nearly 3:00 a.m. in Tampa.

"Yeah," the person sitting next to him said. "That might seem a little desperate."

The group dispersed for bed shortly after, their unease growing. With the morning came an even scarier turn for the Yankees. *Time* magazine dropped a cover story naming Judge its Athlete of the Year. The piece, written by Sean Gregory, contained a quote that stunned the Yankees.

"In fact his wife, high school sweetheart Samantha Bracksieck, reminded him of a prediction he made in 2010, his senior year at Linden High School. 'I said, in 10 years, I'll be married to Sam,' says Judge, 'and playing for the San Francisco Giants.' Judge smiles. 'I was like, that'd better not get out.'"

And playing . . . for the . . . San Francisco . . . Giants?

Holy shit. What a thing to read at the beginning of a day that might bring Judge's decision.

Yankee officials had never experienced anything like this article in a negotiation. Was it part of a strategy to announce Judge's signing with San Francisco? (It wasn't; in reality, Judge was displeased that an interview he had granted earlier in the offseason dropped on that sensitive day.)

For the first time, the front office discussed among themselves the notion that perhaps Judge was done as a Yankee. Maybe he did not want the pressure of a massive contract in New York and preferred to play out his years in the relative quiet of his native California?

Just as Yankee leadership was making this mental adjustment, the

New York Post baseball columnist and MLB Network insider Jon Heyman posted a tweet that appeared to confirm their fears.

"Arson Judge appears headed to the Giants," Heyman wrote at 2:20 p.m. Pacific time, his report including a typo (Arson) that lent an air of absurdity to the already frenzied moment.

Upstairs in the Yankees' suite, Cashman and his lieutenants fell silent. A few dropped their heads into their hands.

They had not yet received word from Judge or Odle that they were out of the running, but Heyman was one of the top news breakers in the business.

In his room nearby, Boone stepped out of the shower and began to dress for a scheduled media availability. As he pulled a gray-and-white-checkered blazer and blue dress shirt from his closet, Boone noticed a series of texts on his phone about Judge and the Giants from friends and reporters.

"What's goin on?" he responded to one of them.

Before receiving an answer, Boone called Cashman with the same question.

"Nothing," Cashman said, having just been told by Odle that Judge had not yet made a decision.

Back in the Yankee suite, scouts and front-office officials tried to distract themselves by working on other projects, but the room was funereal: there was quiet typing, the occasional sigh, and the heavy feel of dejection.

After seven minutes, Heyman walked back his report and apologized, saying that the Giants had not heard from Judge. The mood in the suite lightened a bit, but the team still feared that the report was based in reality. And—still—they had no idea where Judge himself was. That's not usually the case when you're about to sign a guy.

Some of the reporters at the hotel did notice an online record of a private flight that had left Tampa earlier that day and was set to land in San Diego shortly after 4:00 p.m. PT. No one with the Yanks knew it at the time, but Aaron and Samantha Judge were indeed on that aircraft.

At the dinner hour in San Diego, Judge had still not been spotted. A pair of Yankee executives passed through the lobby of the Hyatt, their shoulders sagging, their mouths turned downward.

I saw them and asked, "How you feeling?"

"Well, you know," one of the executives said, shrugging before shuffling off for a glum meal.

Meanwhile, while all of baseball speculated on the competition between the Yankees and the Giants, Judge was in town, meeting with . . . the Padres.

"*What?*" a wide-eyed Yankee official said when I caught wind of that late in the night and passed it along.

The Padres, a late, surprise entrant into the Judge sweepstakes, were offering a contract worth more than $400 million. At the time, the Yankees' bid stood at eight years and $320 million.

"It was a crazy night," Judge told me the following spring. "I was at a Monday Night Football game, watching the Bucs play, and my agent called me to say, 'Yo, the Padres have offered this. We've got to get you on a plane.'"

As night drifted into early morning, some Yankee officials distracted themselves with work, while others achieved the same effect with wine.

The Manchester Grand Hyatt has two bars: one in the lobby, where the group had gathered the night before, and a more private location on the fortieth floor.

In that fortieth-floor bar, sitting on couches that sat low to the ground, some in the front office began to speculate on next steps after Judge left. Would it be better to sign the next-best free agent (at that moment, shortstop Carlos Correa) and try to chase a championship, or reset the organization for a year or two and play rookies and prospects?

The latter course was tempting, but didn't match up with the prime years of Gerrit Cole, the $324 million ace who would turn thirty-three the following season. Maybe the Yankees should sign the center fielder Brandon Nimmo and as much pitching as they could gather?

This is how uncertain the future of the Yankees became at that moment. Hypothetical paths now seemed like concrete possibilities.

Cashman did not participate in this gathering. Wary of being seen by the public with a drink in his hand when news broke that Judge was signing elsewhere—how would *that* go over with an already angry fan base?—he remained in the suite. He spoke to Odle, then finally made contact via text with Judge.

Boone, meanwhile, was with the group on the fortieth floor. He asked his colleagues if they thought he should call Judge, a discussion that had begun a few hours earlier at dinner.

Jim Hendry, a gravel-voiced former GM of the Chicago Cubs and friend of Cashman's who now worked in the Yankees' front office, spoke the loudest.

"What the fuck—call him!" Hendry said. "Fucking call him! You're the goddamn manager of the New York Yankees! You don't want to wake up tomorrow and see he's signed with someone else and you didn't call!"

Boone, who would have done so anyway, ducked out of the bar and down a hallway that led to the men's room. Finding a quiet spot, he dialed. Judge picked up.

Boone made it clear to Judge how much he appreciated him and wanted him back, and suggested that Judge and Steinbrenner connect. Soon after, Steinbrenner began texting Judge from a vacation in Italy. Around 3:00 a.m. PT, they spoke.

"What makes you and your family happy?" Steinbrenner asked. "Do you want to be a Yankee?"

Judge said that he did want to stay—clarity, at last!—but needed Steinbrenner to offer a ninth year.

The Yankees pushed their bid to nine years and $360 million. Cashman, Steinbrenner, Judge, and Odle hammered out details. They closed the deal at 3:30 a.m. Judge informed a few friends on the team, then continued with Samantha on to Hawaii for vacation.

Boone and the entire glum group had left the bar after 1:00 a.m. They woke less than five hours later to calls and texts from well-wishers who had seen the news.

Boone called Cashman.

"Is this real?" he asked.

It was. The entire Yankees organization could exhale. They had kept their icon, their marketable Ruth/DiMaggio/Mantle/Jeter. By the skin of their teeth, they had managed to remain the big, bad New York Yankees.

33

One Last Bit of Business to Resolve

"Is It Really Worth It?"

T HAT 2022 OFFSEASON BROUGHT one more bit of significant Yankee business, less headline grabbing but arguably as significant: Brian Cashman's contract was set to expire on October 31. He and Hal Steinbrenner had to decide whether to continue their partnership.

In the days after the ALCS loss to Houston, fans and columnists piled on Cashman and the Yankees with even more bloodlust than before. The October 24 edition of the *New York Post* in particular caught the Yankees' attention.

That paper contained a column by longtime baseball writer Joel Sherman headlined: "Everything Must Be in Play as Current Yankees Prove They're Not Good Enough."

It began with an unforgiving lede.

"Everything has to be in play now," Sherman wrote. "Hal Steinbrenner can't just offer familiar blather about not meeting the ultimate goal and being disappointed to fail the fans and promise to redouble efforts in the quest for a 28th championship. Then after a cooling-off period, have essentially all the same people back to do all the same things."

This seemed like a call for change in the Yankee front office, perhaps even its longtime leader.

In the same edition of the paper, the columnist Ian O'Connor published an item headlined "Hal Steinbrenner Lucky He Can't Be Fired for Yankees' Repeated Failures."

"The same paying customers who booed Steinbrenner at ceremonies honoring Paul O'Neill and Derek Jeter are sick and tired of the Yankees saying they willingly signed up to be judged in October, only to repeatedly fail in October," O'Connor wrote. "Those fans are sick and tired of an organization that has spent as much time embracing excuses as it does seeking solutions.

"They are sick and tired of Hal Steinbrenner's leadership."

Cashman felt loyal to Hal and defensive on his behalf. He briefly wondered if he shouldn't fall on his sword and leave, in order to spare his boss the criticism related to re-upping him.

Inside the Yankee offices, as the Astros played in and eventually won the World Series, it was a tortured few weeks.

"The media was just feeding the gaping maw," says Jean Afterman. "They were just giving the public what they wanted. The ones that call for Brian's head, they may believe it. But they're just giving the public what they want to read."

Most fans and reporters assumed that Cashman's return was a mere formality. After all, he hadn't seriously considered leaving in more than a decade. But Cashman's closest friends knew that nothing was certain.

"I think he was very discouraged and disturbed at the fan and media reaction," Afterman says. "I think he wondered, 'Is it really worth it?'"

Did Cashman think he might be done as a Yankee—after twenty-five seasons as GM and thirty-six years after first walking in the door as an intern?

"I didn't know," Cashman says. "I just didn't know what was going to happen. My eyes weren't set on anything other than 'Let's see how this plays out.'

"I enjoy [the job], just the backlash—the success that we're having despite not winning a championship, which is not automatic, you know? I was a little bit caught off guard by how things were playing out publicly, despite the amount of success we were having."

Cashman reveals that a representative from the management consulting firm Korn Ferry—known for helping teams with executive searches—contacted him, and he did choose to engage. He makes clear that he did not seek this outreach but was the recipient of a cold call.

"I had somebody that was talking to me," Cashman says. "There was an agent out there. But we never got down the path. We had a lot of conversations, like would you ever leave and blah, blah, blah."

If Cashman worked for a different boss, perhaps he would have left. But he still enjoyed the work culture under the current Steinbrenner.

"He and Hal have a great relationship, and I don't think he wanted to leave Hal in the lurch," Afterman says. "And I think one of Hal's strong suits is that he likes continuity. Everybody used to joke behind George's back that George would have been better suited to football, where you have just one game a week and you live and die on that one game. In baseball you can't live and die on just an individual game. Hal is perfectly suited for baseball. He understands 162 games. He's not going to rise and fall on one game over another."

I ask Hal Steinbrenner if he thought there was a chance he would lose Cashman after the 2022 season. He begins by listing qualities in his GM that he admires.

"Cash is very intelligent," Steinbrenner says. "He's a good leader. He listens to his people. He's not afraid to hear opinions that are different from his own. And like me, I think it's very well balanced. Understanding that this is not just about pro scouting and boots on the ground or this is not just about analytics. It's about both.

"And now it's about biomechanics, performance science. And we look at every trade, every potential free agent signing—we look at it in a very balanced way, and he is aligned with me on that. We have a very good relationship. We communicate very well together.

"I never had a thought he would not want to come back, because we've discussed it from time to time. He loves New York. He loves being a Yankee. His family loves New York. So no, I did not. I did not think—but having said that, I didn't know."

After briefly marinating in the disappointment of another play-off loss and the defensiveness brought on by severe public criticism, Cashman dove back into the game.

He conducted his annual postseason news conference at Yankee Stadium. He engaged Aaron Judge's team in negotiations. He attended the November GM meetings in Las Vegas.

Cashman was still working without a new contract, but at fifty-five years old he had stepped back into the stream that had carried him since he was nineteen. He was a Yankee. The connection ran deep.

As he put it shortly after, "I still haven't decided what I want to be when I grow up."

On December 5, the Yankees announced that they had signed Cashman to a new four-year contract. Some friends in the organization speculated that it would be his last. When I mentioned this to Cashman one day in his office in 2023, he gave a small shrug.

A few weeks later, asked more directly about it in the Yankee dugout during batting practice, he said, "The way I have always looked at it, I don't know what's going to happen a few years from now or ten years from now. I could get let go during this deal."

Considering the extent to which Hal Steinbrenner values continuity, the most likely future of Yankees leadership involves a promotion from within. Inside the organization, Kevin Reese is viewed as the leading candidate, the one whom Cashman would recommend to Steinbrenner if he were ever dismissed or decided to kick himself upstairs into an advisory role.

Reese is a former outfielder whose MLB career spanned twelve games for the Yankees in 2005 and 2006. After retiring, he took a job in Billy Eppler's pro scouting department, then succeeded Eppler as pro scouting director.

In 2023 he was running player development for the organization, the role in which Bill Livesey made his greatest impact more than a generation earlier. Because of his playing experience and openness to analytics and tech, Reese fits the combo mold that Cashman admired in Gene Michael and Tim Naehring. The job might be Reese's one day. Or Cashman's hunger for the work might continue unabated into another decade.

While the team's news release announcing his 2022 extension noted the many accomplishments that will land Cashman in the Hall of Fame—the five championships, the thirty-one consecutive winning seasons (twenty-six as GM) the most by any franchise at any point in their history, and so on and so on—it left out the one detail that drove Yankee fans crazy, and, let's be honest, tortures Cashman, too: They want to taste another championship. Then another. Then another.

That craving remained unsatisfied after a 2023 season that pushed the Yankees even further from their ultimate goal. Beset with injuries and poor performances, the team entered the year with championship aspirations and finished with an 82–80 record, missing the playoffs altogether.

The disappointment fueled fan and media criticism about Cashman's recent string of unsuccessful moves. In 2021, he acquired outfielder Joey Gallo from the Texas Rangers; the sensitive Gallo turned out to be ill-equipped for the pressures of New York. In 2022, he traded for Oakland ace Frankie Montas, only to lose Montas for most of the next year and a half to a shoulder injury. After that season, the Yankees awarded free agent pitcher Carlos Rodón a six-year, $162 million contract—then watched as Rodon went 3-8 with a 6.85 ERA in an injury-plagued debut season.

For the sake of his own mental health, Cashman tried to pull back from reading Twitter and newspapers. The television that was mounted to the wall in his Yankee Stadium office, which for years had showed sports programming, now rested on CNN, because seething over what he considered unfair commentary did not help his job performance. He engaged with reporters less frequently than ever, rarely returning their calls.

Still, enough of the coverage filtered his way—underlings and family members often pointed it out to him—to cause his frustration to mount. Cashman was proud of his record, and even more proud of his staff. Michael Fishman, Tim Naehring, and others had been knocked around for too long, he felt.

Cashman had in the past year convinced Brian Sabean, the legendary San Francisco Giants executive who long ago had helped build the Yankee dynasty, to return as an advisor. He had also hired former Mets GM Omar Minaya, a longtime friend and respected scout. Happy with the intellectual diversity of his front-office staff, Cashman was beginning to feel more pugnacious about defending his people.

The 2023 GM meetings convened on November 6 at the same Omni resort in Scottsdale, Arizona, that hosted the event in 2019, when news of the Houston Astros cheating scandal broke. On the second day of the 2023 meetings, MLB required all American League general managers to participate in a media availability.

It was a hot week, even for Arizona, with near-record temperatures in the eighties and nineties. The reporters and executives were already sweating when Cashman, dressed in a salmon button-down shirt and aviator sunglasses, strode into view with his head of communications, Jason Zillo. As a scrum gathered between palm trees on the outdoor stone patio, Cashman told Zillo that he might let it fly and say what had long been on his mind.

Almost from the beginning, the session was combative. In a setting typically defined by bland corporate-speak and talk of adding a starting pitcher or outfielder in free agency, Cashman unleashed a few "bullshits"—uncommon enough with notebooks out and cameras rolling. He sparred loudly with his questioners, then dropped the most famous front office f-bomb since Cashman himself said a decade earlier that Alex Rodriguez should "shut the fuck up."

"We've got good people," Cashman said. "I'm proud of our people, and I'm proud of our process. Doesn't mean we're firing on all cylinders, doesn't mean we're the best in class, but I think we're pretty fucking good, personally, and I'm proud of our people."

This was not normal for an on-record baseball news conference. The back-and-forth lasted for sixty-seven riveting minutes, and when Zillo announced that time was up, Cashman felt surprise. This had been a virtually out-of-body experience for him, seeming to race by.

Later that night, Cashman held a group dinner with his front office, then went to bed. Afterwards, four of his top lieutenants—Sabean, Naehring, Minaya, and former Cubs GM Jim Hendry—retreated to the resort's bar and expressed to one another their gratitude that Cashman had come to their defense. They talked about how the reserved Fishman had been loyal to Cashman for nearly two decades and said that Cashman wanted to stick up for him.

There was also a sense of sympathy among Cashman's friends that, while he still loved leading the baseball operations department and being a Yankee, he was not having fun dealing with the constant assaults on his people or his legacy.

Later, at a far corner of the bar, two championship-winning general managers and one reporter sipped red wine and listed the recent executives who they believed would land in the Hall of Fame: Cashman; Sabean; longtime Marlins, Tigers, Red Sox, and Phillies head of baseball Dave Dombrowski; and Theo Epstein.

That list, while likely accurate, would have provided no comfort to Cashman or Yankee fans. The pursuit of excellence means constant disappointment and only occasional satisfaction.

This game is a monster, as Sabean once put it. You can wrestle it to the ground, but it always gets up to crush you again. And then for some reason you want more.

Jean Afterman puts it more succinctly.

"I think," she says, "Brian feels that he has more to accomplish as a Yankee."

Acknowledgments

Neither Brian Cashman nor his right-hand man on communications, Jason Zillo, seemed particularly enthused by the idea of this book when I first proposed it. I wouldn't have been surprised if both hoped I would forget it and move on.

But ultimately, both were extremely generous with their time and access, which is all the more appreciated given their reservations. Cashman submitted to what became years, plural, of frequent interviews, and Zillo facilitated contacts on every level of the organization. These are busy people, and I'm grateful for their time.

Actually, pretty much everyone has a busy life, which is why I'm moved when anyone agrees to be interviewed at length. Thank you to every single source who spoke on or off the record for this book.

Here is a list of folks who were so giving of their time, insights, memories, or feedback that they deserve special mention: Jean Afterman, Billy Eppler, Tim Naehring, Buck Showalter, Bill Livesey, and Tim Brown. Thanks for dealing with calls and texts that must have seemed as if they would never stop.

Thanks also to Michael Margolis, Kaitlyn Brennan, and the rest of the Yankees' PR staff for general daily helpfulness.

Thanks to Chris Carlin for years of friendship and steadfast backing.

Joaquin Tianga and Henry Martino worked as research assistants, and George Henn as a fact-checker. Thanks to all three of you.

Brian Jacobs and Esther Newberg at CAA and Jason Kaufman at

Doubleday shepherded me into the book business, making a dream come true.

Steve Raab, Brad Como, Matt Dunn, and Amara Grautski at SNY provided support and trust as I pursued book projects. Dave Mandel, Gerard Guilfoyle, Doug Williams, Sal Licata, and the entire production crew of *Baseball Night in New York* have created a fun but purposeful working environment day in and day out.

Dael and Kelly Oates were interested, supportive, and fun throughout the process. Jesse Rosser and Warner Wada lent me a house on the ocean to write significant chunks of this and two other books.

Ruby Rosser's extremely hard work in our home—which came on top of her extremely hard work at, you know, *work*—created the space to do this.

The aforementioned Henry Martino's burgeoning interest in baseball helped spark my interest in this project.

Violet Martino was a really fun baby while I was working on this book.

My late grandfather, Raymond Martino, was in my thoughts during the Billy Martin sections. He sometimes insisted, without evidence, that Martin was his cousin. All the way back to Tony Lazzeri, Joe DiMaggio, Yogi Berra, and Phil Rizzuto, the Yankees have held a special place in the imaginations of many first- and second-generation Italian Americans. This entire project carried extra meaning for me because of that.

My parents, Jeannie and Ray Martino, showed me how to be a spouse, parent, professional, and human in this world. Other than that, nothing much.

Bibliography

BOOKS

Appel, Marty. *Pinstripe Empire.* New York: Bloomsbury, 2012.

Creamer, Robert. *Babe: The Legend Comes to Life.* New York: Simon & Schuster, 1974.

Curry, Jack. *The 1998 Yankees: The Inside Story of the Greatest Baseball Team Ever.* New York: Twelve, 2023.

Feinsand, Mark, and Bryan Hoch. *Mission 27: A New Boss, a New Ballpark, and One Last Ring for the Yankees' Core Four.* Chicago: Triumph, 2019.

Geivett, Bill. *Do You Want to Work in Baseball?* New Jersey: BookBaby, 2017.

Hoch, Bryan. *62: Aaron Judge, the New York Yankees, and the Pursuit of Greatness.* New York: Atria, 2023.

Klapisch, Bob and Solotaroff, Paul. *Inside The Empire: The True Power Behind the New York Yankees.* New York: Mariner Books, 2019.

Levitt, Daniel R. *Ed Barrow: The Bulldog Who Built the Yankees' First Dynasty.* Lincoln: University of Nebraska Press, 2008.

Lewis, Michael. *Moneyball.* New York: W. W. Norton, 2003.

Madden, Bill. *Steinbrenner: The Last Lion of Baseball.* New York: Harper, 2010.

Madden, Bill, and Moss Klein. *Damned Yankees: Chaos, Confusion, and Craziness in the Steinbrenner Era.* Chicago: Triumph Books, 1990.

Mann, Jack. *The Decline and Fall of the New York Yankees.* New York: Simon & Schuster, 1967.

O'Connor, Ian. *The Captain.* New York: Mariner, 2012.

Olney, Buster. *The Last Night of the Yankee Dynasty: The Game, the Team, and the Cost of Greatness.* New York: Ecco, 2004.

Pennington, Bill. *Billy Martin: Baseball's Flawed Genius.* New York: Mariner Books, 2016.

———. *Chumps to Champs: How the Worst Teams in Yankees History Led to the Dynasty.* New York: Mariner, 2019.

Roberts, Selena. *A-Rod: The Many Lives of Alex Rodriguez.* New York: Harper, 2009.

Sherman, Joel. *Birth of a Dynasty: Behind the Pinstripes with the 1996 Yankees.* New York: Rodale, 2006.

Torre, Joe. *Chasing the Dream: My Lifelong Journey to the World Series.* With Tom Verducci. New York: Bantam, 1997.

Torre, Joe, and Tom Verducci. *The Yankee Years.* New York: Doubleday, 2009.

ARTICLES

Anderson, Dave. "Sports of the Times; The Yankees Stick Is Standing Tall." *New York Times,* Aug. 30, 1981.

Armour, Mark. "The CBS Era Yankees." 2018. National Pastime Museum. thenationalpastimemuseum.com.

———. "Lee McPhail." Sabr.org.

Asher, Mark. "Yanks' New GM Got Good Jump at Catholic." *Washington Post,* Feb. 4, 1998.

Bradley, Jeff. "Don Mattingly Reaches Postseason for First Time as Yankees Clinch Wild Card." New York *Daily News,* Sept. 30, 1995.

Chass, Murray. "Yanks Dismiss Michael After Losing Doubleheader." *New York Times,* Aug. 4, 1982.

———. "Yanks Fire 3 Top Minor League Officials." *New York Times,* Sept. 20, 1995.

Curry, Jack. "Baseball; Yankees Trade Roberto Kelly to Reds for O'Neill." *New York Times,* Nov. 4, 1992.

———. "Hal Steinbrenner Becomes Yankees Boss." *New York Times,* Nov. 20, 2008.

Fast, Mike. "What the Heck Is Pitchf/x?" In *Hardball Times Baseball Annual, 2010* (Skokie, Ill.: Acta Sports, 2009).

Gregory, Sean. "Aaron Judge: Athlete of the Year." *Time,* Dec. 6, 2022.

Harness Racing Museum and Hall of Fame. "Frederick L. Van Lennep." harnessmuseum.com.

Kepner, Tyler. "Swindal Divorce Shakes Up Yankee Hierarchy." *New York Times,* March 29, 2007.

Kirschenbaum, Jerry. "Freddie Is Setting the Pace." *Sports Illustrated,* April 9, 1973.

Leiber, Jill. "Will the Boss Behave Himself?" *Sports Illustrated,* March 1, 1993.

Lewiston *Sun Journal.* "Standout Maine Coach Killed in Auto Crash." Nov. 17, 1979.

Lindbergh, Ben. "Moneyball with Money: How Billy Beane and Brian Cashman Became Friends, Won Games, and Influenced People." *Ringer,* April 21, 2021.

Lupica, Mike. "When Don Mattingly Recaptured Donnie Baseball in 1995: 'I Was Me Again.'" MLB.com, Feb. 9, 2022. mlb.com.

Marchand, Andrew. "Will Jean Afterman Be Baseball's First Female GM? The Sport Should Be So Lucky." ESPNNewYork.com, April 12, 2017. espn.com.

Martinez, Michael. "No Regrets for Thrift." *New York Times,* Sept. 24, 1998.

Matthews, Wallace. "Rough Seas Ahead for Captain, Yanks?" ESPNNewYork .com, Nov. 17, 2010. espn.com.

McCaffrey, Jen. "We're Not Going to Be Pushed Around Anymore: Oral History of the A-Rod/Jason Varitek Fight." *Athletic,* July 19, 2019.

McCarron, Anthony. "Randy Levine Says Wearing Pinstripes Aided Derek Jeter; Captain Free to Test Free Agent Waters." New York *Daily News,* Nov. 18, 2010.

Nelson, John. "The Punch: Martin's Victim Tells His Side of the Story." *Beaver County Times,* Oct. 31, 1979.

O'Connor, Ian. "How to Survive 22 Years as Yankees GM? Brian Cashman Can Thank His Hall of Fame Father." ESPN, Sept. 25, 2019. espn.com.

Olney, Buster. "How the Yankees Inked Aaron Judge: Inside a Wild 24 Hours in San Diego." ESPN, Dec. 14, 2022. espn.com.

———. "No Need for a Foe When A-Rod Is a Friend." *New York Times,* March 3, 2001.

———. "Yankees Subtract a Star but Add a Legend." *New York Times,* Feb. 19, 1999.

Parker, Kathy. "End of an Era: Pompano Park." Harness Racing Fan Zone, May 31, 2022.

Price, S. L. "Brian Cashman: Yankees GM Is an Iconic and Fearless Figure." SI.com, Aug. 25, 2015.

Reid, Tony. "Billy Martin Killed in Fiery Crash." *Washington Post,* Dec. 26, 1989.

Sherman, Joel. "George Steinbrenner's Obsession with Dave Winfield Changed Yankees Forever." *New York Post,* June 2, 2020.

———. "Yankees Prepared to Brush Jeter Back." *New York Post,* Nov. 17, 2010.

Shusterman, Jordan. "Yankees GM Brian Cashman Revisits His College Days at HOF Induction." Foxsports.com, April 11, 2022.

Spence, Harlan. "Paul O'Neill and the Trade That Changed Everything." Pinstripe Alley, Aug. 8, 2014. pinstripealley.com.

Unruh, Jacob. "Meet Dick Groch, the Scout Who Signed Derek Jeter." *Oklahoman,* June 27, 2015.

Wagner, James. "Meet the Biggest Prankster in Baseball: Yankees GM Brian Cashman." *New York Times,* Sept. 29, 2020.

Withers, Tom. "Steinbrenner Names Michael GM in His Final Hours." UPI, Aug. 20, 1990.

Television

The Captain. Directed by Randy Wilkins. ESPN Films, 2022.

The Deal. Directed by Colin Barnicle. ESPN Films, 2014.

Four Days in October. Directed by Gary Waksman. ESPN Films and MLB Productions, 2010.

60 Minutes. CBS. Jan. 12, 2014.

Index

Illustration Credits

About the Author

ANDY MARTINO has written about sports, culture, and entertainment, and has covered Major League Baseball for more than a decade. A former staff writer at *The Philadelphia Inquirer* and the New York *Daily News,* he is currently a reporter and analyst covering MLB for the SNY network in New York.

Illustration Credits

About the Author

ANDY MARTINO has written about sports, culture, and entertainment, and has covered Major League Baseball for more than a decade. A former staff writer at *The Philadelphia Inquirer* and the New York *Daily News,* he is currently a reporter and analyst covering MLB for the SNY network in New York.